THE BLACKS
of
PICKAWAY COUNTY OHIO
in the
NINETEENTH CENTURY

Compiled by
James Buchanan

HERITAGE BOOKS
2012

HERITAGE BOOKS

AN IMPRINT OF HERITAGE BOOKS, INC.

Books, CDs, and more—Worldwide

For our listing of thousands of titles see our website
at
www.HeritageBooks.com

Published 2012 by
HERITAGE BOOKS, INC.
Publishing Division
100 Railroad Ave. #104
Westminster, Maryland 21157

International Standard Book Numbers
Paperbound: 978-1-55613-129-5
Clothbound: 978-0-7884-9310-2

INTRODUCTION

Ohio was one of the busiest states on the Underground Railroad as blacks made their way north from the slavery of the South. But Ohio was also a settling place for those black persons freed by their owners. Pickaway County, in south-central Ohio, was one of the early homes for blacks leaving the South and looking for new homes, whether by choice or flight.

In 1803 Ohio became a state and seven years later Pickaway County was formed. By the 1820 census, the county had become the home for twenty-three families listed as mulatto (mixed black and white heritage) or black. The total "colored" population of the county in that census, was 133, most in these few families. These citizens were mainly farm laborers in the townships, being emancipated mainly from Virginia.

During the 1820s and 1830s, not only did the "colored" population of the county grow, but they made their presence known in ways other than in farming. A blacksmith shop was opened in Darvyville in 1826 with Charles McFeeters, a mulatto, as the owner. Eight few years later the first church for black persons of the county was opened in the county seat at Circleville. The African Methodist Episcopal Church, pastored by Rev. L. Davis, had twelve members when the church began as the first black organizational presence in the county.

Between 1830 and 1840 the "colored" population of Pickaway County doubled, and by 1850 there were 185 black persons and 200 mulattos in the county, mainly located in Circleville. The employment picture had changed as the minority was now involved in farm activities, some blacks owning their own farms, while the majority worked as laborers or in service industries. For example, many of the barbers in Pickaway County were blacks. Also during the 1850s the Second Baptists Church (African) was organized by the Rev. William Norman, Lucy Winters, Enoch Weaver and Sarah Hollinsworth, all well-noted blacks in the county.

By 1860 the "colored" population had almost tripled from 1850, with 670 blacks and 285 mulattos in the county. During this decade the black population joined the whites in defending the Union as a number of the black men joined the 5th U.S. Colored Infantry and the 27th U.S. Colored Cavalry. At the end of the war nineteen members were enrolled in the "Colored" Veterans organization and at least three blacks from the county had given their lives.

The population of blacks in the county continued to rise, totaling 1,072 in the 1870 census and 1,328 in the 1880 census. But during the two decades before the next census (the 1890 census records were destroyed in a fire) the "colored" population dropped to 1900. Several factors account for this, the major one being the reclassification of families during the century from "black" to "mulatto" and then to "white" by 1900. The change became evident in the 1900 census as only one mulatto was listed, all of the remaining 737 "colored" were listed as blacks. In addition to this change was the changing employment status of the blacks. Some owned businesses or worked for government agencies. Others provided service in hotels, factories, and shops. A small minority remained as farmers and farm laborers. The population, while smaller, was more diverse in its activities. In addition, a large number were literate, a factor newly reported in the 1900 census.

This book presents the public genealogical records of the black settlers of 19th century Pickaway County, Ohio. The census rolls from 1820 to 1900 are supplemented with the birth and death records from 1867 to 1900. In addition, some of the marriage records from 1811 to date are included. Because these were not identified specifically as "colored", as are the marriage records in many Ohio county records, identification of the marriage of black persons was more difficult. As a result, many of the marriages are noted but without specific dates of marriage from the public records.

The symbols used in this work are meant to simplify the individual records. Most people recognize "b", "d", and "m" for birth, death and marriage. In addition to these symbols, the letters "bl" and "mul" were added to indicate whether the record differentiates the person as black or mulatto. In a few cases, especially those for families which eventually became "white", the various records list the person both as black and mulatto. The state abbreviations are in the old form rather than the modern abbreviations used for the post office.

These, then are the records of Pickaway County's black citizens during the nineteenth century. Descendants of many of the early settlers leaving Virginia remain in the population of the county, especially of those twenty-three families that represented the beginnings of black settlement in Pickaway County.

ADAMS, EDWARD - b. 1799, VA; d. 9 June 1878, Circleville
    of old age. cooper. listed bl & mul. m lst, Celia
    (____); 2nd, Martha (____). (Circleville, 1840-1870)
        Celia - bc 1798, VA. mul. (1850)
        Martha - bc 1822, VA. mul. parents both b VA.
        (1860-1880)
        Edward J. - bc 1856, OH; s/o Edward & Martha Adams.
            blacksmith. (1860-1880)
        Hartley - bc 1859, OH; s/o Edward & Martha Adams.
            (1860)
        King - bc 1827, VA; s/o Edward & Celia Adams. listed
            bl & mul (1850)
        Sarah P. - bc 1858, OH; s/o Edward & Martha Adams.
            (1860)
ADAMS, ELIZA - bc 1828, VA; mul. (1850)
ADAMS, GEORGE - bc 1800, VA; bl farmer. m Maria (____).
    (Wayne Twp., 1840-1860)
        Maria - bc 1810, DEL; bl. (1850-1860)
        George M. - bc 1833, OH; bl. (1850)
        Henry - bc 1832, OH; bl farmer. (1850)
        Isaac - bc 1829, OH; bl farmer. (1850)
        James - bc 1837, OH; bl. (1850)
        John W. - b 1848, Wayne Twp; bl. (1850-1860)
        M. Jane or Jane M. - bc 1844, Wayne Twp. bl. (1850-
            1860)
        Nancy M. - bc 1835, OH; bl. (1850)
        Otoway - b 1841, Wayne Twp. bl. (1850-1860)
        Samuel - bc 1851, Wayne Twp. bl. (1860)
        Smith - bc 1846, Wayne Twp; bl. (1850-1860)
ADAMS, JULIA - bc 1832, OH; mul. (Circleville, 1850)
ADAMS, THEODORE - m Jeanette (Peal) & lived Darby Twp.
    daughter b 1878.
ADKINSON, CHARLES and son, 2 daughters lived in Darby Twp.
    (Darby Twp, 1830)
ADKINSON, SARAH - bc 1816, VA; bl. (Circleville, 1870)
ALEXANDER, THOMAS - b 1831, VA; bl cooper. (Circleville,
    1850)
ALLEN, CHARLES - bc 1836, VA; mul farmer. parents both b
    VA. m Mary (____). (Jackson Twp, 1880)
        Mary - bc 1839, VA; mul. (1880)
        Forest - bc 1868, VA; mul. (1880)
ALLEN, HARRIET m Henry Whittington & lived in Circleville.
ALLEN, HOWARD - bc 1831, VA; mul laborer. (Circleville,
    1870)
ALLEN, JOSEPH - bc 1833, NC; mul farm laborer. m Melissa
    (____). (Muhlenburg Twp., 1870)
        Melissa - bc 1835, NC; mul. (1870)
        Adeline - bc 1855, NC; mul. (1870)

1

Emma - bc 1867, OH; mul. (1870)
Jesse - b 14 Jan 1869, Muhlenburg Twp. mul. (1870)
Sandy - bc 1864, OH; mul. (1870)
Thadeus - bc 1862, OH; mul. (1870)
Webster - bc 1857, NC; mul farm laborer. (1870)
ALLEN, LANDEN - bc 1833, OH; mul. (Muhlenburg Twp, 1850)
ALLEN, LIZZIE - bc 1862, OH; bl school teacher. father b
  KY; mother b VA. (Circleville, 1880)
ALLEN, LUCY LEE (or Louisa or Elizabeth) - all listed as
  m. Adam Redman.
ALLEN, MARY - b VA; d 3 May 1868, Circleville of lung
  affliction. age 50. widow.
ALLEN, PETER - bc 1820 or 1825, VA; bl. m. Elizabeth
  (_____). (Jackson Twp., 1850-1860)
    Elizabeth - bc 1820, VA; bl. (1850)
    James - b 1850, Jackson Twp. bl. (1850)
ANDERSON, JOHN - bc 1840, OH; bl laborer. (Circleville,
  1860)
    Sophia - bc 1852, OH; bl. (1860)
ANDERSON, Q. - b 1832, NC; bl laborer. m Jane (_____).
  (Circleville, 1870)
    Jane - bc 1834, NC; bl. (1870)
    Edward - bc 1858, NC; bl. (1870)
    Israel - bc 1863, NC; bl. (1870)
    John - bc 1853, NC; bl laborer. (1870)
    Peter - bc 1855, NC; bl laborer. (1870)
    Ruben - bc 1866, NC; bl. (1870)
ANDERSON, SARAH - bc 1828, MD; mul. (Circleville, 1850)
ANVIERS, M.S. - b 1854, OH; domestic servant. father b VA;
  mother b OH. (Circleville, 1880)
ARCHER, MAINDIO - bc 1819, NC; bl housemaid. (Circleville,
  1870)
ARLINGTON, WILLIAM m Rachel (_____) & lived Circleville.
  Elizabeth Katie - b 19 Feb 1885, Circleville.
ARMISTEAD, VIOLET m Christopher Hunt and lived in Muhlen-
  burg Twp.
ARMSTRONG, HATTIE - b June 1887, OH. bl. both parents
  b OH. (Circleville, 1900)
ARNOLD, SAMUEL - bc 1833, VA; bl laborer. bl. (Circle-
  ville, 1860). 2nd listing as b 1830, Ireland.
ARNOLD, WILLIAM m Mary E. (Williams) 20 Mar 1864, Circle-
  ville. --on m license William crossed out and Henry
  inserted--
    daughter b 10 Jan 1869.
ARTIST, THOMAS m Alice Thacker and lived Harrison Twp.
    Oscar - b 12 Dec 1872, Harrison Twp.
ASBERRY, WILLIAM - b Mar 1855, NC; bl farm laborer. father
  b NC, mother b VA. (Scioto Twp, 1900)

2

ASBURY, JOHN - bc 1835, OH; bl farm laborer. (Wayne Twp, 1860)

AUSTIN, ANNA C. - b Benford Co, VA.; d 1 Aug 1880, Picka-way Co. of pneumonia. married.

AUSTIN, JOHN - b May 1868, OH; bl farmer. both parents b OH. m Emma (____). (Muhlenburg Twp, 1900)
    Emma - b June 1876, OH. bl. both parents b OH. (1900)
    Hazel M. - b Sept 1898, OH. (1900)
    Ruth M. - b Aug 1896, OH. (1900)

AUSTIN, MANSFIELD - bc 1843, OH; bl farm laborer. father b VA; mother b VA. m Ann (Steptoe). (Muhlenburg Twp, 1870-1880)
    Ann (Steptoe) - b 1847 or 1850, OH; bl. father b IND; mother b OH. (1870-1880)
    Charles - bc 1879, Muhlenburg Twp. bl. (1880)
    Elizabeth - bc 1873, OH; bl. (1880)
    Hope - bc 1871, OH; bl. (1880)
    John P. - b 15 Mar 1876, Muhlenburg Twp. bl. (1880)
    Roxanna - b 1867, OH; bl. (1870-1880)

BAGLEY, ANNA m Caswell Briggs & lived Circleville.

BAILEY, ANNA lived Circleville. son Robert Karey.
    Robert Karey - b 12 Mar 1891, Circleville.

BAILEY, HANNAH m Elisha Lett and lived Circleville, 1870s.

BAIN, MARY - bc 1846, OH; bl housemaid. (Wayne Twp, 1870)

BAKER, ALBERT - bc 1874, OH. bl. father b KY, mother b VA. (Scioto Twp. 1880)

BAKER, HENRY m Mary (Bartlett) & lived Harrison Twp.
    Henry - b 20 Jan 1871, OH.

BAKER, JAMES - bc 1849, OH; bl farm laborer. (Deer Creek Twp, 1870).

BAKER, MARIA - d 15 Oct 1895, Washington Twp. of heart trouble. age 70. house servant.

BANESTER, JOHN - b 1853, KY; bl saloon keeper. mother b NC. (Circleville, 1880)

BANISTER, JOHN H. - bc 1856, OH; bl farm laborer. (Jackson Twp, 1880)

BANISTER, PRESTON - bc 1851, VA; bl farm laborer. (Jackson Twp, 1880)

BANKS, HARVEY and 1 male, 1 female lived in Jackson Twp. (Jackson Twp, 1840)

BANKS, NATHANIEL - b 1820 or 1825, VA; listed bl & mul cook. parents both b VA. m Margaret (Tan) 18 Nov 1855, Circleville. (Circleville, 1880)

Margaret - b 1836 or 1840, NC or SC; d 5 Oct 1889,
Circleville of lung disease. bl domestic ser-
vant. parents both b NC. (1880)
Isabel - b 15 Feb 1871, Circleville. bl. (1880)
Jane - b 1867, OH; bl. (1880)
Mary E. - b 1857, OH; bl cook. (1860-1880)
William - b 6 Dec 1877, Circleville, s/o Mary Banks
& William Paterson. bl day laborer. (1880-1900)
--1900 census lists both parents b VA--
BANMETER, JOHN - b June 1854, OH; bl teamster. both
parents b VA. m Ann (_____). (Circleville, 1900)
Ann - b Dec 1859, OH. bl. father b KY; mother b OH.
(1900)
BANNER, ARRON - bc 1821, OH; bl farm laborer. parents b
OH. (Harrison Twp, 1880)
Lida - bc 1845, OH; farm laborer. parents b OH.
(1880)
BARCHAN, _____ m T.S. Ridgway & lived in Darby Twp, 1880s.
BARNES, MARTHA m William Meredith & lived in Circleville,
1870s.
BARNET, IDA m William Fields 3 Jan 1888, Pickaway Co. &
lived in Circleville, 1890s.
BARNET, JAMES - bc 1850, MD; bl farm laborer. (Deer Creek
Twp, 1870)
BARNET, ROSE m George Stanup & lived in Circleville, 1880s.
BARNETT, GEORGE - bc 1834, VA; d 27 Mar 1895, Circleville
of apoplexy. laborer.
BARNETT, GEORGE L. - bc. 1830, VA; bl farm worker. parents
b VA. m Sarah (_____). (Circleville, 1880) --may be
same as above--
Sarah - bc 1845, OH; bl. father b VA; mother b OH.
(1880)
Ada A. - bc 1867, OH; bl. (1880)
Hattie - b 1873, OH; bl. (1880)
James E. - b 1868, OH; bl. (1880)
Minnie W. - bc 1876, OH; bl. (1880)
Rozilla - bc 1864, OH; bl house servant. (1880)
BARNETT, JAMES - bc 1870, Pike Co.; d 16 Feb 1887, Circle-
ville of consumption. laborer.
BARNEY, JAMES - bc 1847 or 1850, OH; bl laborer in livery
stable. m Ardella (Nickens). (Circleville, 1870-1880)
Ardella (Nickens) - b 1847, Circleville; d 29 Mar
1890, Circleville of inflamation of bowels.
parents b OH. (1870-1880)
Blanche - bc 1875, Circleville; bl. m Lafayette
Coachman & lived in Circleville, 1890s. (1880)
Festus - b 26 July 1880, Circleville.
Idella - b 16 Aug 1869, Circleville

4

James - d 9 Sept 1871, Circleville of typhoid fever.
   age 9 months.
James - b 1874, Circleville; d 25 Aug 1875 of
   cholera.
Millie - b 1869 or 1870, Circleville; bl. (1870)
Nannie - bc 1877, Circleville; bl. (1880)
Nellie - bc 1870, Circleville; bl. (1880)
William - b 6 Sept 1876, Circleville.
infant - b 14 Aug 1884, Circleville.
BARTLETT, HENRY - bc 1839, PA; bl farm laborer. (Deer Creek
   Twp, 1870)
BARTLETT, HENRY - b 1837 or 1845, OH; bl farm laborer.
   (Scioto Twp, 1860, 1880) -- probably same as above--
BARTLETT, MARY m Henry Baker & lived in Harrison Twp,
   1870s.
BARTLETTE, JOHNSON - bc 1843, OH; bl laborer. m Emma
   (____). (Circleville, 1860)
      Emma - listed as Emily (Negress) in birth records -
         b 1844, VA; bl. (1860)
      Arkansas H. - bc 1852, OH; bl. (1860)
      Cassius M. - b 1858, Circleville; bl. (1860)
      Elnora J. - bc 1850, OH; bl. (1860)
      Nebraska - bc 1856, OH; bl. (1860)
      Thomas J. - bc 1849, OH; bl. (1860)
      child - b 25 July 1857, Circleville.
BARTLEY, LAFAYETTE - b 1870, Harrison Twp; bl. (Harrison
   Twp, 1870)
BARTLEY, LEONARD - bc 1820, OH; bl farmer. m Sarah A.
   (____). (Harrison Twp, 1860)
      Sarah A. - bc 1825, OH; bl. (1860)
      Ann W. - b 1860, Harrison Twp; bl. (1860)
      Caroline - b 1853, OH; bl. (1860-1870)
      Ellen - bc 1845, OH; bl. (1860)
      Henry O. - bc 1850, OH; bl. (1860)
      Joana - bc 1857, OH; bl. (1860)
      Leonard - bc 1848, OH; bl. (1860)
      Lydia A. - b 1851, OH; bl domestic servant. (1860-
         1870)
      Mary A. - bc 1846, OH; bl. (1860)
BARTLEY, MENDORA - bc 1864, OH; bl. (Harrison Twp, 1870)
BARTLEY, THOMAS - bc 1849, OH; bl farm laborer. (Harrison
   Twp, 1870)
BASS, CHESTER - b Mar 1862, VA. worked in transferring.
   father b NC; mother b VA. m Tullie (____). (Circle-
   ville, 1900)
      Tullie - b Feb 1869, MO. white. father b Germany,
         mother b ILL. (1900)

BASS, WILLIAM - b May 1832, NC; mul farmer. parents both b
   NC. m Caroline (____). (Jackson Twp, 1880-1900)
      Caroline - b May 1832, VA; bl. both parents b VA.
         (1880)
      Calvin - bc 1870, VA; mul. (1880)
      E. David - b July 1874, VA.
      Emma - bc 1862, VA; mul. (1880)
      Francis - bc 1858, VA; mul. (1880)
      Jesse - bc 1855, VA; mul. (1880)
      Manning - bc 1872, VA; mul. (1880)
      Martha - b Oct 1867, VA; mul. (1880-1900)
      Richard - bc 1868, VA: mul. (1880)
      Susan - bc 1864, W VA; d 19 Jan 1893, Jackson Twp of
         consumption. mul. (1880)
      William - b Mar 1859, VA; mul. (1880) - see below.
BASS, WILLIAM - worked in transportation. m Malinda
   (Wright) (Jackson Twp, 1880-1890; Circleville, 1900)
      Malinda (Wright) - b July 1868, OH. bl. father b
         VA; mother b OH. (1880-1900)
      Chester Henry - b 8 Dec. 1899, Circleville. (1900)
      Jessie - b 29 June 1886, Jackson Twp. (1900)
      Lelia M. - b Mar 1888, Jackson Twp. (1900)
      Margarett - b 20 June 1897, Circleville. (1900)
      Nina L. - b Mar 1892, Circleville. (1900)
      William D. - b 20 June 1897, Circleville. (1900)
BATHEL, JANE - b 10 Mar 1871, Circleville to Sarah Bathel.
BEARD, FLORA - b 1821, Franklin Co; d 2 Aug 1898, Circle-
   ville of consumption. married. domestic servant.
BEARD, MINNIE - b Apr 1894, OH. both parents b OH.
   (Circleville, 1900)
BEARD, RICHARD - bc 1806, VA; bl laborer. m Delilah
   (____). 3 sons and 3 daughters in 1840. (Pickaway
   Twp, 1840-1850)
      Delilah - bc 1797, VA; bl. (1850)
      David - bc 1828, VA; bl laborer. (1850)
      Elizabeth - bc 1831, OH; bl. (1850)
      John - bc 1829, OH; bl. (1850)
BEARD, TORUNY (?) - bc 1833, NC; bl housemaid. (Jackson
   Twp, 1870)
BEAST, RENA - bc 1830, OH; mul servant. parents both b NC.
   (Jackson Twp, 1880)
BECKER, MARTHA m Lewis Smith & lived in Deer Creek, 1880s.
BELL, AGNESS - b Feb 1897, OH. both parents b OH.
   (Circleville, 1900)

6

BELLAMY, GEORGE - bc 1824, GA; mul farmer. m Mahala A.
(_____). Scioto Twp, 1860)
    Mahala A. - bc 1836, GA; mul. (1860)
    Abraham - bc 1858, GA; mul. (1860)
    Franklin - b 1857, GA; listed bl and mul farm
        laborer. (Scioto Twp. 1860-1870)
    George - b 1861, Scioto Twp. bl. (1870)
    Georgiann - b 1854, GA; listed bl & mul. (1860-1870)
    Sarah A. - b 1856, GA; listed bl & mul. (1860-1870)
BELLGREAR, FLORENCE - b 17 Jan 1878, Washington Twp. to
    Ida Dyer.
BENCH, JOHN - bc 1810, VA; mul laborer. (Harrison Twp,
    1850)
    James - b 1849, NC; mulatto. (1850)
BENCO, HANNIBAL - bc 1816, VA; bl carpenter. (Circleville,
    1870)
    Annie - bc 1849, OH; bl. (1870)
BENDER, RICHARD - bc 1839, VA; mul laborer. parents both b
    VA. m Ellen (_____). (Jackson Twp, 1880)
    Ellen - bc 1842, VA; mul. (1880)
    Bertha - bc 1878, VA; mul. (1880)
    Ellen - bc 1874, VA; mul. (1880)
    Hanna - bc 1869, VA; mul. (1880)
    Maggie - bc 1875, VA; mul. (1880)
    Marian - bc 1872, VA; mul. (1880)
    Mary - bc 1862, VA; mul. (1880)
BILLY, JESSE - bc 1803, VA; d 7 Apr 1868, Circleville of
    consumption. laborer. widower.
BINZER, MARY (birth records also spell Binser) - m Ed C.
    Stewart and lived in Circleville, 1880s.
BIRD, ELIAS - bc 1834, NC; bl well digger. m Harriet
    (Day). father b NC, mother b VA. (Circleville, 1880)
    Harriet (Day) - bc 1844, OH; bl. father b OH, mother
        b VA. (1880)
    Caroline - b 27 May 1879, Circleville. bl. (1880)
    Dolly - bc 1864, OH; bl domestic servant. (1880)
    Dorothy - bc 1863, OH; bl domestic servant. (1880)
    Earl - bc 1874, OH; bl. (1880)
    Elias - bc 1876, OH; bl. (1880)
    James E. - b 17 June 1873, Circleville; d 1876,
        Circleville.
    Joseph - bc 1867, OH; bl. (1880)
BIRD, ELIJA m Ella (Vail) & lived in Circleville, 1890s.
    Moretty - b 23 Oct 1899, Circleville.
BIRD, JAMES lived in Madison Twp with 6 females. (Madison
    Twp, 1840).
BIRD, KESSIAH - b 1868, Ross Co; d 8 Nov 1879, Circleville
    of brain fever.

7

BISHOP, ABNER - lived in Washington Twp, 1820 with 1 male
    and 3 females; Circleville in 1840 with 4 males and 4
    females.
BISHOP, ABNER - b 1845, OH; mul. (Deer Creek Twp, 1850)
BISHOP, JOHN - bc 1818, OH; mul barber. m Elizabeth
    (_____). (Circleville, 1850)
        Elizabeth - bc 1824, VA; mul. (1850)
        Alice A. - b 1848, Circleville; mul. (1850)
        Josephine - bc 1838, OH; mul. (1850)
BISHOP, MAHALA - bc 1818, OH; mul. (Circleville 1850)
        Laura - b 1846, Circleville. mul. (1850)
        Sarah - bc 1834, OH; mul. (1850)
BISHOP, REECE - bc 1794, VA; bl. (Circleville, 1860) --
    see also REESA below.
        Charles - bc 1847, OH; mul. (1860)
        James - bc 1835, OH; mul barber. (1860)
BISHOP, REESA - bc 1798, MD; mul. (Circleville, 1850)
        James - bc 1837, OH; mul. (1850)
        Mary - bc 1839, OH; mul. (1850)
BISSELL (also spelled BIZZEL in records)
BISSELL, JOHN - b 1830, NC; mul. (Circleville, 1850)
BISSELL, JOHN - bc 1824, NC; mul drayman. m Julia (_____).
    (Circleville, 1870)
        Julia - bc 1836, OH; mul. (1870)
        Jessie - b 29 Apr 1875, Circleville
        Nettie W. - b May 1869, Circleville; d 9 Aug 1870,
            Circleville of chills. mul. (1870)
        Suszie - b 19 Feb 1871, Circleville
BISSELL, JOSEPH - bc 1843, VA; bl farm laborer. m Margaret
    (_____). (Muhlenburg Twp, 1870)
        Margaret - bc 1845, VA; bl. (1870)
BISSELL, NOAH - b 1845, St. Louis, NC; d 11 May 1871,
    Circleville of consumption. listed as bl barber &
    laborer. m Nancy (_____). (Circleville, 1860-1870)
        Nancy - bc 1849, OH; bl. (1870)
BISSELL, WILLIAM - bc 1805, NC; bl brick mason. m
    Elizabeth (_____). (Circleville, 1860)
        Elizabeth - bc 1820, NC; bl. (1860)
        Abner - bc 1841, NC; bl laborer. (1860)
        John - bc 1839, NC; bl laborer. (1860)
        Noah - b 1843 or 1845, NC; bl barber. (1860-1870) -
            see above.
        Sally A. - bc 1847, NC; bl. (1860)
        Solomon - bc 1849, NC; bl. (1860)
BLACK, JOSEPH - b 1843, VA; bl farm laborer. m Margaret
    (_____). (Muhlenburg Twp, 1870)
        Margaret - bc 1845, VA. bl. (1870)

BLACK, MARTHA m George Brown & lived in Five Points, 1870s.
BLAKE, CHARLES - b Apr 1871, OH. father b VA; mother b OH.
  m Laura (Gibbs) & lived in Circleville. (Circleville,
  1900)
      Laura - b Apr 1871, OH. parents both b OH. (1900)
      C. Henry - b 8 Jan 1895, Circleville
      Charles - b 1 Oct 1899, Circleville. (1900)
      Gale Ruth - b 18 July 1897, Circleville.
      Harry - b Feb 1890, Circleville. (1900)
      Karl - b Jan 1896, Circleville. (1900)
      Scott - b Feb 1890, Circleville. (1900)
BLAKE, GEORGE - b 1841 or 1844, DC; d 13 May 1891, Circleville of cancer. listed bl & mul plasterer. m Sarah A.
  (Dickerson) 12 Feb 1861, Pickaway Co. (Circleville,
  1870-1880)
      Sarah - b 1845, OH; listed bl & mul. parents both b
        VA. (1870-1880)
      Alma - b 26 Jan 1871, Circleville. mul. (1880)
      Charles - b 1862, OH; listed bl & mul laborer.
        (1870-1880) -- see also above
      Harry - b 1867, OH; listed bl & mul laborer. (1870-
        1880)
      Hester - b 1868, Circleville. bl. (1870-1880)
      William - b 1865, OH; listed bl & mul. (1870-1880)
BLAKE, JAMES - b 1800 or 1810, VA; d 4 Dec 1857, of disease
  of stomach. bl cooper. m Hannah (_____). (Circleville
  Twp, 1850)
      Hannah - b 1804 or 1807, MD; bl seamstress. (1850;
        Circleville, 1860)
      Allen J. - b 1834, OH; bl laborer. (1850-1860)
      Clarinda A. - b 1838 or 1840, OH; bl. (1850-1860)
      John A. - bc 1841, OH; bl. (1850)
      Margaret L. - b 1842, OH; bl. (1850-1860)
      William W. - b 1828, OH; bl porter. (1850-1860)
BLAKE, JOHN - bc 1838, OH; bl. (Circleville, 1880)
BLAKE, MARIA - bc 1830, OH; bl. (Circleville, 1850)
      Mary - bc 1831, OH; bl. (Circleville, 1850)
BLOSE, ROSANNA m Mr. Hooser and lived in Darby Twp, 1890s.
BOBO, FANNY - bc 1839, OH; bl cook. m. Milton Kelly, 21
  May 1871, Jackson Twp. (Jackson Twp, 1870)
      Nancy - bc 1867, OH; bl. (1870)
      Sophia - bc 1864, OH; bl. (1870)
BOBO, NANNIE ELIZABETH m Dennis Tann & lived in Circle-
  ville, 1890s.
BOCKLEY, JOSEPHINE m Allen Jones & lived in Walnut Twp,
  1870s.
BOLER, JOHN - bc 1853, OH; bl laborer. (Circleville, 1870)

9

BOLEY, EDWARD - bc 1853; d 1872, Circleville of consumption.
BOLLEY, ALICE - b June 1857, VA. parents both b VA.
  (Circleville, 1900)
      Ada - b Mar 1870, OH. father b W VA; mother b VA,
      (1900)
      Elisabeth - b Aug 1897, OH. parents both b OH.
      (1900)
BOND, CHARLES - d 15 Sept 1876, Circleville of consumption.
  age listed as 9 months, but may be 9 yr old son of
  Solomon & Susan Bond.
BOND, HUSTON - b July 1869, OH. day laborer. m Minnie E.
  (Hackett) 30 Jan 1893, Circleville. (Circleville, 1900)
      Minnie E. - b Dec 1869, OH. seamstress. parents
      both b OH. (1900)
      Beatrice - b 5 Aug 1893, Circleville. (1900)
      Malcomb - b Mar 1869, Circleville. (1900)
BOND, LYFUS (also ELIPHUS and LIFE) - b May 1832, VA; mul
  barber. m Ceresa (Jones). father b MD; mother b MD or
  LA. (Circleville, 1870-1900)
      Cressa (also Ceresa and Chrissie) - b 1846 or 1848,
      NC; mul. parents both b NC. (1870-1880)
      Franklin - bc 1870, Circleville. mul. (1870)
      Hattie - b 9 Oct 1881, Circleville. domestic.
      (1900)
      Henry or Harry - b 10 May 1874, Circleville.
      laborer. (1900)
      Huston - bc 1869, Circleville. (1880) -- see
      separate listing.
      Lyfas - b 10 May 1874, Circleville.
      Pearley - b 8 March 1879, Circleville.
BOND, MARCELLUS - b 1827, VA; d Aug 1875, Circleville. s/o
  Nancy Bond. listed in separate censuses as farmer
  (1850), drayman (1860) and cartman (1870). m Susan
  (_____). (Circleville, 1850-1870) --listed as Solomon
  in 1870 and death record, probably second name.
      Susan - bc 1828, NC; bl. (1860-1870)
      Charles - b 1868, Circleville. bl. (1870)
      James - b 1856 or 1858, Circleville. bl. (1860-
      1870)
      William - b 1853, Circleville. bl. (1860-1870)
BOND, NANCY - bc 1787, VA; d 27 Jan 1875, Circleville of
  old age. widow. lived with 3 daughters in Circleville,
  1840. (Circleville, 1840)
BOND, NANCY - b 1802 or 1805, VA; bl. (Circleville, 1850-
  1870) -- may be same as Nancy listed above with varia-
  tion in birth date.

10

Elisha - bc 1834, OH; bl. (1850-1860)
Marcellus - b 1827, VA; bl farmer. (1850-1860) ---
see also above.
Rhoda - bc 1831, OH; bl. (1850)
BOND, WILLIAM m Nannie (Chapman) 16 Mar 1876, Circleville &
lived in Circleville.
Bessie - b 13 May 1876, Circleville.
BONES, LEVI - bc 1806, VA; bl. father b VA; mother b NC.
(Circleville, 1880)
BOONE, BOWLEN - bc 1822, NC; mul mason. m Elizabeth
(_____). (Circleville, 1850)
Elizabeth - bc 1824, NC; bl. (1850)
BOONE, CORDELIA - bc 1833, VA; mul. (Circleville, 1870)
BOONE, NAPOLEON - b 1832 or 1835, NC; d 6 Sept 1868,
Circleville of accident. bl laborer. m Martha S.
(_____). (Circleville, 1860)
Martha S. - bc 1838, NC; bl. (1860)
Sithegaram (?) - bc 1856, NC; bl. (1860)
BOWEN, RIDELICK - bc 1828, NC; bl laborer. (Circleville,
1860)
BOWERS, HANSON and 2 males lived in Harrison Twp, 1840.
BOWLEY, EDWARD - bc 1858, VA; bl farm laborer. parents both
b VA. m Alice (_____). (Circleville, 1880)
Alice - bc 1855, VA. bl. parents both b VA. (1880)
Ada - b 1880, Circleville. (1880)
BOWSHER, EDWARD - bc 1850, OH; mul farm laborer. (Jackson
Twp, 1870)
BOYDSTON (also BOYD STONE), JOSEPH - b 1825, OH; listed bl &
mul farmer. m Mary A. (_____). (Deer Creek Twp, 1850;
Circleville, 1860)
Mary A. - b 1825 or 1827, VA; listed bl & mul.
(1850-1860)
James W. - b 1854, Circleville. bl. (1860)
BOYER, CHARLES and 3 females lived in Walnut Twp, 1830.
BOYER, JOHN - b 1861, Circleville; d 29 July 1868, Circle-
ville of summer complaint.
BOYLSTON, ISAAC - bc 1802, OH; bl farmer. m Nancy (_____).
(Perry Twp, 1860)
Nancy - bc 1818, OH; bl. (1860)
Emily J. - b 1860, Perry Twp. bl. (1860)
Mary E. - bc 1857, OH; bl. (1860)
Roseanna - bc 1853, OH; bl. (1860)
BRADLEY, DAVID - bc 1828, OH; bl laborer. (Circleville,
1850)
BRADLEY, JOHNSON m Julia Scott & lived in Circleville,
1890s.
Martha - b 12 Dec 1893, Circleville. father b KY;
mother b OH. (Circleville, 1900)

11

BRAXTON, CARL - b June 1849, VA. bl farmer. parents both
b VA. m. Ella (_____). (Perry Twp, 1900)
  Ella - b Oct 1853, OH. parents both b VA. (1900)
  Earl - b Apr 1886, OH. but age listed as 9. (1900)
  John - b Sept 1881, OH. farm laborer. (1900)
  Lizzy - b Feb 1882, OH but age listed as 14. (1900)
  Maude - b July 1888, OH. (1900)
  Moaty (?) - b Feb 1884, OH. farm laborer. (1900)
BRERTY, JEREMIAH and 2 males, 4 females lived in Monroe
Twp, 1820.
BREWER, HENRY E. - b June 1876, OH. farm laborer. father
b NC; mother b OH. (Perry Twp, 1900)
BREWER, WILLIAM - b Oct 1870, OH. farm laborer. father b
NC; mother b OH. m. Ida (_____). (Perry Twp., 1900)
  Ida - b Mar 1873. father b NC; mother b OH. (1900)
  Albert W. - b. Dec 1899, OH. (1900)
  Stella M. - b. Sept 1894, OH. (1900)
BRIGGS, CALVIN - b 1862, Circleville; s/o London & Susan
Briggs. m Sarah Ann (_____). (Circleville, 1870-1880)
  Sarah Ann - bc 1856, OH; bl. father b OH; mother
    b NC. (1880)
  James H. - b 1880, Circleville. bl. (1880)
BRIGGS, CASWELL - b 31 July 1846, Circleville; d 28 Aug
1877, Circleville of consumption. s/o London & Susan
Briggs. mul barber. m Anna (Bagley) (_____). (Circle-
ville, 1850-1860)
  Maggie - b 21 Dec 1876, Circleville.
BRIGGS, EDDIE - bc Dec 1865; d 30 Mar 1868, Circleville of
lung fever.
BRIGGS, GEORGE - bc 1848, VA; bl. (South Bloomfield, 1870)
BRIGGS, GEORGE W. m Julia (Henry) & lived in Circleville,
1890s.
  Ella - b 8 Feb 1892, Circleville.
  Susan - b 8 Feb 1892, Circleville.
BRIGGS, LONDON - b 1816, VA; listed as bl drayman &
laborer. parents both b VA. m Susan (_____). (Circle-
ville, 1850-1880)
  Susan (also Susannah) - bc 1825, Lynchburg, VA; d 1
    Oct 1866, Circleville of heart disease. listed bl
    & mul. parents both b VA. (1850-1860)
  Calvin - b 1862, Circleville. bl. (1870). -- see
    separate listing.
  Caswell - b 31 July 1846, Circleville; mul barber.
    (1850-1860) -- see separate listing
  Ferdinand - b 1857, Circleville; d 16 Aug 1885,
    Circleville of consumption. listed bl & mul.
    (1860-1870)

12

George W. - b 1847, Circleville. listed bl & mul
   farm laborer. (1850-1880) -- see separate listing
Iredell - bc 1852, Circleville. mul. (1860)
James R. - b 1855, Circleville; d 4 July 1875,
   Circleville. listed bl & mul laborer. (1860-
   1870)
Margaret - b 1849, Circleville. listed bl & mul.
   (1850-1870).
Missie - bc 1868, Circleville. bl. (1880)
Peter - b 29 May 1868, Circleville. bl. (1870)
BRIGHT, NICHOLAS - bc 1821, DEL; bl carpenter. m Elizabeth
   (_____). (Wayne Twp, 1870)
   Elizabeth - bc 1840, OH; bl. (1870)
   Charles - bc 1864, OH; bl. (1870)
BRINN, MARIA m William Seward & lived in Darby Twp, 1870s.
BROLLY, ADA m George Harris & lived in Circleville, 1890s.
BROOKS, JAMES - bc 1848, OH; bl farm laborer. (Jackson
   Twp, 1870)
BROSE, MILLIE - bc 1808, VA; d 11 Aug 1868, Circleville of
   flux.
BROWN, ALBERT - bc 1837, KY; bl farm laborer. (Wayne Twp,
   1860)
BROWN, ALEXANDER m Sarah (Spriggs) & lived in Circleville.
   Mattie - b March 1878, Chillicothe.
BROWN, ANNA m Thomas Watson & lived in Madison Twp, 1870s.
BROWN, BEVERLY (male) - bc 1839, VA; bl engineer. (Har-
   rison Twp, 1870)
BROWN, BRADY - b 1878, VA; bl. parents both b VA. (Monroe
   Twp, 1880)
BROWN, CATHERINE - bc 1842, OH; bl. (Circleville, 1870)
   Lilly - b 1870, Circleville. bl. (1870)
BROWN, DANIEL - bc 1837, OH; bl farm laborer. (Jackson
   Twp, 1870)
BROWN, DAVID - bc 1812, Hampshire Co, VA. bl. lived in
   Circleville 1834.
BROWN, DRAPER and 2 males, 2 females lived in Washington
   Twp, 1820; 2 males and 3 females in Circleville, 1830.
BROWN, ELIJAH - bc 1828, OH; bl farmer. m Mary (_____).
   (Circleville, 1850)
   Mary - bc 1828, VA; bl. (1850)
BROWN, ELIZABETH K. - bc 1858, OH; bl. (Circleville, 1850)
BROWN, ERICK - bc 1814, PA; bl farmer. (Deer Creek Twp,
   1850)
   Mary Ann - bc 1847, OH; mul. m Gibson Phillips &
      lived in Circleville, 1870s. (1850)
BROWN, FLORENCE - b 1869, OH; bl. parents both b VA.
   (Muhlenburg Twp, 1880)

13

BROWN, GEORGE m Martha (Black) & lived in Five Points.
    Florence - b 18 May 1879, Five Points.
BROWN, HENRY - bc 1829, OH; bl farm laborer. (Wayne Twp,
    1870)
BROWN, JACK - bc 1836, TENN; bl house servant. (Circle-
    ville, 1870)
BROWN, JAMES - b Jan 1833, GA; day laborer. parents both
    b GA. (Circleville, 1900)
BROWN, JOHN - bc 1813, OH; bl laborer. (Circleville, 1850)
BROWN, JOHN - bc 1810, OH; bl farmer. (Circleville, 1860)
BROWN, LEVI - bc 1809, VA; bl laborer. (Circleville, 1870)
BROWN, LEVI - bc 1841, NC; bl. (Circleville, 1850)
BROWN, LOUISA m Ezra Davis & lived in Monroe Twp, 1880s.
BROWN, MARY - bc 1832, OH; bl. (Wayne Twp, 1870)
BROWN, MARY m Sampson Lack & lived in Circleville, 1850s.
BROWN, NATHAN and 2 females lived in Salt Creek Twp, 1820.
BROWN, NOFLITE (?) - b July 1841, VA. mul farm laborer.
    parents both b VA. (Walnut Twp, 1900)
BROWN, NORRIS - bc 1840, VA; bl servant. parents both b
    VA. (Harrison Twp, 1880)
BROWN, SAM - bc 1834, OH; bl. (Scioto Twp, 1860)
BROWN, SIDNEY & 1 male, 3 females lived in Circleville,
    1840.
BROWN, THOMAS - bc 1842, OH; bl farmer. (Wayne Twp, 1870)
BROWNE, G. W. - bc 1845, OH; bl farm laborer. parents both
    b OH. (Monroe Twp, 1880)
BRUCE, HANNAH - b 1813; d 14 Apr 1878, Circleville. widow.
BRUSER, _____ - b 1865; d 14 Aug 1867, Circleville of
    summer complaint. c/o John Bruser.
BUINICHER, NEIDA - bc 1849, VA; bl farm laborer. (Jackson
    Twp, 1880)
BUNCH, WADE - bc 1856, VA; mul farm laborer. parents both
    b VA. (Muhlenburg Twp, 1880)
BUNDLES, CLEMENTINE m Ballard P. Stewart & lived in Wayne
    Twp, 1870s.
BUNDY, MARTHA m Nathaniel Johnson & lived in Circleville,
    1870s.
BUNDY, SALLIE m Robert Fowler & lived in Muhlenburg Twp,
    1880s.
BUNDY, SPENCER - bc 1857, VA; bl farm laborer. parents
    both b VA. (Muhlenburg Twp, 1880)
BURLIN, SUMPTER - bc 1860, VA; mul laborer. parents both b
    VA. (Jackson Twp, 1880)
BURNETT, JOHN - bc 1837, VA; bl farm laborer. (Wayne Twp,
    1860)
BURNS, THOMAS - b Mar 1840, VA. bl farmer. parents both
    b VA. m Mattie (_____). (Muhlenburg Twp, 1900)
    Mattie - b Sept 1852, VA. parents both b VA. (1900)
    Burtie M. - b May 1886, OH. (1900)

14

BURR, HANEY - bc 1857, VA; bl farm laborer. parents both b
VA. (Jackson Twp, 1880)
BUTLER, FRANK- bc 1845, KY; bl servant. m Henrietta
(____). parents both b KY. (Pickaway Twp, 1880)
    Henrietta - bc 1845, KY; bl servant. parents both b
    KY. (1880)
BUTLER, SUSAN m. Lawrence Gauer c. 1870.
BYERS, THOMAS m Maria (Lewis) & lived in Circleville,
1860s-1870s.
    Martha A. - b 21 Sept 1869, Circleville; d 17 July
        1870, Circleville of fever.
BYERS, THOMAS and Bias (____).
    daughter - b 10 Aug 1867, Circleville
    son - b 8 June 1868, Circleville
BYRD (also spelled BIRD)
BYRD, ELIAS - b Aug 1830, NC. bl day laborer. parents
both b VA. m. Harriet (____). (Circleville, 1900)
    Harriet - b May 1842, OH. parents both b OH. (1900)
    Callie - b May 1879, OH. bl. (1900)
    Elias - b. Mar 1875, OH. bl. (1900) - see separate
        listing
    Everett - b. Mar 1872, OH. bl. (1900) - see
        separate listing
    Hattie - b Aug 1887, OH. bl. (1900)
    William - b. Aug 1878, OH. bl. (1900)
BYRD, ELIAS - b Mar 1875, OH. bl. m Ella (____).
(Circleville, 1900)
    Ella - b Feb 1880, OH. parents both b IND. (1900)
    Marie- b Oct 1899, Circleville
BYRD, ELSIE - b Aug 1861, OH. bl farm laborer. parents
both b OH. (Monroe Twp, 1900)
BYRD, EVERETT - b Mar 1872, OH. bl day laborer. m.
Adaline (Winner) 24 May 1892, Circleville. --birth
records also list a spouse as Anna (May)
    Adaline - b Sept 1878, VA. parents both b VA.
        (1900)
    Bethel - b 16 Apr 1898, Circleville. (1900)
    Charles - b Jan 1896, Circleville. (1900)
    John - b. 18 Oct 1899, Circleville. (1900)

CABLE, JAKE - b 1841, W VA; d 25 Feb 1876, Harrison Twp. of
    dropsey.
CAIN, JESSE - b 1815, Hocking Co; d 27 Dec 1898, Washington
    Twp. Infirmary of Brights Disease. pauper.
CALAWAY, ROBIN - bc 1862, OH; bl servant/farm worker.
    (Walnut Twp, 1880)
CAMPBELL, ELIZA - bc 1829, VA; bl housemaid. (Circleville,
    1870)

15

CAMPBELL, ELIZA - bc 1815, SC; bl. parents both b SC.
(Circleville, 1880)
      Lizzie - bc 1861, VA; bl servant. (1880)
CANNON, NOAH C - bc 1790. freed by J.H. Millechop of Kent
   Co, DEL and lived in Pickaway Co, 1820s.
CAPITO, ELNORA - b Sept 1874, NC. bl cook. parents both b
   NC. (Circleville, 1900)
CARDOFF, JOHN & 3 males, 4 females in Washington Twp, 1820.
CARNES, LAWRENCE - bc 1839, OH; bl laborer. m Susan
   (_____). (Circleville, 1870)
      Susan - bc 1855, OH; bl. (1870)
      Olive - b 7 Aug 1867, Circleville. bl. (1870)
CARNES, THOMAS - bc 1839, OH; bl teamster. m Annie
   (_____). (Circleville, 1870)
      Annie - bc 1849, NC; bl. (1870)
      Clara - b 1 May 1868, OH; bl. (1870)
CARTER, BRITAIN - bc 1815, NC; bl farmer. m Pricilla
   (_____). (Monroe Twp, 1860)
      Pricilla - bc 1820, NC. bl. (1860)
      Candus - bc 1850, NC; bl. (1860)
      Clark - bc 1844, NC; bl. (1860)
      James H. - bc 1852, NC; bl. (1860)
      John - bc 1845, NC; bl day laborer. (1860)
      Lucinda - bc 1856, OH; bl. (1860)
      Marinda Y. - bc 1854, OH; bl. (1860)
      Mary J. - bc 1846, NC; bl. (1860)
      Oscar - bc 1853, OH; bl. (1860)
CARTER, MARY - b 1827, Smith Co, VA; d 6 March 1886,
   Circleville of consumption. widow.
CARTER, MARY - bc 1854, VA; mul. (Circleville, 1850)
CASE, JASIN - bc 1840, OH. mul. (Wayne Twp, 1850)
CASSEL, JAMES - bc 1834, OH; mul farm laborer. m Rebecca
   A. (_____). (Jackson Twp, 1860)
      Rebecca A. - bc 1837, OH; mul. (1860)
      William A. - bc 1856, OH; mul. (1860)
CASSELS, JOSEPH - bc 1815, OH; mul farmer. m Julia A.
   (_____). Jackson Twp, 1850)
      Julia A. - bc 1820, OH; mul. (1850)
      Albert - bc 1838, OH; mul. (1850)
      Charles W. - bc 1845, OH; mul. (1850)
      Eliza A. - bc 1841, OH; mul. (1850)
      Golden - bc 1847, OH; mul. (1850)
      Jesse L. - b 1850, Jackson Twp. mul. (1850)
      Rachele M. - bc 1844, OH; mul. (1850)
      Reason Y. - bc 1849; Jackson Twp; d 9 Sept 1857,
         Jackson Twp. mul. (1850)
      Rebecca - bc 1850, OH; mul. (1850)

CESAER, JAMEY - b Feb 1862, OH. bl laborer. parents both
  b VA. m Rosa (____). (Circleville, 1900)
     Rosa - b Dec 1860, OH. both parents b VA. (1900)
     Martha - b July 1894, OH. (1900)
     Mary - b May 1892, OH. (1900)
CHAFERS, OLIVE - b Sept 1870, Circleville; d 4 Mar 1872,
  Circleville of brain fever. d/o Kesiah Chafers and John
  Blake.
CHAFERS, SARAH - b Aug 1867, Ross Co; d 25 Feb 1871, Cir-
  cleville of brain fever.
CHAIS (poss. CHAVIS), Ann - bc 1790, VA; mul. (Jackson
  Twp, 1860)
     Ann - bc 1830, VA; mul. (1860)
CHAPMAN (also listed CHATMAN)
CHAPMAN, ALBERT m Maggie (Collins) & lived in Circleville,
  1870s, Wayne Twp, 1880s.
     Lucinda - b 2 Sept 1888, Wayne Twp.
     Nannie - b 8 Mar 1889, Circleville
CHAPMAN, AMANDA - b 1847, OH; mul. m Brittain Tan & lived
  in Circleville, 1870s-1880s. (Wayne Twp, 1860)
CHAPMAN, ANN - bc 1799, VA; bl. (Circleville, 1870)
     William - bc 1839, VA; bl laborer. (1870)
     Charles - bc 1863, OH; bl. (1870)
     Ella - bc 1865, OH; bl. (1870)
CHAPMAN, EDWARD - bc 1863, OH; bl laborer. father b VA;
  mother b OH. (Circleville, 1880)
CHAPMAN, EDWARD or EDWIN - b 1819, VA; d 4 June 1879, Wayne
  Twp. of spinal disease. bl farmer. m Lucinda (____).
  (Wayne Twp, 1870)
  2nd listing EDWIN - mul farm laborer. (Wayne Twp, 1860)
     Lucinda D. - b Oct 1824, VA; listed bl & mul.
        parents both b VA. (Wayne Twp, 1860-1880)
     Alfred C. - b 1855 or 1856, Wayne Twp. listed bl &
        mul. (1860-1870)
     Edward - bc 1858, Wayne Twp. mul. (1860)
     Emily - bc 1852, VA; mul. (1860)
     Henry S. - bc 1865, OH; bl laborer. (1880)
     James A. - b 1862, Wayne Twp. bl laborer. (1870-1880)
     Lucinda - b 1860, Wayne Twp. mul. (1860)
     Nancy - b 1856 or 1857, Wayne Twp. listed bl & mul.
        m John Douglas & lived in Wayne Twp, 1880s.
        (1860-1870)
     Polly - bc 1847, VA; mul. (1860)
     Sherman - b Nov 1864, Wayne Twp. bl. (1870)
     William D. - bc 1843, VA; mul. (1860)
CHAPMAN, EMMA m John Weaver & lived in Circleville 1870s.
CHAPMAN, JOHN H. - b Feb 1869, Wayne Twp; d 8 May 1869,
  Wayne Twp. of pneumonia.

CHAPMAN, MARY - b 1867, Circleville; d May 1870, Circleville of fever.
CHAPMAN, MARY m Richard Redman & lived in Wayne Twp, 1870s.
CHAPMAN, N. - b 1844, Circleville; d 14 Jan 1879, Circleville
CHAPMAN, SHERMAN - b Nov 1864, OD. bl day laborer. (Circleville, 1900) -- probably s/o Edward & Lucinda Chapman.
 Lucinda - b Sept 1888, OH. (1900)
 Nancy - b Oct 1890, OH. (1900)
CHAPMAN, WILLIAM - bc 1840, VA; mul laborer. parents both b VA. (Circleville, 1880)
 William - bc 1872, OH; bl. father b VA; mother b OH. (1880)
CHARLTON, ISABELLA - b 1798; d Sept 1868, Circleville of apoplexy.
CHAVIS, ALICE - b Nov 1870 to Alice Chavis.
CHAVIS, JAMESON - bc 1814, VA; mul farmer. m Ann (_____). (Jackson Twp, 1860)
 Ann - bc 1813, VA; mul. (1860)
 Alex - bc 1838, VA; mul. (1860)
 Drury M. - bc 1853, VA; mul. (1860)
 Edward T. - bc 1849, VA; mul. (1860)
 Martha G. - bc 1851, VA; mul. (1860)
 Mary E. - bc 1847, VA; mul. (1860)
 Matilda A. - bc 1842, VA; mul. (1860)
 Sarah F. - bc 1843, VA; mul. (1860)
 William F. - bc 1845, VA; mul. (1860)
CHAVISH, REBECCA m Peter Montgomery & lived in Circleville, 1870s.
CHEATHAM, EDWARD - b 1853, MO; bl farm laborer. parents both b MO. (Muhlenburg Twp, 1880)
 2nd listing - b 1855, MO; bl hostler. (Muhlenburg Twp, 1870)
CHEATWOOD, CELIA - bc 1855, OH; bl. father b VA; mother b OH. (Circleville, 1880)
 twin daughters - b 27 Jan 1869, Jackson Twp.
CHEATWOOD, EDMAN or EDWIN - b 1790 or 1975, VA; bl. (Muhlenburg, 1850; Jackson Twp, 1860)
 Eliza - bc 1815, OH; bl. (1860)
CHEATWOOD, FANNY - bc 1866, OH; bl. (Jackson Twp, 1870)
CHEATWOOD, SULLY - bc 1847, OH; bl. (Circleville, 1860)
CHERRY, ALFRED - b Jan 1879, OH. bl farm laborer. parents both b OH. (Jackson Twp, 1900)
CHESTER, BENJAMIN and 6 females lived in Wayne Twp, 1840.
CHIM, SUSAN - b Mar 1825, VA. parents both b VA. (Circleville, 1900)
CISCO, MARTHA - bc 1843, OH; mul. (Jackson Twp, 1850)
CLAIR, JIANNIE (?) - b Apr 1866, OH. bl nurse. parents both b OH. (Circleville, 1900)

Charles - b Sept 1888, OH. (1900)
James - b Apr 1890, OH. (1900)
William - b June 1887, OH. (1900)
CLARK, JOHN - bc 1859, VA; mul laborer. parents both b VA.
(Jackson Twp, 1880)
CLARK, MARTHA - bc 1838, NC; mul. parents both b VA.
(Circleville, 1880)
CLARK, WILLIAM - bc 1803, VA; bl. m. Rachel (_____).
(Jackson Twp, 1860)
    Rachel - bc 1809, MD; mul. (1860)
    Charles - bc 1842, OH; bl. (1860)
    Christopher - bc 1846, OH; mul. (1860)
    Clifford - bc 1848, OH; mul. (1860)
    Emily A. - bc 1856, OH; mul. (1860)
    William W. - bc 1844, OH; bl. (1860)
CLIFFORD, ISAIAH - b 1815, W VA; d 21 Sept 1898, Circle-
ville of typhoid pneumonia. married laborer.
COACHMAN, KESIAH - bc 1851, OH; bl cook. parents both b
NC. (Circleville, 1880)
    Lafayette - bc 1853, OH. --see separate listing--
COACHMAN, LAFAYETTE - b Oct 1872, OH; bl. porter at hotel.
father b KY; mother b NC. m. Blanche (Barney).
(Circleville, 1900)
    Blanche - b Dec 1873, OH. parents both b OH. (1900)
    Bernice - b 20 Oct 1898, Circleville
COBO, DUKE - bc 1825, GA; bl farm laborer. (Deer Creek,
1870)
COLE, BERTHA m Arthur Dickerson & lived in Circleville,
1890s.
COLE, HENLOW m Perry (Jones) & lived in Pickaway Twp, 1850s
    Minni - b 2 Feb 1857, Pickaway Twp.
COLE, JAMES H. - b 1831, VA; bl blacksmith. (Muhlenburg
Twp, 1860; Jackson Twp, 1870)
    Martha - bc 1851, OH; bl. (1870)
    Nancy - bc 1837, OH; bl servant. (1860)
    Robert - b 1870, Jackson Twp. bl. (1870)
COLE, OLLIE (f) - b. Sept 1888, OH. parents both b OH.
(Circleville, 1900)
COLE, ROBERT B. - b 1827, VA; bl blacksmith. m Mary A.
(_____). (Muhlenburg Twp, 1860; Circleville, 1870-1880)
    Mary A. - b 1833 or Jan 1838, VA; listed bl & mul.
    parents both b VA. (1860-1880)
    Alice - b 1859, Muhlenburg Twp. mul. (1860)
    Laura - bc 1867, Circleville; bl. (1870-1880)
    Mary - b 1852 or 1854, Muhlenburg Twp. bl. (1870-
    1880)
    Robert J. - b 1856, OH; worked in blacksmith shop. listed
    bl & mul. (1860-1880)

Roberta - b 1855 or 1857, OH; school teacher. listed
    bl & mul. (1860-1880)
Sarah A. - b Apr 1851, OH; dressmaker & school
    teacher. listed bl & mul. (1860-1880)
COLEMAN, ALFORD - bc 1842, MICH; bl laborer and porter. m
  Sarah (Turner). father b KY; mother b OH. (Circle-
  ville, 1860-1900) -- listed as Albert in 1870, b. 1839,
  OH; Alfred in 1880, b. 1846, Canada.
    Sarah (Turner) - b 1845 or 1852, OH; bl. father b
      Canada. (1870-1900)
    Alfred - b 2 Aug 1876, Circleville. bl. (1880)
    Catherine - b 21 May 1874, Circleville.
    Katie - bc 1873, Circleville. bl. (1880)
    Oliver - b 1870, Circleville. bl. (1870-1880)
    Surepta - b 1857, OH; d 28 July 1887, Circleville.
    William - b 20 Dec 1871, Circleville; d 2 Aug 1881,
      Circleville of spinal disease.
    William Allen - b 19 June 1869, Circleville; bl. (1880)
COLEMAN, ALONZO - b Jan 1879, VA. bl farm laborer.
  parents both b VA. (Jackson Twp, 1900)
COLEMAN, ANDREW B. - b Nov 1864, VA. bl minister. parents
  both b VA. m. Ona (____). (Circleville, 1900)
    Ona - b July 1868, VA. parents both b VA. (1900)
    Andrew H. - b 1900, Circleville. (1900)
    Anna - b May 1893, W VA. (1900)
    Cordelia - b. Jan 1886, W VA. (1900)
    Mary H. - b Jan 1891, PA. (1900)
    Ona G. - b Aug 1895, OH. (1900)
COLEMAN, JOHN - b Apr 1870, OH. bl barber. parents both b
  VA. m. Lizzie (____). (Circleville, 1900)
    Lizzie - b Aug 1876, OH. parents both b OH. (1900)
    John - b May 1895, OH. (1900)
COLES, ALWIDA (?) m Morris Garland & lived in Muhlenburg
  Twp, 1880s.
COLIER, REBECCA - b June 1854, OH. parents both b VA.
  (Circleville, 1900)
    Mary - b Aug 1884, OH. father b OH; mother b MO.
      (1900)
COLLIER, EDWARD - b 1844, MO; d 2 Mar 1894, Circleville of
  consumption. bl laborer. m Mary (____). (Circle-
  ville, 1870-1880)
    Mary - b 1829 or 1840, VA; bl. parents both b VA.
      (1870-1880)
COLLIER, GEORGE - b 1880, Circleville; d 8 Aug 1893, Cir-
  cleville of typhoid fever.
COLLINS, JAMES - b 1857 or 1862, Athens Co; d 8 Feb 1892,
  Circleville of brain fever. bl barber. m Louisa
  (Smith). (Circleville, 1870)
    John - b 7 Aug 1889, Circleville

COLLINS, JENNIE m Reuben Peterson & lived in Circleville, 1890s.

COLLINS, LILLIE (____) - b Sept 1871, OH. father b VA; mother b OH. m. Charles Collins, white man. (Circleville, 1900)

COLLINS, NETTIE - b Dec 1849, VA. bl washerwoman. parents both b VA. (Circleville, 1900)

COLLINS, OPLE - b Jan 1899, Circleville; d 12 May 1899, Circleville of cholera inflamation.

COLLINS, WILLIAM - b 1835, VA; bl laborer. m 1st, Ann E. (____); 2nd Mary (Turney). parents both b VA. (Circleville, 1860-1880)

 Ann E. - bc 1829, PA; bl. (1860)

 Mary (Turney) - b 1839, OH; d 14 Oct 1890, Circleville of paralysis. bl. parents both b OH. (1870-1880) -- censuses list b OH; death records list b Hagerstown, MD--

 Amanda - b 1858 or 1862, Circleville; listed bl & mul domestic servant. (1870-1880)

 Charles - b 20 June 1895, Circleville

 Emma - b 31 Mar 1876, Circleville. mul. (1880)

 Frank - bc 1872, Circleville. mul. (1880)

 Harriet - bc 1857, Circleville. bl. (1870) --may be Hattie listed below--

 Hattie - bc 1856, Circleville. bl cook. m James Combs. (Circleville, 1900)

 Hattie - b 1 Nov 1879, Circleville.

 Ida May - b 1854, Circleville. bl. m Daniel Hughes (1860-1870)

 James - b 1857 or 1862, -- see separate listing --

 Maggie - b 1869, Circleville; listed bl & mul. m Albert Chatman and lived in Wayne Twp, 1880s. (1870-1880)

 Marley E. - b 12 Apr 1878, Circleville; d 14 Sept 1878, Circleville.

 Mary - bc 1849, OH; d 2 Sept 1888, Wayne Twp. murdered. bl. (1860)

 Minnie - b 23 March 1874, Circleville. mul. (1880)

 Ordina - b 1880, Circleville. mul. (1880)

 Otis - bc 1858, Circleville. bl. (1860)

 Theodore - bc 1863 or 1865, Circleville. listed bl & mul. (1870-1880)

 William - bc 1858, Circleville. mul laborer. (1880)

 William - b 3 Dec 1871, Circleville.

 NANNA - b 1775, VA; mul parents both b VA. (1880)

COMBS, ELIZA m Alexander Rice & lived in Circleville, 1870s.

COMBS, JACOB and 1 male, 4 females lived in Scioto Twp,
 1830; with 2 males, 1 female in Jackson Twp, 1840.
COMBS, JAMES m Hattie (Collins) & lived in Circleville,
 1870s.
    Carrie - b 24 June 1874, Circleville.
COOK, CATHARINE - b 1799, OH; bl. (Circleville, 1870)
COOPER, AARON - b 1843, 1846 or 1849, OH; s/o John & Amelia
 Cooper. mul plasterer. m Lydia (_____). (Circleville,
 1880)
    Lydia - bc 1849, NC; mul. parents both b NC. (1880)
    George - bc 1875, Circleville; mul. (1880)
    Jane - b 1880, Circleville; mul. (1880)
    Mary - b 1 July 1870, Circleville; mul. (1880)
    William - bc 1872, Circleville; mul. (1880)
COOPER, EDWARD - b Jan 1850, VA. bl day laborer. parents
 both b VA. m. Mary (_____). (Circleville, 1900)
    Mary - b Oct 1859, OH. father b Canada; mother b VA.
     (1900)
    Charles - b Nov 1888, OH. (1900)
    Eddie - b Jan 1885, OH. (1900)
    Elmer - b Sept 1879, OH. (1900)
    Frank - b May 1889, OH. (1900)
    Fred - b 1892, Circleville; d 22 or 26 Apr 1898,
     Circleville of measles.
    George - b Aug 1876, OH. (1900)
    John - b Aug 1883, OH. (1900)
    Rozie - b Feb 1881, OH. (1900)
    Willis - b Oct 1877, OH. (1900)
COOPER, GEORGE - bc 1871, OH; bl. parents both b VA.
 (Circleville, 1880)
COOPER, JAMES lived in Circleville, 1880s
    Dora - b 29 Feb 1884, Circleville.
COOPER, JAMES m Rosa (Peterson) & lived in Circleville,
 1890s.
    James Charles - b 6 Feb 1897, Circleville; d 11 Feb
     1898, Circleville of croup.
COOPER, JOHN - b 1809, 1813 or 1820, VA; mul plasterer.
 parents both b VA. m. Amelia (_____). (Circleville,
 1860-1880)
    Amelia (also Milly) - b 1816, 1818 or 1820, VA; mul.
     parents both b VA. (1860-1880)
    Aaron - b 1843, 1846 or 1849, OH. --see separate
     listing--
    Alice - b 1858, Circleville. mul. (1860-1870)
    Eddie - b 1857, Circleville. mul. (1860)
    Eliza - bc 1871, OH; mul. (1880)
    Hoyt - bc 1874, OH; mul. (1880)

22

James - b 1855 or 1856, OH; mul farm laborer. (1860-1880)

Jane - b 24 Apr 1854, OH; d 9 Aug 1875, Circleville of childbed fever. mul housemaid. (1870)

John - b 1849, OH; mul laborer. (1860-1870)

Josephine - b 1851, OH; mul housemaid. m John Douglas & lived in Circleville, 1870s. (1860-1870)

Martha (also Mattie) - b 1865, Circleville. mul. (1870-1880)

Mary - b 1848, OH; mul. (1860)

Mary - b 1869, Circleville. mul. (1870)

COOPER, JOHN - bc 1852, OH; mul plasterer. parents both b VA. m Lucy (_____). (Circleville, 1880) --possibly John s/o John and Amelia--

Lucy - bc 1858, OH; bl. parents both b NC. (1880)

John, Jr. - b 1879, Circleville; bl. (1880)

COOPER, JOHN - b Mar 1860, OH. bl day laborer. parents both b OH. m. Sarah (Tann). (Circleville, 1900)

Sarah - b Oct 1857, OH. bl. father b Canada; mother b VA. (1900)

Ethel - b Feb 1892, Circleville. (1900)

Laverta - b 30 May 1891, Circleville. (1900)

Margaret - b Sept 1893, Circleville. (1900)

Sarah - b. 1882, Circleville. (1900)

COOPER, JOHN m Margarette (Inyers) & lived in Salt Creek Twp, 1890s.

Ada Belle - b 14 Sept 1895, Salt Creek Twp.

COOPER, JOSEPH - b 1841; d 19 Nov 1894, Circleville of consumption. m. laborer.

COOPER, JOSEPHINE - b Feb 1880, Circleville; d 30 Sept 1880, Circleville of consumption.

COOPER, RHODA - b 1833 or 1835, OH or KY; d 13 Jan 1899, Washington Twp, Infirmary of asthma. bl pauper. parents both b VA. (Circleville, 1870-1880)

Estella - b 1863, Circleville; d 2 June 1881, Circleville of consumption. bl. (1870-1880)

Nancy - b 1865 or 1867, Circleville. bl. (1870-1880)

COOPER, WILLIAM - bc 1871, OH; bl. parents both b OH. (Circleville, 1880)

COPELAND, NANNA - b 1867 or 1868, Circleville; d 31 Jan 1885, Circleville of consumption.

COPELAND, WASHINGTON - bc 1804, VA; bl. m Martha (_____). (Circleville, 1860)

Martha - bc 1827, VA; listed bl & mul. parents both b VA. (Circleville, 1860-1880)

Elmira (also Elmyra) - b 1852, VA; listed bl & mul. (1860-1870)

James - b 1848, CA; listed bl & mul laborer. (1860-1870)

Josephine - b 1855 or 1857, VA; listed bl & mul. (1860-1870)

Rosanna - bc 1857, VA; bl. (1860)

Virginia - b 1854 or 1855, VA; listed bl & mul school teacher. (1860-1880)

son - b 8 May 1868, Circleville.

COTTON, HETTY - bc 1832, NC; mul. (Circleville, 1850)

COX, ALBERT - bc 1834, OH; mul. (Wayne Twp, 1860)

COX, DOLLIE m John P. Redman & lived in Washington Twp, 1890s.

COX, ROBERT - bc 1827, OH; mul farmer. m Dorothea (_____). (Wayne Twp, 1860)

Dorothea - bc 1831, NC; mul. (1860)

Charles E. - bc 1855, Wayne Twp. mul. (1860)

Mary A. - bc 1857, Wayne Twp. mul. (1860)

CRANE, WILLIAM - bc 1837, VA; bl farm laborer. parents both b VA. m Alice A. (_____). (Monroe Twp, 1880)

Alice A. - bc 1850, KAN; bl. parents both b KAN. (1880)

Addison - bc 1872, OH; bl. (1880)

John L. - bc 1865, OH; bl. (1880)

Sarah L. - bc 1868, OH; bl. (1880)

CRAWFORD, MARGARET - bc 1858, OH; mul school teacher. father b KY; mother b VA. (Circleville, 1880)

CRIGER, NANCY m George Nickel & lived in Deer Creek, 1870s.

CROCKETT, OTTO - bc 1879, Weiland; d 5 Feb 1897, Washington Twp, Infirmary of consumption.

CROMLEY, THAD E. m Mary R. (Millar) & lived in Harrison Twp, 1870s.

Charles Edward - b 1 Oct 1872, Harrison Twp.

CROUSE, JANE - bc 1836, OH; bl house servant. (Circleville, 1870)

CROUT, ELIZABETH - bc 1868, OH; mul. (Muhlenburg Twp, 1870)

CRUM, EDWARD and wife lived in Washington Twp, 1820.

CURTIS, GEORGE - bc 1800, VA; bl grocer. (Circleville, 1860)

Alonzo - bc 1846, OH; bl. (1860)

William A. - bc 1836, OH; bl. (1860)

CURTISS, LINA - bc 1859, OH; bl. (Harrison Twp, 1870)

CURTISS, THOMAS - bc 1821, VA; bl farm laborer. m Terusy (_____). (South Bloomfield, 1860)

Terusy - bc 1840, OH; bl. (1860)

Amanda J. - bc 1858, OH. bl. (1860)

Augitruce - b 1860, South Bloomfield. bl. (1860)

Rosetta - bc 1856, OH; bl. (1860)

DADE, ALBERT - b Jan 1847, VA; bl laborer. parents both b
    VA. (Circleville, 1880-1900)
        Frederick - bc 1854, VA; bl laborer. parents both
            b VA. (1880)
        Lizzie - b May 1861, OH; mul. father b OH; mother b
            NC. (1880-1900)
        Nellie D. - b Oct 1872, OH. hair dresser. (1900)
        Nora - b Mar 1889, OH. both parents b OH. (1900)
DADE, EDITH A. m William A. Jones & lived in Circleville,
    1890s.
DADE, ETHEL - b 1884, Circleville; d 27 Nov 1894, Circle-
    ville of typhus fever.
DADE, FRANCES m Albert Smith & lived in Jackson Twp, 1870s.
DADE, GEORGE D. - bc 1856, VA; bl white washer. parents
    both b VA. m Delia (Miles). (Circleville, 1880)
        Delia - bc 1853, OH; bl. father b VA; mother b OH.
            (1880)
        Cornelia J. - b 2 May 1877, OH; bl. (1880)
        Edbert - bc 1871, OH; bl. (1880)
        George W. - bc 1876, OH; bl. (1880)
        James H. - b 1880, Circleville. bl. (1880)
        Rebecca - bc 1868, OH; bl. (1880)
DADE, GEORGE - b Mar 1873, OH. bl day laborer. parents
    both b OH. m. Billie (____). (Circleville, 1900)
        Billie - b Aug 1876, OH. parents both b OH. (1900)
DADE, GODFREY - bc 1830, VA; bl bootmaker. parents both b
    VA. m Martha (____). (Circleville, 1880)
        Martha - bc 1832, VA; mul. parents both b VA. (Cir-
            cleville, 1880)
        Mary - bc 1860, VA; mul. m Frank Stevens & lived in
            Circleville, 1870s. (1880)
        Mattie - bc 1862, VA; mul. (1880)
DADE, JOSHUA - b Feb 1801, VA. bl. parents both b VA.
    (Circleville, 1900)
DADE, MAGGIE - b Feb 1864, OH. bl. parents both b OH.
    (Circleville, 1900)
        Edith - b Sept 1882, OH. parents both b VA. (1900)
        Elmer - b Oct 1891, OH. father b VA; mother b OH.
            (1900)
        Lloyd - b Sept 1899, OH. parents both b OH. (1900)
        Susan - b Nov 1890, OH. parents both b VA. (1900)
DADE, SHIRLEY - b 1887, Circleville; d 11 Mar 1899, Circle-
    ville of spinal trouble.
DALBLEY, JOSEPH - b 1793, VA; d 24 Sept 1876, Darby Twp of
    old age. widower. farmer.
DALTON, DAVID - b 1816, 1824 or 1829, KY; listed bl & mul
    laborer. m Catherine (Peterson). (Circleville, 1860-
    1880)

Catherine - b 1831, 1835 or 1839, VA; bl. parents
both b VA. (1860-1880)
Dayton - b 15 June 1869, Circleville.
Edward - b 1869, Circleville; listed bl & mul.
(1870-1880) -- 1880 census lists age as 8 --
Frances - bc 1862, OH; mul. (1880)
Freddie - bc 1876, Circleville; mul. (1880)
George - b 1860, Circleville; bl. (1860)
John - bc 1858, Circleville; d 30 Dec 1883, Circle-
ville of consumption. bl. (1860-1870)
Joseph - bc 1856, Circleville; bl. (1860)
Marshall - b 1861, Circleville; listed bl & mul.
(1870-1880) --see separate listing--
Mary - bc 1864, Circleville; bl. (1870)
Pricilla - b 1851, OH; bl. (1870)
Thomas - b 1866, Circleville; listed bl & mul.
(1870-1880)
William - b 1869, Circleville; bl. (1870)
DALTON, DAVID m Susan (Hunter) & lived in Circleville,
1870s.
daughter - b 23 July 1875, Circleville.
DALTON, FRANK - b Nov 1860, OH. parents both b OH. (Cir-
cleville, 1900)
Bertha M - b Feb 1892, OH. (1900)
Charles E. - b Sept 1898, OH. (1900)
DALTON, LUTHER - b 1831 or 1835, OH; bl laborer. m Matilda
(_____). (Circleville, 1860-1870)
Matilda - b 1831, 1836 or 1840, OH; bl. (1860-1880)
Edward - bc 1870, Circleville; bl. (1880)
Ellen - b 1858; bl house servant. (1880) - 2nd
listing as living independently, with father b VA;
mother b OH.
Francis - b 1856 or 1858, Circleville; bl. (1860-
1870)
Josephine - bc 1862, Circleville; bl. (1870)
Matilda - b 1860, Circleville. bl. (1860)
Ora - bc 1873, Circleville; bl. (1880)
Sarah J. - b 1855, Circleville; bl. (1860-1870) --
see separate listing--
DALTON, MARSHALL - b 1861, Circleville; s/o David and
Catherine (Peterson) Dalton. m Amanda (Parsons) & lived
in Circleville, 1880s.
Sarah - b 24 Dec 1885, Circleville.
DALTON, ORA R. - b July 1897, Circleville; d 11 March 1898,
Circleville of spinal trouble.
DALTON, SARAH lived in Circleville, 1870s. (Circleville,
1880)
Mary - b 18 Feb 1875, Circleville d/o Sarah Dalton
and Joseph Redman. bl. (1880)

DALTON, WILLIAM - b Oct 1857, OH. bl day laborer. father
    b KY; mother b VA. m Amanda (_____). (Circleville,
    1900)
        Amanda - b Sept 1852, OH. father b VA; mother b NC.
        (1900)
DANGERFIELD, WILLIAM M. and 1 male, 2 females lived in
    Circleville, 1840.
DARING, ARNOLD m Catherine (_____) & lived in Circleville,
    1870s.
        Louis - b 24 July 1870, Circleville.
DAVID, FRANCES m Albert Smith & lived in Circleville,
    1870s.
DAVIDSON, MARY - b 1871; d 23 Mar 1891, Circleville.
DAVIDSON, PINFORD (?) - b 1840, NC. bl barber. m
    Josephine (_____). (Circleville, 1900)
        Josephine - b Nov 1857, MICH. parents both b VA.
        (1900)
DAVIS, ANNA - bc 1835, VA; bl. (Harrison Twp, 1870)
DAVIS, ASA m Lucretia (Brown) & lived in Muhlenburg Twp,
    1880s.
        Laury - b 17 Apr 1881, Muhlenburg Twp.
DAVIS, BIRDY - b 1882, OH. bl house servant. parents both
    b OH. (Circleville, 1900)
DAVIS, EDGAR - bc 1851, OH; bl farm laborer. (Jackson Twp,
    1870)
        John - bc 1849, OH; bl. (1870)
DAVIS, ELIZABETH m James Redmond & lived in Harrison Twp,
    1870s.
DAVIS, EUGENE - bc 1866, OH; bl. father b OH; mother b NC.
    (Circleville, 1880)
DAVIS, EZRA m Louisa (Brown) & lived in Monroe Twp, 1880s
        Arwill A. - b 26 Nov 1883, Monroe Twp.
DAVIS, HENRY - b 1823 or 1828, VA; bl farmer. parents both
    b VA. m Nancy (Stewart). (Harrison Twp, 1870; Scioto
    Twp, 1880)
        Nancy - b 1830, VA; bl. parents both b VA. (1870-
        1880)
        Amanda - b 1859 or 1864, VA; bl. (1870-1880)
        Anderson - bc 1854, VA; bl farm laborer. (1870)
        Arthur W. - b 28 Dec 1871, Harrison Twp.
        Eliza - bc 1856, VA; bl worked by week. (1870-1880)
            --2nd listing for Harrison Twp, 1880
        Margaret - bc 1852, VA; bl domestic servant. m Henry
            Walker & lived in Harrison Twp, 1870s. (Harrison
            Twp, 1870)
        Phillip - b 1858 or 1860, VA; bl farm laborer.
            (1870-1880)
        William - b 1849, VA; farm laborer. (1870-1880)
        SARITY - bc 1795, VA; bl. (1870)

27

DAVIS, JOSEPHINE m Michael Harris & lived in Deer Creek
Twp, 1870s.
DAVIS, LLOYD - b Aug 1861, OH. bl day laborer. parents
both b W VA. m. Maggie (_____). (Williamsport, 1900)
Maggie - b Sept 1855, OH. parents both b OH. (1900)
DAVIS, LUCY m Henry Fowler & lived in Jackson Twp, 1870s
and 1880s.
DAVIS, MARY m Jacob E. Redman & lived in Circleville,
1880s.
DAVIS, PHILIP m Charity (_____) & lived in Harrison Twp,
1840s.
Ann - b 1849, Hardy Co, W VA.; d 25 Feb 1874, Har-
rison Twp of dropsy.
DAVIS, PHILIP - b 1860, VA; s/o Henry & Nancy Davis. bl.
m Eliza (_____). (1900)
Eliza - b 1857 or 1858, VA. bl servant. parents
both b VA. (1900)
DAVIS, RICHARD - bc 1781, VA; bl farm laborer. (Jackson
Twp, 1860)
Mary - bc 1843, VA; mul. (1860)
DAY, GODFREY - bc 1813, VA; bl laborer. m Martha (_____).
(Circleville, 1870)
Martha - bc 1829, VA; bl. (1870)
Joshua - bc 1857, VA; bl. (1870)
Martha - bc 1859, VA; bl. (1870)
Mary - bc 1857, VA; bl. (1870)
DAY, HARRIET m Elias Bird & lived in Circleville, 1870s.
DAY, NORSEY - b 1855; d 1875, Circleville of pneumonia.
DAYSON, JEREMIAH - bc 1801, OH; bl carpenter. m Keziah
(_____). (Scioto Twp, 1870)
Keziah - bc 1810, VA; bl. (1870)
DEARTH, ASA - bc 1816, OH; mul pumpmaker. (Circleville,
1870)
Alexander - bc 1853, OH; mul farm laborer. (1870)
Charles - bc 1848, OH; mul laborer. (1870)
Harriet M. - bc 1856, OH. mul. (1870)
Jacob - bc 1852, OH; mul worker in dyeing mills.
(1870)
Mary J. - bc 1856, OH; mul housemaid. (1870)
DECKER, ELIJAH - bc 1837, OH; mul barber. m Louisa
(_____). (Circleville, 1860)
Louisa - bc 1836, OH; mul. (1860)
Endless J. - b 1860, Circleville. mul. (1860)
DECKER, ISAAC - b 1822 or 1825, OH; bl laborer. m Rhoda
(_____). (Circleville, 1860-1870)
Rhoda - b 1822 or 1829, OH; bl. (1860-1870)
Edward - bc 1848, OH; bl. (1860)
Emma - bc 1861, Circleville. bl. (1870)

Francis - bc 1855, OH; bl. (1860)
Frank - bc 1856, OH; bl. (1870)
George W. - bc 1844, OH; bl laborer. (1860)
Jane - bc 1846, OH; bl. (1860)
John - bc 1863, Circleville. bl. (1870)
Laura - bc 1849, OH; bl. (1860)
Lewis - b 1859, OH; bl. (1860)
Perry - bc 1849, OH. bl. (1870)
Polly - b 1853, OH; bl. (1860-1870)
Robert - b 25 Dec 1857, Muhlenburg Twp. bl. (1860-1870)
William H. - bc 1845, OH; bl laborer. (1860) --see separate listing--
DECKER, ISETTA - b July 1870, Circleville; d Feb 1871, Circleville.
DECKER, ISRAEL - b 1829, VA; d 1 July 1895, Circleville of heart trouble. married laborer.
DECKER, JANE - bc 1849, OH; bl housemaid. (Circleville, 1870)
DECKER, JOHN m Dinah (_____) & lived in Circleville, 1860s. daughter - b 12 July 1868.
DECKER, LAURA m Bird Shaffer & lived in Circleville, 1870s.
DECKER, PHEBE - bc 1818, OH; mul. (Circleville, 1850)
Bartman - bc 1831, OH; mul barber. (1850)
David - bc 1837, OH; mul. (1850)
Elijah - bc 1832, OH; bl barber. (1850) --see separate listing--
James - bc 1846, OH; mul. (1850)
DECKER, WILLIAM and 2 males, 3 females in Circleville, 1830; with 3 males and 1 female in Circleville, 1840.
DECKER, WILLIAM m Roxanna (Turney) & lived in Circleville, 1870s.
Armina - b 5 July 1873, Circleville.
DECKER, _____ - b 1828; d 26 Sept 1876 of typhoid fever.
DELAY, ENOCH and 1 male, 3 females in Pickaway County, 1820.
DELAY, ROSEANNAH - b 1795, MD; bl. lived with 1 male, 3 females in Salt Creek Twp, 1830; with 2 males, 2 females in Salt Creek Twp, 1840. --prob. widow of Enoch--
DENES, MIRANDA m Thomas Davis & lived in Scioto Twp, 1880s.
DENNING, CYRUS - bc 1856, VA; bl farmhand. parents both b VA. (Deer Creek, 1880)
DERVIN (also spelled DIRVIN, DURBIN)
DERVIN, BERTHA - b 1853, Circleville; d 10 June 1878, Circleville of consumption.
DERVIN, KESIAH - b 1858; d 12 June 1891, Circleville of tumor. married.

DERVIN, WILLIAM - b Aug 1843, TENN; mul hosler & laborer.
parents both b TENN. m Parthena (Johnson) (Circleville, 1870-1900)
2nd listing - b.1840, NC; wood carrier. (Circleville,
1880)
    Parthena - bc 1849, NC; mul. (1870-1900)
    Anna - b Dec 1872, Circleville. m George Turner &
       lived in Circleville, 1890s. (sp. Durbin) (1900)
    George Delano - b 2 Dec 1877, Circleville; d 8 July
       1878, Circleville of cholera. (sp. Derwin)
    Harry, Jr. - b 5 Apr 1874, Circleville. (sp. Durbin)
       (1880-1900)
    William - b 18 Apr 1874, Circleville.
DICK, HARRIET - bc 1820, VA; mul. (Circleville, 1850)
DICKERSON, ALVINA m William Garnes & lived in Circleville,
1870s.
DICKERSON, ARTHUR - m Sarah J. (Lucus) and lived in Circle-
ville, 1870s.
    Leroy - b Nov 1874, Circleville.
DICKERSON, ARTHUR - b Mar 1850, VA. bl plasterer. parents
both b VA. m Bertha (Cole) & lived in Circleville.
(Circleville, 1900)
    Bertha - b Sept 1854, VA. parents both b VA. (1900)
    Ethel - b 30 Oct 1891, Circleville.
DICKERSON, C. WAYMAN - b 1878, Circleville; d 29 July 1879,
Circleville.
DICKERSON, ELLEN - bc 1815, MD; bl. (Circleville, 1850)
DICKERSON, FANNIE P. m Joseph P. Norman & lived in Circle-
ville, 1880s.
DICKERSON, GARLAND - b 1801 or 1809, VA; bl farm laborer
and shoe maker. parents both b VA. m Harriet (_____).
(Circleville, 1860-1880)
    Harriet - b 1806, VA; bl. parents both b VA. (1860-
       1880)
    Arthur - b 1849, 1850 or 1852, OH; bl laborer and
       plasterer. (1860-1880) --see separate listing--
    Harriet - bc 1843, OH; bl. (1860)
    John - b 1837, 1838 or 1839, OH; listed bl & mul
       plasterer. (1860-1880) --see separate listing--
    Sarah - bc 1845, OH; bl. m George Blake 12 Feb 1861,
       Pickaway Co. (1860)
    Walter - bc 1840, OH; bl farm laborer. (1860)
DICKERSON, JOHN J. - b 1837, 1838, or 1839, OH; s/o Garland
and Harriet Dickerson. listed bl & mul plasterer and
clergyman. m Mary E. (Ward, Ware or Mason). (Circleville, 1870-1880)
    Mary E. - b 1842, OH. listed bl & mul. parents both
      b VA. (1870-1880) --various birth records for
      the children list the various last names for Mary

30

Clarence - b 15 Nov 1878, Circleville.

Egbert - bc 1872, Circleville; mul. (1880)

Garland - b 30 Sept 1868, Circleville. listed bl &
mul. (1870-1880)

Harriet - b 1864, Circleville; listed bl & mul.
(1870-1880)

Jessie Catherine - b 15 Dec 1875, Circleville. mul.
(1880)

John - b 3 Oct 1863, Circleville; d 4 Oct 1865, Circleville of sore throat.

Rufus A. - b 14 Mar 1877, Circleville. mul. (1880)

DICKERSON, MARY - b June 1856, OH. bl domestic. father b
PA; mother b OH. (Circleville, 1900)

DICKERSON, MORO - bc 1817, VA; bl laborer. mother b VA.
(Circleville, 1880)

Darcy - bc 1853, OH; bl. (1880)

DICKSON, ARTHUR - bc 1853, OH; bl worker on turnpike.
(Muhlenburg Twp, 1870)

DICKSON, ELLEN - b 1807, MD; bl. (Circleville, 1860-1870)

DIXON, ELLEN - b 18 Oct 1873; d 28 Aug 1875, Washington
Twp. Infirmary of pneumonia.

DIXON, RICHARD - b May 1880, TENN. bl servant. parents
both b TENN. (Harrison Twp, 1900)

DIXON, RUTH A. - b July 1898; d 2 Mar 1899, Circleville of
lung fever.

DONALDSON, MARY A. - b 1824, Noble Co, PA; d 30 Dec 1898 of
dropsy. widow.

DORASS, RICHARD - bc 1783, VA; bl farmer. m Larice
(_____). (Jackson Twp, 1840-1850)

Larice - bc 1777, VA; bl. (1850)

DOUGLAS (also DOUGLASS)

DOUGLAS, ADAM - bc 1810, VA; bl laborer. m Eliza (_____).
(Circleville, 1860-1900)

Eliza - b Jan 1811, 1819 or 1820, NC; bl. parents
both b NC. (1860- 1900)

Elisabeth J. - b 1864, OH; bl. (1860-1870)

Frances - bc 1855, OH; bl housemaid. (1870)

James - bc 1843, OH; bl. (1860)

John - bc 1847, OH; bl. (1860) --see separate
listing--

Lavita - b 1860, Circleville; bl. (1860)

Louis - bc 1856, OH; bl. (1860)

Marion - b 1852 or 1853, OH; bl laborer. (1860-1870)
--see separate listing--

Melinda I. (also sp. Malinda) - b 21 May 1857, Jackson Twp; bl. (1860)

Rebecca - b 1849, OH; bl housemaid. (1860-1870)

31

Sarah - b 1855, OH; bl. (1860) --see separate
    listing--
Tabitha - bc 1845, OH; bl. m Barton Hill & lived in
    Muhlenburg and Scioto Twps, 1870s-1880s. (1860)
    -listed as Ellen in two birth records of children-
Virtio - bc 1859, OH; bl. (1870)
DOUGLAS, ALICE - b 1884, Wayne Twp; d 3 Nov 1887, Wayne Twp
of lung fever. --prob. d/o John & Nancy (Chapman)
Douglas.
DOUGLAS, CECIL - b May 1884, OH. bl farm laborer. parents
both b OH. (Darby Twp, 1900)
DOUGLAS, CORA E. m A. G. Hubbard & lived in Circleville,
1880s.
DOUGLAS, ELIZA - bc 1842, Circleville; d 13 Mar 1870, Cir-
cleville of lung fever.
DOUGLAS, ELLEN m William Peterson & lived in Circleville,
1880s.
DOUGLAS, HATTIE - bc 1865, Circleville; d 13 Jan 1870,
Circleville of lung fever.
DOUGLAS, JAMES - bc 1858, Circleville; d 14 Feb 1870,
Circleville of lung fever.
DOUGLAS, JOHN - bc 1846, OH; bl hosler. m Nancy (Chapman).
(Circleville, 1880)
    Nancy - bc 1855, OH; mul. parents both b VA. (1880)
    Edna R. - b 5 Jan 1882, Wayne Twp.
    Myrtel - b 1880, Circleville; mul. (1880)
DOUGLAS, JOHN - bc 1848, OH bl stable worker. father b OH;
mother b VA. (Circleville, 1880)
DOUGLAS, JOHN m Jacqueline (Cooper) & lived in Circleville,
1870s.
    George - b 20 Feb 1872, Circleville.
DOUGLAS, MARION - bc 1855, OH; mul farm laborer. parents
both b VA. m Hattie (Hargrave). (Circleville, 1860-
1880)
    Hattie - bc 1858, OH; mul. parents both b OH.
    (1880)
    Arthur - b 30 Apr 1888, Circleville
    Charlie - b 20 Feb 1885, Circleville
    Charles - b 1880, Circleville. mul. (1880)
    Estella - b 20 Feb 1890, Circleville. (1900)
    Gracey - bc 1877, Circleville. mul. (1880)
    Lillie - b 12 Sept 1875, Circleville
    Minnie - bc 1874, Circleville. mul. (1880)
DOUGLAS, MARY JANE m John McMan & lived in Circleville,
1870s.
DOUGLAS, PARTHENA - bc 1829, VA; housemaid. (Circleville,
1870)
    Ida - bc 1862, OH; bl. (1870)

DOUGLAS, SARAH - b 1855, OH; bl housemaid. (Circleville, 1870)
    Hattie - b 10 Mar 1870, Circleville.
DOWNEY, JENNIE m George Henderson & lived in Circleville, 1880s.
DRUFALL, NEWTON - b Jan 1860, VA. bl farm laborer. parents both b. VA. m. Susa M. (____). (Scioto Twp, 1900)
    Susa M. - b Apr 1878, PA. father b NC; mother b PA. (1900)
DUKE, LAFAYETTE - bc 1851, W VA; bl worker in livery stable. parents both b W VA. (Circleville, 1880)
    Sarah J. - bc 1837, W VA; mul. parents both b W VA. (1880)
DUNLAP, CHARLES H. m Mary E. (McGath) & lived in Walnut and Washington Twps, 1880s.
    Rosa E. - b 1 Dec 1880, Walnut Twp.
    Vina A. - b 12 Feb 1882, Washington Twp.
DUNNING, ELIZA of Champaign Co. m Powhatan B. Hatter of Wayne Twp & lived in Wayne Twp, 1880s.
DUNS, ELIZA m Thomas Runyon & lived in Harrison Twp, 1870s.
DURHAM, CAROLINE m Alex Pattent & lived in Circleville, 1870s.
DURHAM, MARY m Presley Wingo & lived in Darby Twp, 1870s.
DUTTEN, PERCILLA m Andrew Turner & lived in Circleville, 1880s.
DYSON (also DISEN)
DYSON, ISAAC - b 1836 or 1842, OH; bl farm laborer. parents both b OH. m Miranda (Turney). (Harrison Twp, 1870; Walnut Twp, 1880)
    Miranda b 1845, 1847, or June 1850, OH; bl housekeeper. parents both b OH. (1870-1880; Circleville, 1900)
    Albert G. - b 22 Feb 1874, Circleville; bl. (1880)
    Birdie - b 12 Jan 1879, Circleville.
    Finley - b Feb 1879, OH. bl day laborer. (1900)
    Flora B. - bc 1867, OH; bl. (1870-1880)
    Harry - b Mar 1871, OH. bl day laborer. (1900)
    Isaac W. - b 1869, Harrison Twp. bl. (1870-1880)
    James H. - bc 1871, OH; bl. (1880)
    John - b Feb 1866, OH; bl day laborer. (1880-1900)
    Johnny - b 1870, Harrison Twp; bl. (1870)
    Myrtal - b 5 Jan 1885, Circleville.
    Sherman - b 24 May 1882, Circleville.
    Virtue - bc 1878, OH; bl. (1880)

EARLY, JAMES - bc 1788, VA. freed 5 Nov 1811, Franklin Co. VA. lived in Circleville, 1828.

EDWARDS, CHARLES - b 1843 or 1846, OH; d 10 Mar 1872, Circleville of consumption. bl laborer. m Delila (_____).
(Circleville, 1860-1870)
    Delila - b 30 Apr 1849, Pike Co; d 18 July 1878, Circleville of consumption. bl. (1870)
    William - b 1869, Circleville; bl. (1870-1880)
EDWARDS, GLEN - bc 1843, OH; bl. (Muhlenburg Twp, 1850)
EDWARDS, HENRY and 2 females lived in Circleville, 1840.
EDWARDS, JAMES - bc 1840, OH; farmhand. (Muhlenburg Twp, 1860)
    Thomas - bc 1848, OH; bl (1860)
EDWARDS, JANE - bc 1820, OH; bl. (Circleville, 1880)
    Susie - b May 1871, OH; bl housekeeper. (Circleville, 1880-1900) --may be c/o Charles & Delila because Jane was taking care of her and William in 1880)
EDWARDS, JESSIE m M. J. (Sedars) & lived in Monroe Twp, 1880s.
    Phrina - b 15 July 1881, Monroe Twp.
EDWARDS, LOUIS - bc 1848, OH. bl. (Jackson Twp, 1850)
ELIR, SAMUEL- b Mar 1891, OH. mother b OH. (Circleville, 1900)
ELKIN, JANE - b Nov 1825, VA. bl. parents both b VA. (Circleville, 1900)
EMERINE, JACKSON - bc 1836, MD; bl miller. (Wayne Twp, 1860)
ERVING, JACOB m Matilda (Jackson) & lived in Circleville, 1870s.
    Minerva L. - b 18 May 1875, Circleville.
ESTELL, SCOTT - b 17 Sept 1871, OH; d 28 Jan 1872, Ross Co. of fits.
EVANS, CATHERINE m Jack Williams & lived in Circleville, 1870s.
EVANS, MARTHA E. m Robert Julius & lived in Pickaway Twp, 1870s.
EVANS, ROBERT and 7 males, 5 females lived in Pickaway Twp, 1840.
EWING, LAURA m Henry Kelley & lived in Circleville, 1870s.
EWING, LUCY - bc 1857, VA; blk domestic servant. (Circleville, 1880)
    Harry - bc 1876, OH; bl. (1880)
    Sarah - b 1880, Circleville; bl. (1880)
EWING, MARY M. - b 1841, Lee Co, VA; d 17 Sept 1889, Circleville of stomach disease. married.

FALLS, S.H. - bc 1838, OH; bl plasterer. m Mary (_____).
(Circleville, 1860)

34

Mary - bc 1841, OH; bl. (1860)
Alice A. - bc 1858, OH; bl. (1860)
Emma - bc 1857, OH; bl. (1860)
Margaret J. - b 1860, Circleville. bl. (1860)
FARN, MARY - bc 1855, OH; bl waitress. (Circleville, 1870)
FEES, MILES - bc 1826, VA; mul farmer. (Circleville Twp, 1850)
FERGUSON, CHARLES - bc 1865, OH; bl apprentice blacksmith. father b VA; mother b OH. (Circleville, 1880)
Geneva - bc 1869, OH; bl. parents both b OH. (1880)
FERGUSON, JAMES - bc 1843, OH; bl laborer. m Mary Ann (____). (Circleville Twp, 1860)
Willie - b 3 Sept 1867, Circleville.
FIDLER, EDWARD and 2 males, 4 females lived in Washington Twp, 1820.
FIELDS, GEORGIA - bc 1862, OH; bl servant. (Circleville Twp, 1880)
FIELDS, GEORGIA - b Pickaway Twp; d 5 Mar 1878, Pickaway Twp of typhoid fever. --may be second listing of "Jane" below--
FIELDS, MILES - b 1820 or 1830, VA; listed bl & mul black-smith. parents both b VA. m. Jane (____). (Pickaway Twp, 1860-1880)
Jane - b 1813 or 1815, VA; listed bl & mul. father b Scotland; mother b VA. (1860-1880)
George M. - bc 1864, Pickaway Twp; bl farmer. (1880)
Jane - b 14 Jan 1855, OH; d 3 Feb 1878, Pickaway Twp.
Jane - b 1861, Pickaway Twp. bl. (1880)
Mary J. - b 1880, Pickaway Twp. mul. (1880)
Robena A. - bc 1856, OH; d 11 Sept 1878, Pickaway Twp of typhoid. mul. (1860)
Susan A. - bc 1855, OH; mul. (1860)
William - b 1858, Pickaway Twp; listed bl & mul farmer. (1860-1880) --see separate listing--
FIELDS, THOMAS - bc 1824, VA; bl farmhand. (Monroe Twp, 1860) --2nd listing - bc 1835; day laborer. (Muhlen-burg Twp, 1860)
Fawny - bc 1850, OH. bl. (1860)
FIELDS, WILLIAM - b Mar 1851, OH. bl farm laborer. parents both b VA. m. Ida (Barnet) 3 Jan 1888, Pickaway Co. (Jackson Twp, 1880-1900)
Ida - b Aug 1870, OH. parents both b OH. (1900)
Bernice Idell- b 28 Aug 1892, Jackson Twp. (1900)
Capitola - b 7 Jan 1888, Circleville. (1900)
Donald - b 1 Mar 1890, Circleville. (1900)
FISSELL, SARAH A. m William G. Kirkendall & lived in Darby Twp, 1870s.
FODEL, LEUTISHA - bc 1838, OH; mul. (Wayne Twp, 1850)

FOSTER, GEORGE - b 1810, 1820 or 1825, VA; d 25 Apr 1890,
   Circleville of dropsy. listed bl & mul laborer. m 1st,
   Minerva (____); 2nd Eveline (_____). (Circleville,
   1850-1880)
      Minerva - b 1821, 1822 or 1824, VA; bl. (1850-1860)
      2nd listing b 1824, VA; domestic. mul. (Wayne Twp,
         1860)
      Eveline - b 1830, NC; bl. (1870-1880)
      Charles W. - bc 1859, NC; bl. (1870)
      Cornelius - b 1859 or 1861, OH; bl laborer. (1870-
         1880)
      James - b 1866, Circleville; bl. (1870-1880)
      Nelson - b 1838, OH; bl. (1850) --see separate
         listing--
FOSTER, NELSON - b 1838, OH; s/o George & Minerva Foster.
   m Elisabeth (_____). (Circleville, 1860)
      Elisabeth - bc 1841, OH; bl. (1860)
FOSTER, RICHARD lived in Circleville, 1860s.
      infant - b 1865; d 19 Aug 1867, Circleville of summer
         complaint.
FOWLER, ELIZA - b 1844; d 15 Dec 1884, Jackson Twp. of
   consumption.
FOWLER, HENRY - bc 1845, VA; bl farmer. parents both b VA.
   m Lucy (Davis). (Walnut Twp, 1880)
      Lucy - bc 1844, VA; bl. parents both b VA. (1880)
      America - bc 1869, VA; bl. (1880)
      Callie - bc 1868, VA; bl. (1880)
      Charles W. - bc 1875, VA; bl. (1880)
      Floid - bc 1873, VA; bl. (1880)
      Francis - bc 1866, Walnut Twp. bl. (1880)
      Hattie - b 25 Jan 1881, Walnut Twp.
      Henryetta - b 25 Nov 1877, Jackson Twp. bl. (1880)
      Julius Hunter - b 28 Dec 1882, Walnut Twp.
      Mattie - bc 1865, VA; bl. (1880)
      Sandes (male) - bc 1870, VA; bl. (1880)
FOWLER, JUNE - bc 1871, Jackson Twp; d 20 Apr 1885, Jackson
   Twp of measles.
FOWLER, MARY - b 31 July 1875, VA; d 3 Apr 1876, Circle-
   ville of diarrhea.
FOWLER, ROBERT - bc 1852, VA; bl farm laborer. parents
   both b VA. m Frances (Whittaker). (Muhlenburg Twp,
   1880)
      Frances - bc 1853, Smyth Co, VA; d 27 Aug 1880, Muh-
         lenburg Twp. of pneumonia. bl. parents both b
         VA. (1880) --2nd listing - d 17 Aug 1881,
         Muhlenburg Twp. of consumption.
      Alice H. or R. - b 27 Oct 1878, Muhlenburg Twp; bl.
         (1880)

John H. - bc 1877, OH; bl. (1880)
Martha A. - bc 1873, VA; bl. (1880)
Mary V. - bc 1872, VA; bl. (1880)
William A. - b 5 May 1880, Muhlenburg Twp. bl.
   (1880)
ELIZA - bc 1824, VA; parents both b VA. bl. (1880)
FOWLER, ROBERT m Sallie (Bundy) & lived in Muhlenburg Twp,
   1880s. --possibly same as above--
   Dotty - b 13 Oct 1881, Muhlenburg Twp.
   Ellen - b 3 July 1883, Muhlenburg Twp.
FOWLER, SOLOMON - bc 1844, W VA; bl farm laborer. m
   Elizabeth (_____). (Scioto Twp, 1870)
   Elizabeth - bc 1845, W VA; bl. (1870)
   David - bc 1869, Circleville; bl. (1870)
   Sarah - bc 1867, OH; bl. (1870)
FOWLER, WILLIAM. - bc 1868; d 20 Feb 1885, Jackson Twp. of
   burns.
FOX, FRANK - bc 1842, VA; bl farm laborer. m Rebecca
   (_____). (Wayne Twp, 1870)
   Rebecca - bc 1843, OH; bl. (1870)
   Elitha - bc 1865, OH; bl. (1870)
   Sammy - bc 1864, OH; bl. (1870)
   son - b 2 Nov 1870, Wayne Twp.
FOX, HENRY - b 1841, VA; bl farmer. parents both b VA. m
   Elizabeth (Watson). (Harrison Twp, 1870-1880)
   Elizabeth - b 1842, VA; bl. parents both b VA.
      (1870-1880)
   Harrison - b 1 Apr 1870, Harrison Twp; bl farm
      laborer. (1870-1880)
   Malinda - b 1862, OH; listed bl & mul farm laborer.
      (1870-1880) --also listed in Circleville, 1880
   Mercades - b 1858, OH; bl farm laborer. (1870-1880)
   William - b 1860 or 1862, OH; bl. (1870-1880)
FRANKLIN, MATTIE m James Sample & lived in Circleville,
   1870s.
FRANKLIN, WADE - bc 1854, VA; bl farm laborer. parents
   both b VA. (Muhlenburg Twp, 1880)
FRANKS, ELLA m Jerry Wyatt & lived in Circleville, 1880s.
FREEMAN, ADAM and 2 females lived in Washington Twp, 1820;
   with 5 females lived in Circleville, 1830.
FREEMAN, JAMES - b May 1867, OH. bl doctor's servant.
   parents both b S.C. (Circleville, 1900)
FREEMAN, NANCY - bc 1780, VA; bl. (Circleville, 1840-1850)
   --prob. wife of Adam.
   Ann - bc 1828, OH; bl. (1850)
FREEMAN, OBADIAH - bc 1800, VA; bl laborer. (Circleville,
   1860)

FRY, JANE - bc 1846, KY; bl. (Pickaway Twp, 1870)
    Ellen - bc 1865, KY; bl. (1870)
FRY, WILLIAM H. and 1 male, 2 females lived in Pickaway
    Twp, 1840.
FULLER, RICHARD m Margaret E. (Keys) & lived in Darbyville,
    1870s.
    Nancy E. - b 30 Sept 1871, Darbyville.
FUNK, HARRY - b Jan 1866, OH; bl day laborer. parents
    both b OH. m Jennie (____). (Circleville, 1900)
    Jennie - b Jan 1855, OH. father b OH; mother b VA.
        (1900)
FURBIN, ISAAC - bc 1828, OH; bl farmer. (Deer Creek, 1850)

GALBERT, FRANK lived in Circleville, 1870s.
    Frank - b 20 Mar 1874, Circleville
    Harry - b 20 Mar 1874, Circleville.
GALES, GEORGE W. - b 1840 or 1841, OH; bl farm laborer.
    (Jackson Twp, 1870)
    Mary - bc 1836, NC; bl farmhand. (1870)
GAM, FRANCES - bc 1844, OH; bl domestic. (Jackson Twp,
    1860)
GANAWAY, HENRY - bc 1855, VA; mul omnibus driver. parents
    both b VA. m Frances (____). (Circleville, 1880)
    Frances - b Feb 1860, VA; mul. parents both b VA.
        (Circleville, 1880-1900)
    Arthur - b 2 Sept 1888, Circleville.
    George - b 11 Dec 1885, Circleville.
    William M. - b 22 Nov 1877, Circleville; d 4 Dec
        1894, Circleville of typhoid fever. mul porter.
        married. (1880)
GARDENER, ANDERSON - bc 1854, TENN; bl farm laborer.
    (Darby Twp, 1870)
GARLAND, MORRIS m Alvida (Coles) & lived in Muhlenburg Twp,
    1880s.
    Walter - b 31 Dec 1882, Muhlenburg Twp.
GARNES (often listed as Carnes with intertwining citations)
GARNES, ABNER - bc 1820, OH; bl waiter. (Circleville,
    1870)
GARNES, ALBERT - bc 1838, OH; bl. (Circleville, 1860)
GARNES, ALVIRA - b 1818, VA; d 10 Sept 1897 of fat.
GARNES, ANASTASIA - bc 1851, NC; bl. (Circleville, 1860)
GARNES, ELMER - b 1888, Circleville; d 7 Nov 1898, Circle-
    ville of typhoid fever.
GARNES, JOHN - bc 1815, VA; bl clergyman. m Melissa
    (____). (Circleville, 1860)
    Melissa - bc 1822, VA; bl. (1860)
GARNES, LAWRENCE - b 1839, NC; listed bl & mul laborer in
    livery stables. parents both b NC. m Susan (____).
    (Circleville, 1860-1900)

38

Susan - b Mar 1844, OH; mul housekeeper. mother b
VA. (1880-1900)
Ernest - bc 1874, Circleville; mul. (1880)
Grafton - bc 1872, Circleville. bl. (1880)
Ollie - bc 1868, Circleville. bl housekeeper.
(1880-1900)
GARNES, MARY - bc 1841, NC; bl. (Circleville, 1860)
GARNES, MARY - b Oct 1869, OH. bl housekeeper. father b
NC; mother b OH. (Circleville, 1900)
GARNES, MINERVA - bc 1844, NC; bl. m George Hackett &
lived in Circleville, 1870s and 1880s. (Circleville,
1860)
GARNES, NAPHALET (?) - b. 1848, NC; bl laborer. parents
both b NC. m Jennie (_____). (Circleville, 1880)
Jennie - bc 1852, W VA.; bl. parents both b W VA.
(1880)
Minnie - bc 1876, OH; bl. (1880)
Naphalet - bc 1877, OH; bl. (1880)
GARNES, NOAH - b 1814, 1816 or 1819, NC; d Aug 1878,
Circleville of scarlet fever. bl drayman. m Jean or
June (_____). (Circleville, 1860-1870)
Jean or June - b c. 1816 or 1819, OH; bl. (1860-
1870)
Abner - b 1845, NC; bl laborer. (1860-1870)
Euclid - bc 1852, NC; bl. (1860)
James - bc 1844, NC; bl laborer. (1860)
John - bc 1840, NC; bl laborer. (1860)
Ludwig - bc 1860, NC; bl. (1860)
Margaret - bc 1857, OH; bl. (1860)
William - bc 1843, NC; bl laborer. (1860)
GARNES, SALLY lived in Circleville, 1890s.
Nellie - b 28 Feb 1892, Circleville
GARNES, WILLIAM - bc 1835, NC; bl. (Circleville, 1860)
GARNES, WILLIAM - b Apr 1839, NC; bl cartman. parents both
b NC. m Alvira (Dickerson). (Circleville, 1870-1900)
Alvira - b 1835 or 1837, VA; bl. parents both b VA.
(1870-1880)
Harriet - bc 1848, OH; bl. (1870)
Mary - b 1858, Circleville; bl. (1870-1880)
Sally - bc 1860, Circleville; bl. (1880) --see
separate listing--
Sarah - b 5 Oct 1869, Circleville
Walter - bc 1873, OH; bl. (1880)
GATES, MAGGIE m George H. Maxwell & lived in Circleville,
1880s.
GIBBS, AMBROSE m Dell (Turney) & lived in Circleville,
1880s.
Floyd - b 16 Aug 1886, Ross Co.

GIBBS, LAURA m Charles Blake & lived in Circleville, 1890s.
GIBBS, NATHAN - b Sept 1872, OH. bl farm laborer. parents
    both b OH. m Ella (_____). (Perry Twp, 1900)
        Ella - b Apr 1871, OH. parents both b VA. (1900)
        Edgar - b June 1894, OH. (1900)
        Jennie - b Nov 1890, OH. (1900)
GIBBS, SCOTT - b Dec 1859, OH. bl farm laborer. parents
    both b OH. m Sarah Ellen (Turney) Gibbs. (Perry Twp,
    1880; Williamsport, 1900)
        Sarah - b Feb 1867, OH. parents both b OH. (1900)
        Allen F. - b Dec 1894, OH. (1900)
        Cuba - b May 1898, OH. (1900
        Goldie May - b. 10 Feb 1889, Perry Twp. (1900)
        Helen B. - b Mar 1892, OH. (1900)
        Scott - b June 1893, OH. (1900)
        Susan - b Feb 1887, OH. (1900)
GILBERT, JEFFERSON - bc 1844, OH; bl laborer. m Jane
    (_____). (Circleville, 1870)
        Jane - bc 1846, OH; bl. (1870)
GILES, JOHN - bc 1820, OH; bl laborer. m Melissa (_____).
    (Circleville, 1860)
        Melissa - bc 1824, OH; bl. (1860)
GILLESPIE, ANN - bc 1820, OH; mul. (Circleville, 1850)
GILLIS, CHARLES - b 1864 or 1866, OH; bl farm laborer.
    (Scioto Twp, 1870-1880)
GILLIS, MARY - bc 1865, OH; bl. (Muhlenburg Twp, 1870)
GLASWELL, GRACE - b 1803, Cecil Co, MD; d 27 Feb 1886, Cir-
    cleville of consumption. widow.
GOFF, CHARLES - bc 1846, VA; bl farm laborer. m Henrietta
    (Weaver). (Jackson Twp, 1870)
        Henrietta - bc 1851, NC; bl. (1870)
        Elizabeth - b 8 Nov 1870, Wayne Twp.
        Eugene - bc 1868, OH; bl. (1870)
GOINES, FRANCES lived in Circleville, 1880s.
        Alice - b 4 July 1889, Westerville.
GOINZ, JOHN and 3 males, 2 females lived in Harrison Twp,
    1840.
GOLDEN, CARRY (male) - b VA. bl laborer. parents both b
    VA. (Muhlenburg Twp., 1880)
GOODRICH, NATHANIEL - bc 1841, VA; bl farm laborer. m Ann
    (Lowery). (Wayne Twp, 1870)
        Ann J. or M. - bc 1856, VA; bl. (1870)
        Elias - b 11 May 1869, Wayne Twp. bl. (1870)
        John - bc 1868, Wayne Twp. bl. (1870)
GOWENS, MARY - bc 1842, OH; mul. (Monroe Twp, 1860)
GORMAN, JOHN m Mary (_____) & lived in Circleville, 1870s.
        infant - b Circleville; d 17 Jan 1870, Circleville.

40

GRAHAM, JAMES H. - bc 1844, NC; bl farm laborer. (Jackson
    Twp, 1860)
        Lucretia - bc 1846, OH; bl. (1860)
GRANT, HIRAM - bc 1824, OH; mul. m Rachel (_____). (Cir-
    cleville, 1850)
        Rachel - bc 1823, OH; mul. (1850)
        Alfred - bc 1847, OH; bl. (1850)
GRANT, JAMES - b 1833, VA; bl day laborer. parents both b
    VA. m Elizabeth (_____). (Circleville, 1860-1880)
        Elizabeth - b 1834, or 1836, Bedford, PA; d 1 Feb
            1875, Circleville of consumption. bl. (1860-
            1870)
        Margaret - b 1864, Circleville. bl. (1870-1880)
        Marion - b 1859 or 1860, Circleville. bl. (1860-1870)
        Susan - b 1852 or 1853, PA; bl. (1860-1870)
        WINIFRED - bc 1801, VA; bl. parents both b VA.
            (1880)
GRANT, LILLIE E. m George R. Kelley & lived in Muhlenburg
    Twp, 1880s. --2nd listing as Ettie L. Grant--
GREEN, ALAN - b Mar 1827, VA; bl drayman. parents both b
    VA. (Circleville, 1900)
GREEN, ALBERT - b 1844, OH; bl laborer. parents both b VA.
    m Jane (_____). (Circleville, 1870) -1880 census lists
    as b. 1848, VA; car man--
        Jane - b 1840 or 1845, VA; bl. parents both b VA.
            (1870-1880)
GREEN, ALICE - bc 1850, OH; bl laborer. parents both b VA.
    (Wayne Twp, 1880)
GREEN, ELIZA - bc 1860, OH; mul. (Jackson Twp, 1860)
GREEN, FRANK - bc 1854, VA; bl farm worker. parents both b
    VA. m Delila (Thacker). (Walnut Twp, 1880)
        Delila - bc 1854, OH; mul. father b VA; mother b OH.
            (1880)
        Ardie - b 1880, Walnut Twp; bl. (1880)
        Elisabeth - b July 1875, OH; bl cook. (1880;
            Circleville, 1900)
        John - bc 1878, Walnut Twp; bl. (1880)
        Sarah A. - bc 1872, OH; bl. (1880)
GREEN, JOHN - b Mar 1840, OH; bl day laborer. parents both
    b OH. (Circleville, 1900)
GREEN, LEWIS - bc 1822, OH; bl laborer. (Circleville,
    1870)
GREEN, LEWIS - b Mar 1829, VA; bl plasterer. parents both
    b VA. m 1st , Susan (Russell); 2nd, Martha (_____).
    (Circleville, 1870-1900)
        Susan - bc 1848, OH; bl. (1870)
        Martha - bc 1851, VA; bl. parents both b VA. (1880)

41

Cora - b 1870, Circleville. bl. (1870)
Eliza - bc 1857, OH; bl. (1870)
Ellen - b 30 Aug 1873, Circleville.
Minnie - bc 1868, Circleville. bl. (1870)
infant - b 1880, Circleville. (1880)
infant - b 1865; d 30 Sept 1867, Chillicothe of
    throat disease.
GREEN, LEWIS - bc 1833, VA; bl farmhand. m Dorcas (_____).
  (Circleville, 1860)
    Dorcas - bc 1833, VA; bl. (1860)
    Eliza J. - bc 1855, OH; bl. (1860)
GREEN, LEWIS - b 1848, OH; bl. (Circleville, 1860)
GREEN, MATHEW - bc 1853, OH. mul. (Wayne Twp, 1860)
GREEN, THOMAS - b Mar 1859, W VA; bl day laborer. parents
  both b VA. m. H. (_____). (Circleville, 1900)
    Heur--- - b Nov 1870, OH. parents both b KY. (1900)
    Bessie - b June 1888, OH. (1900)
    Cora - b Jan 1899, OH. (1900)
    Mable - b June 1886, OH. (1900)
GREEN, THORNTON - bc 1854, VA; mul laborer. parents both b
  VA. (Muhlenburg Twp, 1880)
GREEN, WAYNE - bc 1853, OH; mul. (Jackson Twp, 1860)
GREEN, WILLIAM - b Sept 1863, VA; bl day laborer. parents
  both b VA. (Circleville, 1900)
GREENE, JAMES - bc 1844, OH; bl farmer. parents both b OH.
  m Susan C. (_____). (Monroe Twp, 1880)
    Susan C. - bc 1854, VA; bl. parents both b VA.
      (1880)
    Amanda - b 1879, Monroe Twp; bl. (1880)
    Elizabeth - bc 1874, OH; bl. (1880)
    John S. - bc 1869, OH; bl. (1880)
GREGORY, FRANCIS - b. c. 1790, VA; black. lived with 3
  males and 6 females in Perry Twp, 1830; with 1 male, 4
  females in Perry Twp, 1840. (Deer Creek, 1850)
    Matilda - bc 1832, OH; mul. (1850)
    William - bc 1815, VA; mul farmer. (1850)
GREGORY, JOSEPH - bc 1810, VA; bl farmer. m Elvira
  (_____). (Monroe Twp, 1860)
    Elvira - bc 1810, OH; bl. (1860)
    Ellen - bc 1842, OH; bl. (1860)
    Francis - bc 1845, OH; bl. (1860)
    Isabella - bc 1848, OH; bl. (1860)
    Phiomelia - bc 1857, OH; bl. (1860)
    Sarah - bc 1837, OH; bl. (1860)
    William S. - bc 1856, OH; bl. (1860)
GREGORY, LUCINDA m Thomas Smithson & lived in Monroe Twp,
  1850s
GREGORY, ROSA - bc 1819, VA; mul. (Circleville, 1870)

GREGORY, ROSANNA - b 1815 or 1817, VA; d Oct 1875, Circle-
ville. black. (Circleville, 1860)
 Walter - bc 1857, OH; bl. (1860)
GRIMES, ELIZA - bc 1841, OH; bl. (Deer Creek, 1850)
GRIMES, GABRIEL - bc 1798. lived in Pickaway Co, 1827. m.
Melody (_____).
 Melody - bc 1804.
 Catharine - bc 1825.
 Eleanor- b June 1827.
 Elizabeth - bc 1822.
 Mary - bc 1817.
GRIMES, MINERVA - bc 1840, OH; mul. (Circleville, 1860)
GUNS, NANCY - bc 1832, VA; mul. (Jackson Twp, 1850)

HACKER, CHARLES m Margaret Hacker & lived in Circleville,
1860s.
 E. M. Anderson - b 17 Aug 1867, Circleville
HACKETT, GEORGE - b Dec 1845, OH; bl barber. father b PA;
mother b OH. m Minerva (Garnes). (Circleville, 1880-
1900)
 Minerva - b Mar 1848, NC; mul. parents both b NC.
  (1880-1900)
 Calvin - b June 1867, OH; mul day laborer. (1880-
  1900)
 Carrie - bc 1875, Circleville; mul. (1880)
 Charles - bc 1866, OH; mul. (1880)
 George - bc 1873, Circleville; mul. (1880)
 Lillie A. - b 1 Sept 1869, Circleville; mul. (1880)
 Maud - b 8 Sept 1882, Circleville. (1900)
 Minnie Ellen - b 1 Sept 1869, Circleville; mul. m
  Huston Bond 30 Jan 1893, Circleville, (1880-1900)
 Myrtle M. - b Aug 1890, OH. (1900)
 Nellie - bc 1878, Circleville; mul. (1880)
 Roy - b June 1887, Circleville. (1900)
 William - bc 1864, OH; mul apprentice blacksmith.
  (1880)
HACKETT, GEORGE - b May 1882, Circleville; d 3 Nov 1882,
Circleville.
HAGEN, EDWARD - b 1800 or 1801, VA; bl farmer. (Muhlenburg
Twp, 1860)
 Elisabeth - bc 1785, VA; bl. (1860)
HAGER, CHARLES - bc 1849, OH; bl farm laborer. (Jackson
Twp, 1870)
HAIR, JAMES lived in Walnut Twp, 1820.
HAITHCOCK (also HACOCK)
HAITHCOCK, AUGUSTUS - b 1835, NC; listed bl & mul plas-
terer. parents both b NC. m Violet (_____). (Circle-
ville, 1860-1880)

Violet (listed in 1870 as Frances) - b 1839, 1842 or
   1846, VA; listed bl & mul. parents both b VA.
   (1860-1880)
Emma - bc 1865, Circleville. bl. (1880)
Frederick - bc 1866, Circleville. bl. (1870)
Ida (listed as Ada in 1880) - b 1869, Circleville.
   bl. (1870-1880)
Laura - b 1860, Circleville. bl. (1860)
Mary E. - bc 1858, Circleville. bl. (1860)
Netta - bc 1864, Circleville. bl. (1870)
HAITHCOCK, WILLIS - bc 1839, OH; bl plasterer. father b
   KY; mother b VA. m Laura C. (Tibbs). (Circleville,
   1880)
Laura C. - bc 1853, OH. bl. (1880)
Anna M. - bc 1874, OH; bl. (1880)
Bertha L. - bc 1871, OH; bl. (1880)
Daniel or David L. - b 4 June 1877, Circleville. bl.
   (1880)
John C. - bc 1869, OH; bl. (1880)
Kittie - bc 1879, Circleville. bl. (1880)
Minnie C. - bc 1863, OH; bl. (1880)
Sarah C. - bc 1872, OH; bl. (1880)
HALEY, WILLIAM - b Dec 1842, VA; bl farm laborer. parents
   both b VA. m Sarah (Sanders). (Wayne Twp, 1870; Cir-
   cleville, 1900)
Dolly R. - b 16 Oct 1873, Wayne Twp.
HALL, SARAH - b 1801 or 1803, OH; bl housemaid. parents
   both b VA. (Circleville, 1870)
HAMMINS, LANDEN - bc 1830 OH; bl laborer. (Muhlenburg, 1860)
HAMMOND, LANGDON - bc 1835, OH; bl laborer in rubber works.
   (Circleville, 1880) --may be same as above--
HANTON, IDA m Andrew Mayo & lived in Williamsport, 1880s.
HARGIS, PHILLIP - b Mar 1864, OH; bl farm laborer. parents
   both b VA. m Mary (_____). (Scioto Twp, 1900)
Mary - b Sept 1859, OH. parents both b VA. (1900)
HARGO (also HARGA and HARGRO)
HARGO, BENAJMIN - b Jan 1850, OH. parents both b OH.
   (Circleville, 1900)
HARGO, FENNEL - b 1826, OH; bl farmer. m Elisabeth
   (_____). (Jackson Twp, 1860; Muhlenburg Twp, 1860)
Elisabeth - b 1827, OH; bl. (1860-1870)
Charles E. - b 1858, OH; bl. (1860-1870)
Lucinda - bc 1864, OH; bl. (1870)
Mary Jane - b 1843, OH; bl. (1860-1870)
Nancy - b 1856, OH; bl. (1860-1870)
Samantha - bc 1860, OH; bl. (1870)
HARGO, GABRIEL - b 1779 or 1783, VA; bl farmer. (Jackson
   Twp, 1850-1860)

Agnes - bc 1839, OH; bl. (1850)
Benjamin - bc 1851, Jackson Twp. bl farmhand.
    (1860)
Charlotte - b 1844, OH; bl. (1850-1860)
Elija - bc 1830, OH; bl farmer. (1850)
Elizabeth - bc 1832, OH; bl. (1850)
Franklin - b 1845, OH; bl farmhand. (1860)
George - b 1841 or 1843, OH; bl farmhand. (1850-
    1860)
Jeremiah - bc 1835, OH; bl farmer. (1850) --see
    separate listing--
Lewis - b 1859, Jackson Twp. bl. (1850-1860)
Margaret - bc 1836, OH; bl. (1850)
Maria - bc 1808, VA bl. (1860) --possibly wife--
Mary Ann - bc 1826, OH; bl. (1850-1860) --listed as
    Marilla in 1860--
Sarah - bc 1871, Jackson Twp. bl. m Hope Stepter
    and lived in Adelphi, 1880s. (1860)
Thomas - b 1847, OH; bl. (1850-1860)
HARGO, GEORGE W. - bc 1854, OH; bl farmhand. parents both
    b OH. (Deer Creek, 1880)
HARGO, HANNAH lived in Deer Creek, 1870s.
    Elizabeth - b 17 Sept 1877, Deer Creek. father was
        John Nickels.
HARGO, IDA - b Feb 1854, OH. father b OH; mother b PA.
    (Washington Twp, 1900)
    Charlie - b Aug 1885, OH; bl farm laborer. (1900)
    Washington - b Mar 1873, OH; bl farmer. (1900)
HARGO, JEREMIAH - b 1835, OH; s/o Gabriel Hargo. bl day
    laborer. m Margaret Ann (Robbins or Robberts).
    (Muhlenburg Twp, 1860-1870)
    Margaret Ann - bc 1851, NC; bl. (1870)
    Eliza - b 7 Oct 1872, Muhlenburg Twp.
    John - b OH; bl. (1870)
    Martha E. - b 30 Apr 1871, Muhlenburg Twp.
    William - b 16 Feb 1876, Scioto Twp.
HARGO, MALINDA m Abraham Nickels & lived in Deer Creek,
    1880s.
HARGRAVE, BENJAMIN - b 1793, 1799, 1803, 1810 or 1815, VA;
    d 19 July 1888, Circleville of dropsey. bl laborer.
    mother b VA. m Harriet (_____). (Circleville, 1850-
    1870) --death record and each census has different age
    listed--
    Harriet - b 1809 or Oct 1819, VA; listed bl & mul.
        parents both b VA. (1850-1870)
    Flora - bc 1861, Circleville. mul. father b VA;
        mother b OH. (1870)

Hattie - b 1858, Circleville. listed bl & mul nurse.
m Marian Douglas & lived in Circleville, 1870s and
1880s. (1860-1870)
John - b 1843, OH; bl. (1850-1860)
Julia - b 1840, OH; listed bl & mul housemaid.
(1850-1870)
Lewis - b 1847, OH; bl. (1850-1860)
Mary E. - b 1845, OH; bl. m Lewis Woodey & lived in
Circleville, 1870s. (1850-1860)
Willie - bc 1851, Circleville. (1860)
HARGRAVE, JUNE - bc 1837, OH; bl cook. (Circleville, 1860)
HARGY, JOHN - bc 1846, OH; bl. (Circleville, 1860)
HARMON, ROBERT - bc 1835, DEL; mul farm laborer. m Nancy
(_____). (Deer Creek, 1860)
    Nancy - bc 1838, DEL; mul. (1860)
    Ann E. - bc 1858, DEL; mul. (1860)
    Walter - bc 1859, DEL; mul. (1860)
HARNESS, RUTH ANN - b 1874, Washington Court House; d 1 May
1886, Deer Creek Twp of consumption.
HARPER, MARY - bc 1857, OH; bl housemaid. (Wayne Twp,
1870)
HARRIS, ABRAM - bc 1848, SC; bl saw mill worker. (Harrison
Twp, 1870)
HARRIS, ALFRED - bc 1825, SC; bl farmhand. (Perry Twp,
1880)
HARRIS, EDWARD - bc 1842, OH; bl. (Pickaway Twp, 1860)
HARRIS, EMMA - bc 1863, KY; bl servant. parents both b KY.
(Pickaway Twp, 1880)
HARRIS, FRANCES m William H. Valentine & lived in Circle-
ville, 1870s.
HARRIS (or HARRISON), GEORGE - bc 1813, Frederick Co, VA;
mul. lived in Pickaway Co, 1831.
HARRIS, GEORGE m Ada (Brolly) & lived in Circleville,
1890s.
    Elizabeth - b 31 July 1897, Circleville.
HARRIS, JOHN - bc 1816, NC; bl farmhand. m Mary (_____).
(Monroe Twp, 1860)
    Mary - bc 1820, NC; bl. (1860)
    Benjamin - bc 1856, OH; bl. (1860)
    Charles - b 1860, Monroe Twp. bl. (1860)
    James - bc 1850, OH; bl. (1860)
    Samuel - bc 1855, OH; bl. (1860)
    Yorilda (male) - bc 1852, OH; bl. (1860)
HARRIS, JOHN - bc 1836, OH; bl farm laborer. m Bunelda
(_____). (Deer Creek, 1860)
    Bunelda - bc 1839, OH; bl. (1860)
    Florada - b 1860, Deer Creek. bl. (1860)

HARRIS, JOHN - bc 1845, OH; bl laborer. m Cyrilda (____).
   (Circleville, 1870) --probably same as above--
      Cyrilda - bc 1845, OH; bl. (1870)
      Abella - bc 1866, OH; bl. (1870)
      Florida - bc 1859, OH; bl. (1870)
      Frederick - bc 1869, Circleville. bl. (1870)
      Jerome - bc 1861, OH; bl. (1870)
HARRIS, JOHN - bc 1845, NC; bl farm laborer. parents both
   b NC. m Sarah A. (____). (Monroe Twp, 1880)
      Sarah A. - bc 1852, OH; bl. father b MD; mother b
         VA. (1880)
      John W. - b 1877, OH; bl. (1880)
      Lilly Belle - b 21 Apr 1879, Monroe Twp. bl. (1880)
      Mary F. - bc 1876, OH; bl. (1880)
      Ruth A. - bc 1872, OH; bl. (1880)
HARRIS, JOHN m Zelda (Turney) & lived in Circleville,
   1870s.
      Albert - b 10 Jan 1872, Circleville.
HARRIS, JOHN m Agnes (Nicolas) & lived in Deer Creek,
   1880s.
      Abraham - b 2 Aug 1886, Deer Creek; d 15 Feb 1887,
         Deer Creek Twp.
HARRIS, JORDAN - bc 1835, OH; bl farmer. m Scioto (____).
   (Monroe Twp, 1860)
      Scioto - bc 1841, OH; bl. (1860)
      Joseph - bc 1857, OH; bl. (1860)
HARRIS, LEVI - b Apr 1855, OH; bl barber. father b VA;
   mother b OH. m. Elisabeth (____). (Circleville, 1900)
      Elisabeth - b Apr 1850, OH; bl barber. parents both
         b OH. (1900)
      George - b July 1876, OH; bl barber. (1900)
HARRIS, MARY - bc 1856, VA; mul. (Circleville, 1870)
HARRIS, MICHAEL- bc 1850, OH; mul farm laborer. m
   Josephine (Davis). (Monroe Twp, 1870)
      Josephine - bc 1851, OH; mul. (1870)
      Margaret Alice - b 15 Feb 1871, Deer Creek Twp.
HARRIS, REBECCA - b 1844, OH; listed bl & mul domestic.
   (Circleville, 1850-1860)
HARRIS, RHODA - bc 1829, OH; mul washerwoman. (Circle-
   ville, 1870)
      Stillman - bc 1867, OH; mul. (1870)
HARRIS, RICHARD - b 1815, VA; listed bl & mul drayman. m
   Rebecca J. (Street). (Circleville, 1860-1880)
      Rebecca J. - b 1838, OH; listed bl & mul. (1860-
         1880)
      Audelbert - bc 1864, Circleville. mul laborer.
         (1880)
      Bucyrus - b 1861 or 1862, Circleville. listed bl &
         mul. (1870-1880)

Clarence - b 11 Sept, 1874, Circleville. mul.
(1880)
Eliza J. - b 1858, OH; bl. (1860-1870)
Ida M. (also listed as Idoline) - b 1855, OH; bl.
(1860-1870)
James W. - b 24 Mar 1870, Circleville. (1870)
Lenora Bell - b 26 July 1872, Circleville.
Lucinda - b 19 Feb 1882, Circleville.
Minnie - b 1880, Circleville. mul. (1880)
Nellie A. - b 1866, Circleville; d 23 July 1874,
Circleville. (1870)
Richard E. - bc 1865, Circleville. (1870)
William - bc 1869, Circleville. bl. (1880)
OPHILIA - b 1799 or 1803, VA; d 24 Oct 1878, Wash-
ington Twp. of old age. bl. (1860-1870)
HARRIS, ROSA ANN - bc 1863, VA; mul. parents both b VA. m
Isaac Seward & lived in Harrisburg, 1880s. (Circle-
ville, 1880)
HARRIS, ROSEANN m Ausy Souers & lived in Muhlenburg Twp,
1870s.
HARRISON, HARVEY - bc 1845, OH; bl house servant. (Circle-
ville, 1870)
HARRISON, THOMAS - bc 1829, KY; bl farm laborer. m Mary
(_____). (Muhlenburg Twp, 1870)
Mary - bc 1840, VA; mul. (1870)
HART, GEORGE - bc 1846, OH; bl barber. m Manerva (_____).
(Circleville, 1870)
Manerva - bc 1848, OH; bl. (1870)
Calvin - bc 1867, OH; bl. (1870)
Charles - bc 1865, OH; bl. (1870)
Lilly - b 1870, Circleville. bl. (1870)
Minnie - b 1870, Circleville. bl. (1870)
William - bc 1863, OH; bl. (1870)
HARVEY, HARRIET - b 1830 or 1831, SC; bl. parents both b
SC. (Circleville, 1870-1880)
Burny - b 1869, Circleville. bl. (1870)
Ernest - bc 1865, OH; bl. (1870)
Henry - b 1 Feb 1869 to Harriet and Henry Harvey.
Horace - bc 1843, VA; bl laborer. (1870) --see
separate listing--
John W. - bc 1845, VA; d 26 July 1887, Circleville of
brain fever. bl laborer. (1870) --see separate
listing--
Paul - bc 1857, OH; bl laborer. (1870-1880)
Ulesses - bc 1869, Circleville. bl. (1880)
William - bc 1857, OH; bl. (1870)
HARVEY, HORACE - bc 1846, VA; bl groomsman. parents both b
VA. m Roxanna (Shepherd). (Circleville, 1880)

Roxanna - bc 1841, NC; bl. parents both b NC.
(1880)
Alice - bc 1866, OH; bl. (1880)
Delano - b 10 July 1878, Circleville. bl. (1880)
Elinor - bc 1867, OH; bl. (1880)
Helen - b 30 Nov 1875, Circleville.
HARVEY, JOHN - bc. 1847, VA; bl laborer. parents both b
VA. m Virginia (____). (Circleville, 1880)
Virginia - bc 1853, VA; bl. parents both b VA.
(1880)
Mary C. - b 6 Jan 1874, Circleville. houseworker.
(1880-1900)
HATTMAN, NANNIE m Britt Tan & lived in Circleville, 1870s.
HAWKINS, NED - bc 1792, Richmond, VA. freed by Peter
Hawkins 5 Feb 1806. lived in Pickaway Co, 1826.
HAYES, FRANK - bc 1863, VA; mul laborer. parents both b
VA. (Jackson Twp, 1880)
HAYES, FRANKLIN - bc 1847, OH; bl farm laborer. parents
both b OH. (Muhlenburg Twp, 1880)
HAYES, GEORGE - b Apr 1890, OH; bl day laborer. parents
both b OH. (Circleville, 1900)
HAYES, HOWARD - bc 1861, OH; bl laborer. father b OH;
mother b VA. (Jackson Twp, 1880)
HAYES, NAOMA - b 1868, Jackson Twp; d 30 June 1887, Circle-
ville of typhoid fever. married.
HAZLEWOOD, AD-- - bc 1845, VA; mul blacksmith. m Lizzie
(____). (Circleville, 1880)
Lizzie - bc 1854, OH; mul. parents both b VA.
(1880)
HAZLEWOOD, ANNA m Joseph Wilson & lived in Circleville,
1890s.
HAZLEWOOD, ELISHA - b Sept 1846, NC; bl blacksmith. father
b NC; mother b SC. m Frances (____). (Circleville,
1900)
Frances - b Dec 1849, OH. parents both b VA. (1900)
Earl - b Jan 1886, OH; bl miller. (1900)
Maud - b Dec 1876, OH; bl confectionary salesperson.
(1900)
HAZLEWOOD, NETTIE m Harry Whittington & lived in Circle-
ville, 1890s.
HEIM, JANE m Paris Negro & lived in Circleville, 1860s.
HEIRS, ELIAS and wife lived in Madison Twp, 1840.
HENDERSON, ANNIE - b Nov 1878, KY; bl servant. parents
both b KY. (Circleville, 1900)
HENDERSON, GEORGE - b May 1856, OH; bl drayman. m Jennie
(Dormey). (Circleville, 1880-1900)
Jennie - b Apr 1858, KY; bl. parents both b KY.
(1900)

49

Ann Mary - b 1 June 1884, Circleville; d 6 Nov 1867, Circleville.

William A. - b 16 Sept 1888, Circleville. (1900)

MARY ANN - b July 1825, VA. bl. (1900)

HENDERSON, JEREMIAH - bc 1807 or 1809, Washington Co, VA; d 26 Mar 1898, Circleville of old age. bl drayman or laborer. mother b VA. m Mary F. (_____). (Circleville, 1860-1880)

Mary A. or F. - bc 1813 or 1817, VA; bl. mother b VA. (1860-1880)

Arthur - bc 1859, Circleville. bl. (1860)

Benjamin Franklin - bc 1845, VA; bl laborer. (1860)

Eliza J. - bc 1853, OH; bl. (1860)

George E. - b 1850, OH; bl drayman. (1860-1880) -- see separate listing--

Mary E. - bc 1858, OH; bl. (1860)

Sarah C. - b 1847 or 1849, OH; bl housemaid. (1860-1870)

William - b 1854, OH; bl laborer. (1860-1870) --see separate listing--

HENDERSON, JOHN - bc 1839, VA; bl farm laborer. (Deer Creek Twp, 1870)

HENDERSON, JOHN - bc 1849, KY; bl saw mill worker. (Harrison Twp, 1870)

HENDERSON, JOHN - b June 1867, Circleville; d 16 Sept 1868, Circleville of brain fever.

HENDERSON, WILLIAM - b 1854 or 1856, OH; bl barber. parents both b VA. m Cornelia (_____). (Circleville, 1880)

Cornelia - bc 1858, OH; mul. parents both b OH. (1880)

HENGES, JAMES - bc 1837, OH; mul farm laborer. (Pickaway Twp, 1860)

HENRY, ISABEL - bc 1858, OH; bl. (Circleville, 1870)

HENRY, JULIA m George W. Briggs & lived in Circleville, 1890s.

HENRY, MARY - b 1825 or 1828, OH; bl house servant. parents both b OH. (Circleville, 1870-1880)

Belle - b 1860, OH; bl domestic servant. (1870-1880)

Ellen - bc 1854, OH; bl house servant. (1870)

Judith - b 1853, OH; bl house servant. parents both b OH. (Jackson Twp, 1860; Circleville, 1870-1880)

Sarah - bc 1851, OH; bl housemaid. (1870)

HENRY, SALLY - bc 1841, OH; bl house servant. (Circleville, 1870)

HICKEM, ABRAM - bc 1865, VA; bl farm laborer. parents both b VA. (Scioto Twp, 1880)

HIGHTREE, EDMOND - bc 1864, OH; bl. (Harrison Twp, 1870)
HIGHWANDER, ABEDNEGO and 2 males, 2 females in Walnut Twp,
    1820; with 2 males, 3 females in Walnut Twp, 1830.
HIGHWANDER, ISAAC - b 1822 or 1825, PA; bl laborer. m Mary
    A. (_____). (Circleville, 1850-1860)
        Mary A. - bc 1840, VA; bl. (1860)
        Clark - bc 1852, OH; bl. (1860)
        Willis - bc 1855, OH; bl. (1860)
HILL, ANNA m William Jackson & lived in Harrison Twp,
    1870s.
HILL, BARTON - b 1821, 1823 or 1825, OH; bl. m lst, Martha
    (_____); 2nd or 3rd, Tabitha (Douglass). (Jackson Twp,
    1860; Deer Creek, 1870; Scioto Twp, 1880)
        Martha A. - bc 1833, OH or VA; mul. (1860)
        Tabitha (Douglass) -
        Amanda - b 1864, OH; bl. m James Weinman & lived in
            Circleville, 1880s. (1870-1880)
        Barton, Jr. - b 1867, OH; bl. (1870-1880)
        Eldora - b 27 Oct 1881, Scioto Twp.
        Elias - b 26 July 1857, Jackson Twp. listed
            bl & mul farm laborer. (1860-1880; Jackson Twp,
            1900)
        Ellen - b 1840 or 1846, OH; bl. father b VA; mother
            b NC. (1870-1880) --possibly second wife--
        Emmora - b 27 Oct 1881, Scioto Twp.
        Ezra - bc 1871, OH; bl day laborer. (1880-1900)
        Frank - b 7 Aug 1874, OH; bl. (1880)
        John - b. 1877, OH; black. (1880)
        Martha - bc 1862, OH; bl. (1870)
        Mary - b 1876, OH; bl. (1880)
        Noah - b Mar 1890, OH. (1900) -probably s/o Thomas
            Hill--
        Simon - b 1880, Scioto Twp. bl. (1880)
        Thomas - b 1869 or June 1872, OH; bl blacksmith.
            (1870-1880; Jackson Twp, 1900)
        Vinton - b 1852 or 1855, Jackson Twp. listed bl &
            mul farm laborer. (Jackson Twp, 1860; Muhlenburg
            Twp, 1870)
    William A. - b. 1860, Jackson Twp. mulatto. (1860)
HILL, ELLA m David Jones & lived in Deer Creek Twp, 1880s.
HILL, ELLA - b Oct 1881, OH. parents both b OH.
    (Washington Twp, 1900)
HILL, HARRY - May 1870, OH; bl farm laborer. parents both
    b OH. m. lst, Sarah (Williams) and lived in Deer Creek
    Twp, 1880s; 2nd Elizabeth (Short) and lived in Darby
    Twp. (Darby Twp, 1900)
        Elizabeth - b Jan 1875, OH. parents both b OH.
            (1900)
        Burr___ - b. June 1892, OH. (1900)

Ella - b 10 Aug 1894, Darby Twp; d 16 Aug 1894,
　　Darby Twp.
Harrison - b 1 Oct 1888, Deer Creek Twp.
Jennie - b Oct 1897, OH. (1900)
Myrtle - b Oct 1890, OH. (1900)
HILL, HARVEY - b 1885, Circleville; d 3 June 1887, Circle-
ville.
HILL, JAMES - b 1864, VA; d 4 Dec 1895, Circleville of
consumption. married. laborer.
HILL, JOHN - bc 1838, OH; bl farm laborer. (Deer Creek,
1850; Jackson Twp, 1860)
HILL, LINCOLN - b 1834 or 1840, OH; bl farm laborer.
father b DEL; mother b OH. m Ellen (Jackson). (Jackson
Twp, 1860; Deer Creek Twp, 1870-1880)
　　Ellen - b June 1839, VA; listed bl & mul. father b
　　　　VA; mother b NC. (1860-1870)
　　Aaron - b 1879, Deer Creek. bl. (1880)
　　Chestle or Chester - b 1859, Jackson Twp; listed bl &
　　　　mul farm laborer. (1860-1870)
　　Emily - bc 1863, OH; bl. (1870)
　　Harry - b 1868, OH; bl. (1870-1880) --see separate
　　　　listing--
　　James - bc 1861, OH; bl. (Deer Creek, 1870)
　　Mary - b 1880, Deer Creek; bl. (1880)
　　Mary Ellen - bc 1865, OH; bl. (1870)
　　Phoebe - b 1838, OH; bl. both parents b OH. (1880)
HILL, LIZZIE - b Nov 1873, ILL; bl servant. parents both b
ILL. (Washington Twp, 1900)
HILL, MATHIAS - bc 1845, OH; bl farm laborer. m. Mary
(＿＿＿). (Deer Creek, 1870)
　　Mary - bc 1841, OH; bl. (1870)
　　Floyd - bc 1858, OH; bl. (1870)
HILL, NATHANIEL - bc 1861, OH; bl barber. (Circleville,
1880)
HILL, PHOEBE - b 1858, Deer Creek; d 18 July 1887, Deer
Creek of sunstroke. married. laborer.
HILL, SAMUEL - bc 1795, VA; mul. m Patsey (＿＿＿).
(Jackson Twp, 1850)
　　Patsey - bc 1805, OH; mul. (1850)
　　Bartin - bc 1821 or 1823, OH; mul laborer. (1850) --
　　　　see separate listing--
　　Mary Ann - bc 1845, OH; mul. (1850)
HILL, SIMON - bc 1833, VA; bl farm laborer. m Elizabeth
(＿＿＿). (Wayne Twp, 1860)
　　Elizabeth - bc 1835, OH; bl. (1860)
HIMP, CHARLES - b 1807, VA; d 28 Aug 1891, Washington Twp.
of paralysis. married. laborer.

HINES, MINGLE - bc 1847, NC; bl farm laborer. (Jackson
    Twp, 1870)
HINKLEY, SARAH E. m Jeff Turner & lived in Circleville,
    1890s.
HIRT, ANDREW m Lizzie (Wolf) & lived in Circleville, 1880s.
    Anna - b 1 Nov 1883, Circleville.
HODGE, R. R. - bc 1815, KY; mul shoemaker. m Mary (_____).
    (Circleville, 1850)
        Mary - bc 1818, VA; mul. (1850)
        Ashton - bc 1845, OH; mul. (1850)
        Lucy A. - bc 1848, OH; mul. (1850)
HOLLINGSWORTH, MARY - bc 1811, VA; bl. (Circleville, 1870)
HOLLINGSWORTH, ROBERT - b 1847, OH; s/o Sarah Hollings-
    worth. bl laborer. m Missouri (_____). parents both b
    VA. (Circleville, 1870-1880)
        Missouri - b 1857, OH; bl housemaid. (1870-1880)
        Abraham Lincoln - b 20 Nov 1879, Circleville. bl.
            (1880)
        Bell - b 1869, Circleville. bl. (1870-1880)
        Charles - b 29 Dec 1873, Circleville. bl. (1880;
            Muhlenburg Twp, 1900)
        Daniel - b 20 Nov 1879, Circleville. bl. (1880)
        Fannie - bc 1877, Circleville. bl. (1880)
        Mary - bc 1871, Circleville. bl. (1880)
        Robert - bc 1876, Circleville. bl. (1880)
        William - bc 1872, Circleville. bl. (1880)
HOLLINGSWORTH, ROBERT - b Feb 1892, OH; bl bootblack.
    parents both b OH. (Circleville, 1900)
HOLLINGSWORTH, SARAH - b 1809 or 1822, VA; bl. lived with
    Robert & Missouri in 1880. (Circleville, 1850-1880)
        John - b 1845, OH; bl house servant. (1850-1870)
        Robert - b 1847, OH; bl. (1850) --see separate
            listing--
HOLMES, AUZ (?) - bc 1842, OH; bl plasterer. m Polly
    (_____). (Circleville, 1880)
        Polly - bc 1845, OH; bl. parents both b OH. (1880)
        Frances - bc 1867, OH; bl. (1880)
        William - bc 1875, OH; bl. (1880)
HOLMES, HENRY - bc 1849, OH; bl laborer. m Sophia (_____).
    (Circleville, 1870)
        Sophia - bc 1851, NC; bl house servant. (1870)
HOLMES, HENRY - bc 1847, OH; bl day laborer. parents both
    b VA. m Angeline (_____). (Circleville, 1900)
        Angeline - b Dec 1860, OH. parents both b OH.
            (1900)
HOLMES, HENRY - bc 1851, OH; bl farm laborer. parents both
    b VA. m Marion (_____). (Circleville, 1880)

53

Marion - bc 1860, OH; bl. father b OH; mother b PA. (1880)
HOLMES, JOHN - bc 1850, KY; bl day laborer. parents both b KY. m Margaret (____). (Scioto Twp, 1880)
    Maggie - bc 1853, OH; bl. parents both b VA. (1880)
    John - bc 1878, OH; bl. (1880)
    Mary - bc 1875, OH; bl. (1880)
    William - bc 1878, OH; bl. (1880)
HOLMES, LIZZIE - bc 1877, OH; bl. parents both b OH. (Circleville, 1880)
HOLMES, LOTTA m George Wyatt in Circleville, 1870s.
HOLMES, MARTHA - bc 1848, OH; bl. (Circleville, 1860)
HOLMES, MARY - bc 1842, VA; bl. (Circleville, 1860)
HOLMES, MARY m Reuben Peterson & lived in Circleville, 1870s.
HOLMES, MATTIE - bc 1875, OH; bl. father b OH; mother b VA. (Circleville, 1880)
HOLMES, MINNIE - bc 1873, OH; mul. parents both b VA. (Circleville, 1880)
HOLMES, ROSA - b 1806 or 1820, KY; bl. father b VA; mother b Santo Domingo. (Circleville, 1870-1880)
    Charlott - bc 1848, KY; bl housemaid. (1870)
    Harry - b 1851 or 1853, KY; bl laborer. (1870-1880)
    Harrison - bc 1856, OH; bl laborer. (1870)
    Jack or John - b 1849 or 1851, KY; bl laborer. (1870) --see separate listing--
    Lottie - bc 1846, KY; bl housemaid. (1870)
    Margaret - bc 1841, KY; bl. (1880)
    Sophia - bc 1852, OH; bl housemaid. (1870)
HOLMES, WILBER - b Feb 1876, OH; bl plasterer. parents both b OH. m Graff (____). (Circleville, 1900)
    Graff - b Aug 1881, OH. parents both b OH. (1900)
HOLMES, WILLIAM A. - b Mar 1845, OH; bl plasterer. parents both b VA. m. Sarah (Henry). (Circleville, 1880-1900)
    Sarah - b Apr 1853, OH. parents both b OH. (1900)
    Pearley - b 30 June 1881, Circleville. (1900)
HOMER, WILLIAM - b June 1876, OH; bl farm laborer. parents both b OH. (Harrison Twp, 1900)
HOOKES, SAMUEL - bc 1806, OH; mul farmer. m Elizabeth (____). (Muhlenburg Twp, 1850)
    Elizabeth - bc 1816, OH; mul. (1850)
    Caleb - bc 1847, OH; mul. (1850)
    Hannah E. - bc 1843, OH; mul. (1850)
    Martha E. - bc 1845, OH; mul. (1850)
    Sarah Ann - bc 1840, OH; mul. (1850)
HOOKS, LAVERTA - b Feb 1862, OH; bl laundress. father b VA; mother b NC. (Circleville, 1900)
    Maud - b Apr 1881, OH. (1900)

HOOSER, Mr. m Rosanna (Bloose) & lived in Darby Twp, 1890s.
Abraham - b 14 Jan 1894, Darby Twp.
HOOVER, STEPHEN - bc 1839, OH; bl laborer. (Circleville,
1870)
HORSE, FRANCIS and 1 male, 1 female lived in Washington
Twp, 1820; Circleville, 1830.
HOUSTON, FREDERICK - b June 1877, VA; bl farm laborer.
parents both b VA. (Washington Twp, 1900)
HOWARD, ALLEN - b 1840 or 1832, OH; bl farm laborer. m
Roxanna (_____). (Wayne Twp, 1860; Muhlenburg Twp,
1870)
    Roxanna - bc 1845, OH; bl. (1870)
    Mary - bc 1869, Muhlenburg Twp. bl. (1870)
HOWARD, CHARLES E. - b 15 Feb 1876, Washington Twp. Infir-
mary; s/o Sarah Redman.
HOWARD, ELSIE - bc 1839, OH; bl farm laborer. m Martha
(_____). (Monroe Twp, 1870)
    Martha - bc 1843, OH; mul. (1870)
    Joseph - bc 1862, OH; mul. (1870)
    Martha - bc 1866, OH; mul. (1870)
    Mary - b 1 June 1868, Monroe Twp. mul. (1870)
    Nelly - bc 1864, OH; mul. (1870)
HOWARD, JOHN - bc 1861, OH; bl laborer. father b OH;
mother b VA. (Jackson Twp, 1880)
HOWARD, NATHANIEL - b 1844 or 1846, OH; mul farm laborer.
parents both b VA. m. Sophia (_____). (Circleville,
1870-1900)
    Sophia - b Mar 1852, KY; mul. parents both b KY.
    (1880-1900)
HOWELL, ARTHUR - bc 1811, GA; bl clergyman. m Winnie
(_____). (Circleville, 1860)
    Winnie - bc 1812, GA; bl. (1860)
HOWELL, EDWARD - bc 1877, OH; mul. parents both b VA.
(Circleville, 1880)
HUBBARD, A. G. m Cora E. (Douglass) & lived in Circleville,
1880s.
    Edith C. - b 31 Dec 1883, Circleville.
HUDSON, BENJAMIN - b 1807, 1809 or 1815, VA; d 12 May 1895,
Washington Twp. of heart trouble. bl blacksmith. m
Delia (_____). (Circleville, 1850-1870)
    Delia - b 1819 or 1820, VA; bl. (1850-1880) --listed
        in 1860 and 1870 as Mary - b. 1823, OH--
    Gasaway - b 1849, Circleville. bl blacksmith.
        (1850-1870)
    Henry - bc 1840, OH; bl blacksmith. (1850-1870) --
        see separate listing--
    Howard D. - b 24 Dec 1857, Circleville. bl laborer.
        (1860-1870)

Mary - b 1842, OH; bl. (1850-1870)
Noah - b 1850, Circleville. bl blacksmith. (1860-1870) --see separate listing--
HUDSON, CYNTHIA - b Nov 1852, OH. parents both b OH. (Circleville, 1900)
    Benjamin H. - b Feb 1889, OH. (1900)
    Mary - b Apr 1883, OH. (1900)
    Sarah - b Apr 1881, OH. (1900)
HUDSON, ELIZABETH - b 31 Aug 1874, Circleville; d 6 Apr 1875, Circleville.
HUDSON, HENRY S. - b 1842, Lancaster, OH; d 18 Nov 1894, Circleville of heart failure. blacksmith. m Narcissa (Redman). (Circleville, 1880) --probably s/o Benjamin Hudson--
    Narcissa - bc 1850, OH; bl. (1880)
    Mabel - b 31 July 1877, Circleville; d 12 Nov 1878, Circleville of brain fever.
HUDSON, NANCY - b 1820 or 1825, VA; bl. (Circleville 1850) --two listings with varying age--
HUDSON, NOAH - b 1852, OH; d 16 Dec 1894, Circleville of Bright's Disease. bl blacksmith. father b VA; mother b OH. m Dolly (Patten). (Circleville, 1880)
    Dolly (also DRUSILLA) - bc 1854, ALAB; mul domestic. parents both b ALAB. (1880-1900) --1900 census lists b May 1836
    Amos G. - bc 1876, Circleville. bl. (1880)
    Clara M. - b 16 July 1884, Circleville.
    Cora - b 1880, Circleville. bl. (1880)
    Ella N. - bc 1874, Circleville. bl. (1880)
    Elnora - b 12 Sept 1875, Circleville.
    Emma - b 30 Nov 1880, Circleville.
    Eva - b 6 Oct 1890, Circleville. (1900)
    Gracie B. - b 20 Mar 1883, Circleville.
    Hartley - b 10 Apr 1878, Circleville; d 13 July 1878, Circleville of pneumonia.
    Margie - b Aug 1892, Circleville. (1900)
    Mina - b Jan 1889, Circleville. (1900)
    Noah G. - b 5 Nov 1894, Circleville; d 28 Feb 1896, Circleville of congestion.
    Robert - b 30 Sept 1886, Circleville. (1900)
HUGHES, DANIEL - b Aug 1845, VA; bl house servant. parents both b VA. (Circleville, 1870-1900)
HUGHES, JAMES L. - bc 1827, VA; bl plasterer. m Lucy (____). (Circleville, 1860)
    Lucy - bc 1838, OH; mul. (1860)
    Alexander- bc 1857, OH; mul. (1860)
    William H. - - bc 1858, OH; mul. (1860)

HUNT, CHRISTOPHER - b Jan 1838, VA; bl laborer. parents
both b VA. m. Violet (Armistead) & lived in Muhlenburg
Twp, 1880s. (Circleville, 1900)
    Violet - b Jan 1851, VA. parents both b. VA. (1900)
    Elmer - b 17 Sept 1885, Darbyville. (1900)
    Ham - b Feb 1889, OH. (1900)
HUNT, HATTIE - b 1771; d June 1884, Darbyville.
HUNTER, JULIUS - bc 1843, VA; bl laborer. mother b VA. m
Eliza (_____). (Circleville, 1880)
    Eliza - bc 1855, OH; bl. father b VA; mother b OH.
        (1880)
HUNTER, PRISCILLA - b 1791 or 1799, VA; bl. mother b VA.
(Circleville, 1860-1880)
    Henry - b 1839 or 1841, VA; laborer. (1870)
HUNTER, SUSAN m David Dalton & lived in Circleville, 1870s.
HURNY, BILLIE - b Mar 1861, OH; bl houseworker. father b
VA; mother b OH. (Circleville, 1900)
    Jay - b July 1882, OH; bl day laborer. parents both
        b OH. (1900)
HUSTICK, JENNIE m William H. Johnson & lived in Circle-
ville, 1880s.
HYMAN, EPHRAIM - b June 1849, VA; bl brick molder and ser-
vant. parents both b VA. m Georgia A. (Malone).
(Circleville, 1870-1900)
    Georgia A. -
    Fannie - b 29 Aug 1875, Circleville.
    George L. - b 12 Nov 1878, Circleville
    Lina - b Sept 1861, OH. father b KY; mother b VA.
        (1900)
HYMAN, GEORGIANNA - b 1860, Wayne Twp; d 10 Dec 1878,
Circleville of confinement.
HYMAN, JAMES OLIVER - b 1855, Circleville; d 15 Nov 1878,
Circleville. married.
INYERS, MARGARETTA m John Cooper & lived in Salt Creek Twp,
1890s.
IRVING (alternatively listed as IRVIN or IRWIN in 1820-1850
censuses)
IRVING, CHARLES - b 1803, VA; listed bl & mul carpenter.
parents both b VA. m Nancy (_____). (Circleville,
1850-1880)
    Nancy - b 1803 or 1805, VA; listed bl & mul. parents
        both b VA. (1850-1880)
    Henry - bc 1828, VA; mul. (1850)
    Richard - b 1832, VA; listed bl & mul blacksmith.
        (1850-1880) --see separate listing--
IRVING, CHARLES - bc 1844, VA; bl plasterer. parents both
b VA. m Mary (Hacker). (Circleville, 1880)

Mary - bc 1851, OH; mul. parents both b VA. (1880)
Catherine - b 30 June 1875, Circleville. mul. (1880)
Dolly - bc 1879, Circleville. mul. (1880)
Eda - bc 1887, Circleville. mul. (1880)
IRVING, EPH--- - b 1875, Circleville; d Mar 1890, Circle-
ville of lung disease.
IRVIN, FRANCES - b Mar 1891, OH; parents both b OH.
(Washington Twp, 1900)
IRVING, HARRIET - d 10 Aug 1870, Circleville.
IRVING, PALESTINE - b 1845, OH; mul carpenter. parents
both b VA. m Ellen (Thomas). (Circleville, 1870-1880)
    Ellen - b 1848 or 1850, OH; mul operated notion
        store. (1870-1880)
    Charles - b 27 Nov 1870, Circleville. mul. (1880)
    Edith - b 23 Dec 1874, Circleville. mul. (1880)
    Ella - b Jan 1852, VA; bl cook at hotel. parents
        both b VA. (Circleville, 1900) --may be Ellen--
    Estella - b 6 Aug 1877, Circleville. mul house-
        keeper. (1880-1900)
    Homer - bc 1868, Circleville. mul. (1870)
    Palestine - b 16 Aug 1883, Circleville; mul day
        laborer. (Circleville, 1900)
    Thaddeus - b 27 Nov 1872, Circleville. mul. (1880)
    Theodosia - b 8 Aug 1880, Circleville. (1900)
IRVING, RICHARD - b 1832, VA; d 9 Sept 1898, Washington
Twp. Infirmary of epilepsy. blacksmith. m Mildred
(Walker). died as pauper. (Circleville, 1860-1880)
    Mildred - b 1842, VA; mul. (1870-1880)
    Charles - b 30 Mar 1877, Circleville
    E. H. - b 5 Jan 1879, Circleville.
    Earnest W. - b 9 Aug 1869, Circleville. mul. (1870-
        1880)
    Gracie - bc 1879, Circleville. mul. (1880)
    Mabel C. - b 4 Nov 1883, Circleville. (1900)
    Maude - b 31 July 1872, Circleville.
    Miller - b 3 Dec 1874, Circleville.
    Minnie - bc 1875, Circleville. mul. (1880)
    Richard H. - b 19 July 1876, Circleville. mul.
        (1880)
    Rosa - b 1864, Circleville; d 5 Feb 1893, Circleville
        of lung disease. mul. (1870-1880)
    Sarah A. (also Sally) - b 1866, Circleville. mul.
        (1870-1880)
IRVING, SIMON - bc 1855, TENN; bl laborer. (Circleville,
1870)
IRVING, THOMAS - bc 1845, OH; bl. (Circleville, 1860)
IRWIN, DANDRIDGE and 1 male, 2 females in Circleville,
1840.

IRWIN, ROSINA - bc 1817, VA; mul. (Circleville, 1850)
    Millstand - bc 1847, OH; mul. (1850)
IRWIN, VINCENT - b Oct 1845, OH; bl hosler. parents both b
    VA. (Circleville, 1900)
IZARD, NORFTIH (?) - bc 1848, NC; bl. (Circleville, 1860)

JACKSON, ANN - bc 1812, Ross Co; d 12 Mar 1877, Circleville
    of tumor. widow.
JACKSON, BENNETT - b Feb 1870, Circleville; d 10 Dec 1880,
    Circleville of consumption.
JACKSON, BESSIE N. - bc 1881, Circleville; d 11 Jan 1895,
    Circleville of consumption.
JACKSON, CHARLES W. - bc 1862, Circleville; d 28 Feb 1871,
    Circleville. of consumption.
JACKSON, EDSON m Sallie (Sampson) & lived in Circleville,
    1880s.
    Henry - b 9 Mar 1883, Circleville.
JACKSON, ELIJAH - b Mar 1862, OH; laborer. mul brick
    mason. parents both b OH. m. Jennie J. (_____).
    (Jackson Twp, 1880; Circleville, 1900)
    Jennie - b May 1866, OH. father b OH; mother b VA.
        (1900)
    Charles V. - b 7 Oct 1897, Circleville. (1900)
    Clara - b May 1880, OH. (1900)
    Edgar M. - b 10 July 1891, Circleville. (1900)
    Ethel - b 5 May 1899, Circleville
    George - b Feb 1890, OH. (1900)
    Harry B. - b Nov 1895, OH. (1900)
    James - b Feb 1893, OH. (1900)
    Laverta - b 6 Oct 1888, Circleville. (1900)
    Sister - b May 1899, OH. (1900)
JACKSON, ELIZABETH - bc 1834, OH; bl farm laborer. (Jack-
    son Twp, 1860)
    Sarah - bc 1841, VA; mul. (1860)
    Martha - bc 1859, OH; mul. (1860)
JACKSON, ELLEN m Lincoln Hill & lived in Deer Creek Twp,
    1870s.
JACKSON, EMMA - bc 1853, Circleville; d 28 Mar 1871, Cir-
    cleville of consumption.
JACKSON, EVELINE m Thomas Lucas & lived in Circleville,
    1880s.
JACKSON, EVERETTE - bc 1844, OH; bl farmer. parents both b
    VA. m Mary (Nickels). (Muhlenburg Twp, 1880)
    Mary - bc 1847, OH; bl. parents both b OH. (1880)
    Arabella - bc 1868, OH; bl. (1880)
    George E. - bc 1870, OH; bl. (1880)
    Harriette A. - bc 1874, OH; bl. (1880)
    Lawrence - b 15 Feb 1883, Muhlenburg Twp.

Mary A. - bc 1878, OH; bl. (1880)
Robert - bc 1872, OH; bl. (1880)
Sarah A. - bc 1865, OH; bl. (1880)
JACKSON, FREDERICK - b Feb 1885, OH; bl farm laborer.
parents both b OH. (Washington Twp, 1900)
JACKSON, G.F. m Hattie (_____) & lived in Darby Twp, 1890s.
David - b 17 Dec 1894, Darby Twp.
JACKSON, HARRY - b 1842, Darbyville; d 16 Oct 1884, Circle-
ville of consumption. married. cooper.
JACKSON, HARTWELL - bc 1837, OH; bl farm laborer. (Wayne
Twp, 1860)
JACKSON, HARVEY - b 1818 or 1820, VA; bl farmer and shingle
maker. mother b VA. m 1st, Pollie (_____); 2nd, Mary
(Williams). (Muhlenburg Twp, 1860; Circleville, 1870-
1880)
Pollie (or Polly) - b 1828 or 1834, VA; listed bl &
mul. (1860-1870)
Mary - bc 1835, VA; bl. mother b VA. (1880)
Alice - b 1862 or 1865, OH; bl domestic servant.
(1870)
M. Aveline (also Eva) - b 21 Jan 1870, Circleville.
bl. (1870)
Bud - bc 1856, VA; shingle maker. (1880)
Eliza - b 1848 or 1849, VA; bl housemaid. (1870)
Francis - bc 1850, VA; mul. (1860)
Kate - b 1861, OH; bl domestic servant. (1870)
Margaret - bc 1845, VA; mul. (1860)
Richard - bc 1853, VA; bl laborer. (1870)
Tilley - bc 1858, OH; bl nurse. (1870)
JACKSON, HENRY - b Nov 1894, Circleville; d 19 Feb 1895,
Circleville of cholera.
JACKSON, ISAAC - bc 1845, OH; bl farm laborer. parents
both b VA. (Muhlenburg Twp, 1880)
JACKSON, JAMES - b 1830, VA; listed bl & mul farmer. m Ann
(_____). (Jackson Twp, 1850; Muhlenburg Twp, 1860)
Ann - bc 1823, OH; bl. (1860)
JACKSON, JAMES W. - b 1833, Fayette Co; d 30 Oct 1896,
Circleville of heart trouble. s/o William and Elizabeth
Jackson. listed bl & mul carpenter and plasterer.
father b Scotland; mother b VA. m Laverta (Whittington)
(Circleville, 1860-1880)
Laverta - b 1838, OH; listed bl & mul. parents both
b VA. (1870-1880)
Charles - bc 1877, Circleville. mul. (1880)
Clarence - bc 1877, Circleville. mul. (1880)
Harriet - b 28 Oct 1873, Circleville.
Hattie - bc 1874, Circleville. mul. (1880)
James W. - b 1864, Circleville. bl. (1870-1880)

60

C. Jennetta - b 1866, Circleville. bl. (1870-1880)
J.N. - bc 1872, Circleville. mul. (1880)
Lizzie - bc 1867, Circleville. bl. (1870)
M. - b 1880, Circleville. mul. (1880)
Thomas - bc 1875, Circleville. mul. (1880)
JACKSON, JAMES - bc 1848, OH; bl. (Muhlenburg Twp, 1860)
JACKSON, JAMES - bc 1857, OH; farm laborer. parents both b
OH. (Muhlenburg Twp, 1880)
JACKSON, JAMES - b May 1870, OH; bl farmer. parents both b
OH. m. Mary J. (_____). (Scioto Twp, 1900)
Mary J. - b Aug 1873, OH; parents both b OH. (1900)
Aulty - b Oct 1896, OH. (1900)
Ray - b July 1894, OH. (1900)
JACKSON, JAMES m Mary Ann (_____) & lived in Circleville,
1860s.
daughter - b 12 Nov 1867, Circleville.
JACKSON, JAMES m (_____) (Runnels) and lived in Circle-
ville, 1870s.
James - b 15 Mar 1877, Circleville.
JACKSON, JOHN - bc 1817, VA; d 15 Feb 1869, Circleville of
consumption.
JACKSON, JOHN - bc 1850, OH; bl farm laborer. (Jackson
Twp, 1870)
Sarah - bc 1849, OH; bl housemaid. (1870) --possibly
spouse but listed separately--
Nancy - bc 1868, OH; bl. (1870)
JACKSON, JOHN - b 1867; d 1 Feb 1868, Circleville of lung
fever.
JACKSON, JOHN H. - b Apr 1874, OH; bl carpenter. parents
both b OH. m. Julia (_____). (Circleville, 1900)
Julia - b Aug 1873, OH. parents both b OH. (1900)
Mary E. - b May 1898, OH. (1900)
JACKSON, JUNE - b 1852, NC; d 20 Oct 1877, Muhlenburg Twp.
of consumption. married.
JACKSON, LOUISA - b Apr 1850, VA. parents both b VA.
(Circleville, 1900)
Charles - b Oct 1877; bl farm laborer. (1900)
Clarence - b Mar 1876, OH; bl farm laborer. (1900)
Harry - b July 1874, OH; bl carpenter. (1900)
JACKSON, M.M. - b 1864; d 20 Feb 1869, Circleville.
JACKSON, MARGARET m William Redman & lived in Wayne Twp,
1870s.
JACKSON, MARTHA m Homer Steward & lived in Muhlenburg Twp,
1870s.
JACKSON, MARTHA m Robert Robison & lived in Circleville,
1870s.
JACKSON, MARTHA m George Mayson & lived in Circleville,
1880s.

JACKSON, MATILDA m Jacob Erving & lived in Circleville, 1870s.
JACKSON, MARY - bc 1853, OH; bl housemaid. (Circleville, 1870) --possibly d/o Richard & Ardena Jackson--
JACKSON, MARY - bc 1826, NC; bl. father b VA; mother b N.C. (Circleville, 1880)
JACKSON, MARY - bc 1827, OH; bl servant. (Circleville, 1870)
     Mary E. - bc 1852, OH; bl housemaid. (1870) --
         possibly same as above--
     Lucinda - bc 1858, OH; bl house servant. (1870)
JACKSON, MERVIL - b 12 Sept 1898, Circleville to Clara Jackson.
JACKSON, PARTHENA m William Dervin & lived in Circleville, 1870s.
JACKSON, PHILISTINE - bc 1768 , SC; mul. (Circleville, 1850)
JACKSON, PRISCILLA - bc 1849, OH; bl. m Andrew Turney & lived in Circleville, 1890s. (Circleville, 1860)
JACKSON, REDICK - bc 1839, OH; bl farm laborer. (Wayne Twp, 1860)
JACKSON, RICHARD - bc 1820, OH; bl farmhand. m Ardena (____). (Muhlenburg Twp, 1860)
     Ardena - bc 1828, OH; bl. (1860)
     Grury (?) - bc 1854, OH; bl. (1860)
     John - bc 1857, OH; bl. (1860)
     Mary A. - bc 1852, OH; bl. (1860)
JACKSON, RICHARD - bc 1843, OH; bl laborer. m Frances (____). (Circleville, 1870)
     Frances - bc 1839, OH; bl. (1870)
     Cordelia - bc 1851, OH; bl. (1870)
JACKSON, RICHARD E. - b Feb 1861, OH. parents both b OH. m Hester E. (Miller). (Darby Twp, 1900)
     Hester - b Feb 1864, OH. parents both b OH. (1900)
     Arthur James - b 28 Nov 1893, Darby Twp.
     Clessa M.- b Apr 1898, Darby Twp. (1900)
     Harrison - b Oct 1889, Darby Twp. (1900)
     Nevada - b Mar 1892, Darby Twp. (1900)
     Sara - b Feb 1884, Darby Twp. (1900)
JACKSON, ROBERT - bc 1857, OH; bl farm laborer. (Muhlenburg Twp, 1870)
JACKSON, SALLIE (also listed as ALICE) m James Redick & lived in Circleville, 1880s.
JACKSON, SAMUEL - bc 1840, OH; bl day laborer. (Muhlenburg Twp, 1860)
SARAH ANN m Samuel Seward & lived in Darbyville, 1890s.
JACKSON, STEPHEN - b Apr 1851, OH; bl drayman and delivery wagon driver. parents both b VA. m Sally (____). (Circleville, 1880-1900)

Sally - b Aug 1858, W VA; bl. parents both b VA.
(1880 -1900)
Harry - b Mar 1883, OH. (1900)
John - b 1880, Circleville. bl. (1880-1900)
JACKSON, THOMAS - bc 1858, OH; bl farm laborer. father b
VA; mother b OH. (Harrison Twp, 1880)
JACKSON, WILLIAM - bc 1811, Scotland; mul foundryman. m
Elizabeth (____). (Circleville, 1850)
    Elizabeth - bc 1818, VA; mul. (1850)
    Thomas - bc 1848, Circleville. mul. (1850)
    William - bc 1841, OH; mul. (1850)
JACKSON, WILLIAM - bc 1822, OH; bl. (Circleville, 1870)
JACKSON, WILLIAM - bc 1826, VA; mul laborer. m Narissa
(____). (Circleville, 1860)
    Narissa - bc 1830, VA; mul. (1860)
    Carry - bc 1848, OH; mul. (1860)
    John - bc 1857, OH; mul. (1860)
    Melissa - bc 1844, OH: mul. (1860)
    Plassy (?) - bc 1852, OH; mul. (1860)
    William - bc 1850, OH; mul. (1860)
    Winfield - bc 1846, OH; mul. (1860)
JACKSON, WILLIAM - bc 1833, VA; bl farm laborer. (Muhlen-
burg Twp, 1870)
    Augustine - bc 1860, OH; bl. (1870)
    James - bc 1855, OH; bl farm laborer. (1870)
    John - bc 1869, OH; bl. (1870)
    Marietta - bc 1869, OH; bl. (1870)
    Sara - bc 1848, OH; bl. (1870)
    Sarah - bc 1862, OH; bl. (1870)
    Thomas - bc 1857, OH; bl farm laborer. (1870)
JACKSON, WILLIAM - bc 1836, VA; bl farm laborer. (Wayne
Twp, 1860)
JACKSON, WILLIAM m Anna (Hill) & lived in Jackson Twp,
1870s.
    George Edward - b 20 Sept 1873, Circleville.
JACOBS, GABINT (?) - bc 1845, OH; bl laborer. (Circle-
ville, 1870)
    Catherine - bc 1850, OH; bl cook. (1870)
JACOBS, GABRIEL - bc 1841, OH; bl farm laborer. (Jackson
Twp, 1870)
JAMES, CLARA - bc 1816, Circleville; d 19 Jan 1868, Circle-
ville of palsey. married.
JAMES, MARY - b Feb 1819, VA. parents both b VA.
(Circleville, 1900)
    James R.- b Dec 1854, VA; bl plasterer. parents both
        b VA. (1900)
JAMES, TARLTON - bc 1810, VA; bl carpenter. m Eliza
(____). (Circleville, 1860)
    Eliza - bc 1814, VA; bl. (1860)

JAMES, WILLIAM - bc 1848, ALAB; bl farm laborer. (Scioto Twp, 1870)

JAMISON, PATRICK - bc 1806, Botetourt Co, VA. lived in Pickaway Co, 1830.

JEFFERSON, JAMES - bc 1851, TENN; bl saw mill worker. (Harrison Twp, 1870)

JEFFERSON, LUCY m Henry Fowler & lived in Walnut Twp, 1880s.

JENKINS, WILLIAM - bc 1833, OH; bl barber. (Circleville, 1850)

JENSON, DAVID - bc 1847, OH; bl farm laborer. (Wayne Twp, 1870)

JESSUP, ZION - bc 1825, KY; bl domestic. (Circleville, 1860)

JOHNS, GEORGE - b May 1855, OH; bl farm laborer. parents both b VA. m. Mary (____). (Circleville, 1900)
    Mary - b Dec 1857, OH. father b VA; mother b NC. (1900)

JOHNS, MOSES - b Mar 1862, OH; bl day laborer. parents both b VA. m. Martha (____). (Circleville, 1900)
    Martha - b Feb 1845, OH. father b VA; mother b OH. (1900)
    Chester - b Dec 1885, OH. (1900)

JOHNSON, ANNIE - b 1875, Ross Co; d 21 Sept 1894, Circleville of consumption.

JOHNSON, BRECKENRIDGE - bc 1862, OH; bl laborer. parents both b VA. (Circleville, 1880)

JOHNSON, CATHERINE - bc 1850, OH; bl cook. (Circleville, 1870)

JOHNSON, CHENEY - bc 1840, VA; mul laborer. (Circleville Twp, 1860)

JOHNSON, CYRUS - bc 1822, D.C.; mul laborer. m Mary (____). (Circleville, 1870)
    Mary - bc 1839, D.C.; mul. (1870)
    Cyrus M. - bc 1866, OH; mul. (1870)
    Ella - bc 1867, OH; mul. (1870)

JOHNSON, DAVID - bc 1846, KY; bl laborer. (Circleville, 1870)

JOHNSON, DAVID - bc 1874, OH; mul. parents both b OH. (Washington Twp, 1880)
    Susan - bc 1876, OH; mul. (1880)

JOHNSON, ELISHA (or ELIJAH) - b Mar 1861, OH; bl day laborer. parents both b OH. m Rosa (Tann) (Circleville, 1880-1900)
    Rosa - b Feb 1873, OH. parents both b OH. (1900)
    Bessie - b June 1896, OH. (1900)
    Clarence - b Aug 1894, OH. (1900)
    Frances Marilla - b 5 Aug 1889, Circleville.

Frank - b 9 Sept 1898, Circleville. (1900)
    Helen - b Apr 1891, OH. (1900)
    Wilette - b Oct 1892, OH. (1900)
JOHNSON, ELIZABETH - bc 1829, OH; bl house servant. (Circleville, 1870)
    Nellie - b 1870, Circleville. bl. (1870)
    Susan - bc 1855, OH; bl. (1870)
    Victoria - bc 1866, OH; bl. (1870)
JOHNSON, ERIC - bc 1815, MD; bl laborer. m Sandra (_____). (Circleville, 1860)
    Sandra - bc 1804, VA; bl. (1860)
    Catherine - bc 1846, VA; bl. (1860)
    Lewis - bc 1848, MD; bl. (1860)
JOHNSON, FRANCIS - b 1885, Circleville; d 1 Mar 1892, Circleville.
JOHNSON, GEORGE - b Jan 1856, OH; bl saloon keeper. parents both b OH. m. Mary (_____). (Circleville, 1900)
    Mary - b Mar 1858, OH. parents both b OH. (1900)
JOHNSON, HENRY - b 1851, OH; mul horse attendant. m Elizabeth (Satchel). (Circleville, 1880)
    Elizabeth - bc 1857, OH; mul. mother b OH. (1880)
    Charles W. - bc 1878, OH; mul. (1880)
    Elsa Bell - b 16 June 1876, Circleville.
JOHNSON, HENRY - b Apr 1852, OH; bl janitor at bank. parents both b VA. m. Liza (_____). (Circleville, 1900)
    Liza - b Feb 1852, GA. parents both b GA. (1900)
JOHNSON, HENRY - b May 1874, Circleville; d 3 Nov 1874, Circleville of cholera.
JOHNSON, HENRY lived in Circleville, 1890s.
    William G. - b 7 May 1894, Circleville.
JOHNSON, ISABELLA m John Sheridan & lived in Circleville Twp, 1870s.
JOHNSON, JAMES - bc 1843, OH; bl barber. (Circleville, 1860)
JOHNSON, JAMES - bc 1851, Circleville; d 22 Jan 1876, Circleville of consumption.
JOHNSON, JOHN - b Dec 1869, OH; bl porter at hotel. parents both b OH. m. Jennie (_____). (Circleville, 1900)
    Jennie - b Nov 1874, OH. father b OH; mother b KY. (1900)
    Hilderbaum - b Sept 1896, OH. (1900)
    Jennie - b Dec 1894, OH. (1900)
JOHNSON, JOHN WILLIS lived in Circleville, 1870s. --possibly s/o Wilson & Rhoda Johnson.
    Mary - b 29 Sept 1873, Circleville.

JOHNSON, JULIUS - bc 1825, VA; bl farm laborer. m Olive
(_____). (Circleville, 1870)
    Olive - bc 1835, MD; bl farm laborer. (1870)
    Juniper - bc 1858, OH; bl. (1870)
    Kesiah - bc 1848, OH; bl housemaid. (1870)
    Rebecca - bc 1855, OH; bl. (1870)
JOHNSON, LIGETT - b July 1874, OH; bl farm laborer.
parents both b OH. m. Luella (_____). (Pickaway Twp,
1900)
    Luella - b Apr 1876, VA. parents both b VA. (1900)
JOHNSON, LONDON - bc 1809, VA; bl laborer. m Ary (_____).
(Circleville, 1870)
    Ary - bc 1814, MD; bl. (1870)
    Catherine - bc 1848, OH; bl housemaid. (1870)
JOHNSON, LUCY - bc 1858, OH; bl house servant. (Circle-
ville, 1880)
    Ann - bc 1877, Circleville. bl. parents both b OH.
    (1880)
    Mary - bc 1874, OH; bl. (1880)
JOHNSON, MARATH - b 1843; d 8 Jan 1897, Circleville of
heart trouble.
JOHNSON, MARION - b 13 Apr 1877, Circleville; d 29 Sept
1877, Circleville of cholera.
JOHNSON, MARY E. - b 11 or 12 May 1847, Monroe Twp; d 19
Apr 1877, Circleville of confinement. married. --2nd
listing b. Perry Twp.--
JOHNSON, MARY - b 1855, Ross Co; d Mar 1887, Pickaway Co.
JOHNSON, MARY - b. 3 Dec 1876, Washington Twp.
JOHNSON, MARY - b Aug 1880, D.C.; bl house servant.
parents both b VA. (Circleville, 1900)
JOHNSON, MARY - b Dec 1881, OH; bl cook. parents both b
OH. (Circleville, 1900)
JOHNSON, METE - bc 1851, OH; bl. (Circleville, 1860)
JOHNSON, NARISSA - bc 1852, OH; bl housemaid. (Circle-
ville, 1870)
JOHNSON, NATHANIEL m Martha (Bundy) & lived in Circleville,
1870s.
    daughter - b 2 Apr 1876, Circleville.
JOHNSON, RED - b Apr 1844, KY; bl day laborer. parents
both b KY. (Circleville, 1900)
    Bessie - b June 1884, OH. (1900)
    Grace - b Apr 1886, OH. (1900)
JOHNSON, RICHARD - b 1842 or 1844, KY; bl farm laborer.
parents both b KY. m Mary (Todd). (Muhlenburg Twp,
1870-1880)
    Mary - b 1852, OH; listed bl & mul. mother b VA.
    (1870-1880)
    Flora - b 1 Apr 1870, Muhlenburg Twp. bl. (1870)

Mabel J. (also Bell) - b 1868, OH; bl. (1870-1880)
Matilda - bc 1872, Muhlenburg Twp. bl. (1880)
Oddy - bc 1875, Muhlenburg Twp. mul. (1880)
infant - b 1 Feb 1879, Muhlenburg Twp; d 2 Feb 1879,
    Muhlenburg Twp.
infant - b 15 Mar 1886, Muhlenburg Twp.
JOHNSON, ROBERT - b 1856, OH; bl farm laborer. parents
    both b VA. (Muhlenburg Twp, 1800)
JOHNSON, SUSAN - bc 1845, OH; bl. (Circleville, 1870)
    John - bc 1841, OH; bl. (1870) --possibly husband--
JOHNSON, SUSAN m William Williams & lived in Circleville,
    1870s.
JOHNSON, WILLIAM - b 1833, NC; d 12 May 1898, Circleville
    of consumption.
JOHNSON, WILLIAM - b 1845 or 1847, VA; bl farm laborer.
    parents both b VA. m Sarah (_____). (Jackson Twp,
    1870; Circleville Twp, 1880)
    Sarah - bc 1845, VA; bl. parents both b VA. (1880)
    James - bc 1870, OH; bl. (1880)
    Rosa - bc 1876, OH; bl. (1880)
    Willie - bc 1878, OH; bl. (1880)
JOHNSON, WILLIAM - bc 1847, VA; bl laborer. parents both b
    VA. m Laura (_____). (Circleville, 1880) --possibly
    same as above--
    Laura - bc 1847, NC; mul . parents both b NC.
        (1880)
    Leaia - bc 1868, NC; mul. (1880)
    Lydia - bc 1871, NC; mul. (1880)
JOHNSON, WILLIAM L - b May 1857, OH; bl farm. laborer.
    father b NC; mother b OH. (Perry Twp, 1900)
JOHNSON, WILLIAM - b Feb 1862, KY; bl barber. parents both
    b KY. (Circleville, 1900)
    Joseph - b Mar 1861, OH. father b KY; mother b VA.
        (1900)
    Maud - b Aug 1883, OH. mother b. OH. (1900)
JOHNSON, WILLIAM H m. Jennie (Hustick) & lived in Circle-
    ville, 1880s.
    Henry B. - b 11 Nov 1884, Circleville
JOHNSON, WILLIS m Lucy (Winter) & lived in Circleville,
    1870s.
    daughter - b 2 Mar 1876, Circleville
    Mittie - b 21 May 1878, Circleville
JOHNSON, WILSON - bc 1820, NC; mul laborer. m Rhoda
    (_____). (Circleville, 1860)
    Rhoda - bc 1825, NC; mul. (1860)
    Francis - bc 1851, NC; mul. (1860)
    Henry W. - b 1845 or 1849, NC; listed bl & mul
        servant. (1860-1880)

John W. - bc 1847, NC; mul. (1860)
Martha J. - bc 1843, NC; mul. (1860)
Parthena - bc 1849, NC; mul. (1860)
Robert - bc 1855, NC; mul. (1860)
Sarah - bc 1858, NC; mul. (1860)
Surena - bc 1840, NC; mul. (1860)
Susanna - bc 1854, NC; mul. (1860)
William - bc 1841, NC; mul. (1860)
Wilson - bc 1843, NC; mul. (1860)
JOHNSTON, JULIUS - bc 1805, VA; bl. m Olivia (_____).
  (Circleville, 1880)
    Olivia - b Sept 1824, NC; bl. parents both b NC.
      (1880-1900)
    Nellie - bc 1871, VA; bl. (1880)
JOHNSTON, LEWIS and 1 male, 3 females lived in Circleville,
  1840.
JOINER, BARRY - bc 1847, TENN; mul plasterer. parents both
  b TENN. m Nancy (_____). (Circleville, 1880)
    Nancy - bc 1847, MICH; mul. father b VA; mother b
      OH. (1880)
    Freddie - bc 1878, OH; mul. (1880)
    Harry - bc 1875, OH; mul. (1880)
JONES, ABRAHAM and 1 male 2 females lived in Monroe Twp,
  1820; with 1 male 4 females lived in Jackson Twp, 1830.
JONES, ALLEN m Josephine (Stanley) & lived in Walnut Twp,
  1870s.
    Josephine (Stanley) (or Lockley) -
    Lemuel - b 5 Apr 1876, Walnut Twp.
JONES, CHRISSIE m Life Burch & lived in Circleville, 1880s.
JONES, DAVID - b Oct 1859, OH; bl farm laborer. parents
  both b OH. m Ella (Hill). (Deer Creek Twp, 1870-1900)
    Ida Florence - b 22 July 1882, Deer Creek Twp.
JONES, EMIAS and wife lived in Jackson Twp, 1830.
JONES, ESTHER lived in Jackson Twp, 1830.
JONES, HENRY - b Aug 1857, OH; bl farm, laborer. parents
  both b VA. m. Anna (_____). (Perry Twp, 1900)
    Anna - b Feb 1861, NC. parents both b NC. (1900)
    William - b June 1890, OH. (1900)
JONES, HUTSON (or HUDSON) - b July 1868, OH; bl day
  laborer. parents both b W VA. m Dollie (Redman).
  (Darby Twp, 1900)
    Dollie - b Feb 1868, OH. parents both b VA. (1900)
    Arthur N. - b 22 Feb 1892, Darby Twp. (1900)
    Hazel N. - b 29 July 1894, Darby Twp.
JONES, JOHN - b Jan 1845, VA; bl day laborer. parents both
  b VA. m. Elizabeth (_____). (Circleville, 1900)
    Elizabeth - b Apr 1850, OH. father by KY; mother b
      VA. (1900)

JONES, LEONARD - b Mar 1891, Darby Twp; d 19 July 1891, Darby Twp of cholera inflamation.

JONES, MALINDA - b July 1847, OH. parents both b OH. (Circleville, 1900)
    George - b Feb 1891, OH. (1900)
    Henry - b Aug 1888, OH. (1900)
    John - b Feb 1884, OH. (1900)
    Mary - b Apr 1886, OH. (1900)

JONES, NELSON - b Feb 1858, W VA; bl shoemaker. parents both b W VA. (Darby Twp, 1900)

JONES, PERRY m Henlow Cole & lived in Pickaway Twp, 1850s.

JONES, PHILLIP - bc 1851, OH; bl farm laborer. parents both b NC. m Ellen (_____). (Pickaway Twp, 1880)
    Ellen - bc 1853, OH; bl. father b VA; mother b OH. (1880)
    Walter - bc 1878, Pickaway Twp. bl. (1880)

JONES, REBECCA - bc 1838, VA; bl. (Jackson Twp, 1850)

JONES, SAMANTHA J. - bc 1849, Canada; mul. (Circleville, 1860)

JONES, SAMUEL - b Apr 1840, OH; bl day laborer. parents both b VA. (Circleville, 1900)

JONES, STEPHEN A. m Carrie (Trimble) & lived in Jackson Twp, 1890s.
    Arthur F. - b 17 Feb 1899, Jackson Twp.

JONES, TAYLOR - b 1838 or 1846, VA; bl farm laborer. parents both b VA. (Jackson Twp, 1870)
    John - bc 1853, OH; bl farm laborer. (1870)

JONES, WILLIAM - bc 1860, OH; bl. (Wayne Twp, 1870)

JONES, WILLIAM A. m Edith A. (Dade) & lived in Circleville, 1890s.
    Lorried A. - b 12 Sept 1899, Circleville.

JORDAN, ANNA - b 1867, Circleville; d 3 Jan 1869, Circleville of consumption.

JORDAN, JANE - bc 1835, OH; bl cook. (Circleville, 1860)

JORDAN, LEWIS - bc 1793, VA; bl shoemaker. (Circleville, 1850)
    Ellen - bc 1818, VA; bl. (1850)

JUDRICK, GOLD - b 1868, Circleville; d 12 Oct 1869, Circleville; c/o Cecelia Judrick and C.R. Gold.

JULIUS, ROBERT m Martha E. (Evans) & lived in Pickaway Twp, 1870s.
    Walter - b 25 Oct 1877, Pickaway Twp.

JULIUS, SAMUEL - bc 1841, OH; bl farm laborer. (Wayne Twp, 1860)

JUSTICE, DAVID - b 25 July 1882, Washington Twp. Infirmary; d/o Nancy Justice.

KAMBLE, IDA lived in Washington Twp, Infirmary, 1895.
    Philip - b 25 Mar 1895, Washington Twp. Infirmary to
       Ida Kamble and Mr. _____ Radcliff.
KAREY, ROBERT - b 12 Mar 1891, Circleville to Anna Bailey
    and _____ Karey.
KEAL, MELINDA m Robert Lints & lived in Circleville, 1880s.
KEAL, WARREN m Anna (Turney) & lived in Circleville, 1880s-
    1890s.
    Anna - b 6 Aug 1890, Circleville
    Pearly - b 5 Dec 1884, Circleville.
KEITH, SUSAN - bc 1849, OH; bl cook. (Circleville, 1870)
KELLEY, FANNY - b Mar 1835, KY. parents both b KY.
    (Circleville, 1900)
KELLEY, HENRY m Laura (Ewings) & lived in Circleville,
    1870s.
    Idosa Jane - b 12 Feb 1879, Circleville.
KELLEY, SOPHIA - b July 1856, OH; bl housekeeper. parents
    both b KY. (Circleville, 1900) --probably d/o Fanny
    Kelley--
    M----- (f) - b Aug 1881, OH; bl housekeeper. (1900)
    Ruben - b Dec 1886, OH. (1900)
KELLY, GEORGE R. m Ettie Lillie (Grant) & lived in Muhlen-
    burg Twp, 1880s.
    Frederick - b 20 May 1886, Muhlenburg Twp.
    Pearly T. - b 11 Mar 1885, Muhlenburg Twp; d 6 Sept
       1886, of consumption.
KELLY, JOHN R. - b 14 Feb 1886, Circleville to Sophia Kelly
    and John Harbuster.
KELLY, WILLIAM - b May 1880, OH; bl farm laborer. parents
    both b OH. (Jackson Twp, 1900)
KEMPER, NANCY A. m Jackson Redman & lived in Muhlenburg
    Twp, 1870s.
KENT, DAVID - bc 1850, VA; mul laborer. parents both b VA.
    (Jackson Twp, 1880)
KENT, JANE - bc 1851, OH; bl cook. (Circleville, 1870)
KENT, JENNIE - bc 1845, OH; bl housemaid. (Circleville,
    1870)
    Homer - b 3 June 1871, s/o Jennie Kent & George
       Briggs.
KENT, SUSAN - b 1815 or 1819, W VA.; bl cook. parents both
    b VA. (Circleville, 1870)
    Virginia - bc 1852, VA; bl housemaid. (1870)
KEYES, DEMPSEY - b. Dec 1852, ALAB; bl farm laborer and
    fisherman. parents both b ALAB. m Eliza (_____).
    (Jackson Twp, 1870; Circleville, 1880-1900)
    Eliza - bc 1849, OH; bl. father b KY; mother b MD.
       (1880) --also listed as Louisa Nichols in census
       and birth records--

Abraham or Anderson - b 1868, OH; black. (1870-1880)
Dempsey - b Nov 1873, Circleville; d 10 Feb 1876,
    Circleville of diarrhea.
Forest - bc 1877, Circleville; bl. (1880)
James - b 31 Dec 1871, Circleville.
Lucinda - b 12 June 1878, Circleville.
William - bc 1865, OH; bl. (1870)
KEYES, FLORENCE - b Aug 1869, Circleville; d 4 Mar 1877,
    Circleville of consumption.
KEYES, MARGARET E. m Richard D. Fuller & lived in Darby-
    ville, 1870s.
KEYES, WILLIAM - b 28 Dec 1898, Circleville to Maggie Keys.
KINNICKETT, WILLIAM - bc 1843, VA; bl apprentice wagon
    maker. (Muhlenburg Twp, 1860)
KNAPPER, JOHN - bc 1847, OH; mul farmer. parents both b
    OH. m Lilly (____). (Darby Twp, 1880)
    Lilly - bc 1860, OH; mul. parents both b OH. (1880)
    Clifford A. - bc 1877, OH. mul. (1880)
    Nelson - b May 1879, OH. (1880)
    Ralph - b 1880, OH; mul. (1880)
KNAPPER, MARY A. m Jackson Redman & lived in Muhlenburg
    Twp, 1870s.
KREBLE, SARAH lived in Washington Twp. Infirmary, 1890s.
    Jerry - b 25 Feb 1895, Washington Twp. Infirmary.

LACK (or LOCK), SAMPSON m Mary (Brown) & lived in Circle-
    ville, 1850s.
    son - b 31 Jan 1857, Circleville.
LANDS ON CANNAL, JEANS and 1 female lived in Circleville,
    1830s.
LANG, JAMES - bc 1846, OH; bl farm laborer. (Muhlenburg
    Twp, 1870)
LAUGHY, NICHOLAS, JR. and 2 males, 1 female lived in Cir-
    cleville, 1830s.
LAW, BRITTON - bc 1835, NC; mul farm laborer. m Rebecca
    (____). (Pickaway Twp, 1850)
    Rebecca - bc 1841, OH; mul domestic. (1850)
LAWS, GUNTHRIE - bc 1821, PA; bl laborer. m Ann (____).
    (Jackson Twp, 1850)
    Ann - bc 1823, VA; bl. (1850)
    James - bc 1847, Circleville. bl. (1850)
LAWSON, LIZZIE - b 1855, OH; d 14 Oct 1876, Circleville of
    typhoid fever.
LEACHMAN, ROBIN (male) - bc 1845, GA; bl farm laborer.
    (Wayne Twp, 1870)
LEIST, WILSON lived in Washington Twp, 1860s.
    daughter - b 26 July 1868, Washington Twp.

71

LETT, CHARLEY - bc 1865, OH; mul servant. parents both b
OH. (Harrison Twp, 1880)
LETT, ELISHA - b 1820 or 1829, OH; bl laborer. m Hannah
(Bailey). (Circleville, 1860-1870)
    Hannah - b 1825 or 1835, OH; bl. (1860-1870)
    Nettie - b 25 Dec 1875, Circleville.
    Sarah - bc 1861, OH; bl. (1870)
LETT, JENNIE - bc 1860, OH; mul domestic servant. parents
both b OH. (Harrison Twp, 1880)
LEWIS, ALICE - bc 1849, OH; bl housemaid. (Circleville,
1870)
LEWIS, ANNIE - bc 1854, OH; bl house servant. (Circle-
ville, 1870)
LEWIS, ELIZABETH - b 1810, VA; d 15 Dec 1893, Circleville
of old age.
LEWIS, EMMA - bc 1860, KY; bl house servant. parents both
b KY. (Circleville, 1880)
    James B. - b 1879, OH; bl. parents both b KY.
    (1880)
LEWIS, FRANK - bc 1839, VA; bl laborer. m Sarah (____).
(Circleville, 1870)
    Sarah - bc 1846, VA; mul. (1870)
    ISABEL - bc 1809, VA; bl cook. (1870)
LEWIS, FRANK - bc 1843, VA; bl hosler. parents both b VA.
(Circleville, 1870-1880)
    Elizabeth - bc 1825, VA; bl. parents both b VA.
    (1870-1880)
    John W. - bc 1871, OH; bl. (1870-1880)
LEWIS, GEORGE - bc 1855, OH; bl farm laborer. (Circleville
Twp, 1870)
LEWIS, GEORGE - bc 1850, TENN; mul plasterer. parents both
b VA. m Rebecca (____). (Pickaway Twp, 1880)
    Rebecca - bc 1850, OH; mul. father b OH; mother b
    VA. (1880)
LEWIS, HENRY - bc 1839, OH; bl laborer. (Circleville,
1870)
LEWIS, HENRY - bc 1843, TENN; bl farm laborer. (Wayne Twp,
1870)
LEWIS, JOHN lived in Circleville, 1860s.
    child - b 1865; d 30 Sept 1867, Circleville of summer
        complaint.
LEWIS, JOHN - b Sept 1869, OH; bl mail carrier. father b
VA; mother b OH. m. Ettie (____). (Circleville, 1900)
    Ettie - b May 1869, OH. parents both b OH. (1900)
    Frank - b Oct 1894, OH. (1900)
LEWIS, MARIA m Thomas Byer & lived in Circleville, 1860s.
LEWIS, PHEBE - bc 1846, VA; bl domestic servant. (Harrison
Twp, 1870)

LEWIS, WILLIAM - b May 1884, OH; bl. parents both b OH.
(Circleville, 1900)
LINDSAY, CATHERINE m Charles Terry & lived in Washington
Twp, 1880s.
LINDSEY, HENRY - b 1841; d 20 Mar 1872, Circleville of
pneumonia. laborer.
LINTS, ROBERT m Malinda (Keal) & lived in Circleville,
1880s.
    Robert - b 25 Dec 1881, Circleville.
LIONAGE, LEWIS - bc 1830, VA; bl servant. (Circleville,
1860)
LITTINGTON, MILLEY - freed by Andrew Littington in Bath Co,
VA, 12 Oct 1801. lived in Pickaway Co, 1828.
    Ann - bc 1776, Bath Co, VA. lived with 2 sons, 2
        daughters in Pickaway Co, 1828.
LOCKLEY, JOSEPHINE m Allen Jones & lived in Walnut Twp,
1870s.
LOCKLEY, MOSES - bc 1852, OH; bl laborer. (Circleville,
1870)
LOGAN, EMILY m Lawrence Payne & lived in Perry Twp, 1880s.
LOLLS, LEWIS m Nancy (Napper) & lived in Circleville,
1850s.
    George - b 10 Nov 1857.
LOTT, ARTHUR W. - b Jan 1898, Circleville; d 27 Oct 1898,
Circleville of scrofula.
LOWERY, ANN J. m Nathaniel Goodrich & lived in Wayne Twp,
1860s.
LOWERY, JANE - bc 1822, VA; bl housekeeper. (Scioto Twp,
1880)
LOWERY, LEVI - bc 1820, VA; bl farmer. m Maria (_____).
(Harrison Twp, 1870)
    Maria - b 1828 or 1832, VA; bl. parents both b VA.
        (Harrison Twp, 1870; Circleville, 1880)
LOYD, DAVIS - bc 1857, OH; bl farmhand. parents both b OH.
m Maggie (_____). (Deer Creek, 1880)
    Maggie - bc 1857, OH; bl. parents both b OH. (1880)
    John - bc 1870, OH; bl. (1880)
LUCAS, ABRAHAM - b 1829 or 1831, OH; listed bl & mul
farmer. parents both b PA. m 1st, Martha (_____); 2nd,
Sarah Jane (_____). (Circleville, 1850-1880)
    Martha - b Apr 1826, VA; bl. parents both b VA.
        (1870-1900)
    Hattie - b 24 July 1872, Circleville d/o Abraham &
        Sarah Jane Lucas.
    Sarah - b 1853 or 1856, Circleville. bl. (1870-
        1880)
    Thomas - b 1862, Circleville. bl. (1870-1880)

LUCAS, BODEN m Charles Turner & lived in Circleville, 1870s.
LUCAS, CLARA - bc 1862, OH; bl. parents both b OH. (Scioto Twp, 1880)
LUCAS, EFFIE lived in Circleville, 1890s.
    Lucille - b 19 Feb 1892, Circleville.
LUCAS, ELMIRA - bc 1835, OH; mul house servant. (Circleville, 1880)
LUCAS, HAMILTON - bc 1863, OH; mul laborer. parents both b OH. (Darby Twp, 1880)
LUCAS, HENRY - b Jan 1844, OH; mul farm laborer. parents both b OH. m Virginia (_____). (Jackson Twp, 1870; Circleville, 1880-1900)
    Virginia - b 1848 or June 1850, OH; mul. parents both b VA. (1870-1900)
    Ada - b Feb 1878, OH; mul. (1880-1900)
    Allen - b Feb 1878, OH; mul day laborer. (1880-1900)
    Charles - b 20 Dec 1872, OH. mul. (1880)
    Edwin E. - b 1870, Jackson Twp. mul. (1880)
    Elizabeth (also Lizetta) - b 1869, Jackson Twp. mul. (1870-1880)
LUCAS, ISAAC - b Oct 1839, OH; bl plasterer. parents both b OH. m Martha Jane (_____). (Circleville, 1870-1900)
    Martha Jane - b May 1847, PA; bl. father b VA; mother b MD. (1870-1900)
    Daniel - b 20 July 1870, Circleville. bl. (1870-1880)
    Effie - b 17 May 1872, Circleville. bl. (1880)
    Gracie - b 20 Mar 1882, Circleville; bl houseworker. (1900)
    Jessie - b 18 Mar 1877, Circleville; d 19 Mar 1877, Circleville.
    Marshall - b 1879, Circleville. bl. (1880)
    Madaline (also Mattie) - b 15 Nov 1884, Circleville. (1900)
    William - b 1868, Circleville. bl. (1870-1880)
LUCAS, JACOB - b 1817, VA; d 22 Jan 1869, Circleville of consumption.
LUCAS, JAMES F. - bc 1857, OH; laborer. parents both b OH. m Sarah F. (_____). (Darby Twp, 1880)
    Sarah F. - bc 1856, OH; mul. father b VA; mother b OH. (1880)
LUCAS, JOHN - bc 1831, OH; mul farmer. (Circleville, 1850)
LUCAS, JOHN P. m Reacy A. (Napper) & lived in Wayne Twp, 1860s.
    John Ulysses - b 8 Oct 1869, Wayne Twp.
LUCAS, MARY - bc 1848, OH; bl servant. parents both b OH. (Salt Creek Twp, 1880)

LUCAS, MARY L. - b 5 Feb 1889, Circleville; d 26 Feb 1890, Circleville. of consumption.

LUCAS, SARAH J. m Arthur Dickerson & lived in Circleville, 1870s.

LUCAS, THOMAS m Eveline (Jackson) & lived in Circleville, 1880s.

    Mary L. - b 5 Feb 1889, Circleville.

LUCAS, WILLIAM - bc 1797, VA; bl cartman. m Caroline (_____). (Circleville, 1870)

    Caroline - bc 1819, MD; bl. (1870)

    Joseph - bc 1858, OH; bl. (1870)

    Philip - bc 1859, OH; bl. (1870)

LUCAS, WILLIAM - b 1862, Circleville; d 3 July 1868, Circleville of flux.

LUIK, ROBERT - b 1807, VA; d 13 Feb 1891, Washington Twp. of paralysis. married. laborer.

LYNCH, ANSON - bc 1832, OH; bl laborer. (Circleville, 1870

LYNCH, SOLOMON - b 1843, TENN; d 4 Apr 1881, Circleville of consumption. bl cartman. parents both b TENN. m Hester A. (also listed as Ellen) (Redman). (Circleville, 1870-1880)

    Hester A. - b 1843 or 1845, W VA; d 22 June 1898, Circleville of paralysis. bl. parents both b VA. (1870-1880)

    Elizabeth - b 27 Aug 1871, Circleville.

    Josiah - b 14 Mar 1878, Circleville. bl. (1880)

    Lance - b 1869, Circleville. bl. (1870-1880)

    Mary - bc 1872, Circleville. bl. (1880)

    Sol - b 17 Jan 1870, Circleville.

    JANE - b 1803 or 1809, SC or TENN. bl. father b TENN; mother b VA. (1870-1880)

LYND, LUCINDA - bc 1840, OH; bl hotel worker. father b VA; mother b OH. (Circleville, 1880)

LYONS, BROOKENS and wife lived in Washington Twp, 1820. --spelled Liens--

LYONS, CHARLES - bc 1806, OH; bl farmer. m Catherine (_____). (Circleville, 1850)

    Catherine - bc 1808, PA; bl. (1850)

    Margaret - bc 1829, OH; mul. (1850)

    Martha - bc 1835, OH; mul. (1850)

    William - bc 1829, OH; bl farmer. (1850)

    William - bc 1832, OH; mul farmer. (1850)

    William - bc 1836, OH; bl. (1850)

LYONS, ELLEN - bc 1830, OH; bl servant. (Circleville, 1880)

LYONS, FRANK - bc 1851, OH; bl wood carrier. m Mary (_____). (Circleville, 1880)

    Mary - bc 1860, KY; bl. parents both b KY. (1880)

LYONS, FRANK - b Sept 1858, OH; bl day laborer. parents
  both b VA. (Circleville, 1900)
    James - b Apr 1882, OH; bl day laborer. mother b KY.
      (1900)
LYONS, ISAIAH - b 1853, OH; bl farm laborer. (Jackson Twp,
  1860-1870)
LYONS, ISAIAH - bc 1852, VA; bl servant. parents both b
  VA. (Pickaway Twp, 1850)
LYONS, MARCELLA - b 1819, NC; d 29 Aug 1868, Circleville.
  married.
LYONS, WILLIAM - bc 1809, OH; bl laborer. (Circleville,
  1870) --may be same as below--
    Isaiah - bc 1851, OH; bl laborer. (1870)
LYONS, WILLIAM and 2 males, 3 females lived in Circleville,
  1840. --spelled Lions--
LYONS, WILLIAM - b 1820, OH; bl farm laborer. m Martha
  (_____). (Circleville, 1860)
    Martha - bc 1825, NC; bl. (1860)

McATEE, DERIUS m Sarah J. (Muncie) & lived in Wayne Twp,
  1880s.
    Maud - b 13 June 1885, Wayne Twp.
McBRIDE, MAY - b Jan 1875, OH; bl. parents both b VA.
  (Circleville, 1900)
    William - b May 1892, OH. parents both b OH. (1900)
McCLARE, THOMAS - b Sept 1859, VA; bl barber. parents both
  b VA. m Olive (_____). (Circleville, 1900)
    Olive - b Nov 1859, OH. father b VA: mother b OH.
      (1900)
    Laura - b Aug 1890, OH.
McCLAIR, THORNTON m Ollie (Smithen) & lived in Circleville,
  1890s.
    Laura - b 5 Aug 1890, Circleville.
McFEETERS, ADAM - bc 1783, VA; mul laborer. lived with 4
  males and 5 females in Monroe Twp, 1830. m Mary
  (_____). (Monroe Twp, 1830; Darby Twp, 1850)
    Mary - bc 1800, VA; mul. (1850)
    Adam C. - bc 1837, OH; mul. (1850)
    Elizabeth - bc 1826, VA; mul. (1850)
    Hannah - bc 1834, OH; mul. (1850)
    James S. - bc 1835, OH; mul. (1850)
    Mary A. - bc 1843, OH; mul. (1850)
    Matilda - bc 1830, OH; mul. (1850)
    Sarah J. - bc 1845, OH; mul. (1850)
    Wiley - bc 1840, OH; mul. (1850)
    William - bc 1831, OH; mul. (1850)
McFEETERS, CHARLES - bc 1827, OH; mul farmer. (Muhlenburg
  Twp, 1850)

McGATH, MARY E. m Charles H. Dunlap & lived in Washington
Twp, 1880s.
McMANN, CHARLES E. - b 1864, Circleville; d 15 Oct 1867,
Circleville of pneumonia.
McMANN, FRANK - b Feb 1881, OH; bl farm laborer. parents
both b OH. (Scioto Twp, 1900)
McMANN, JENNIE m Edward Seward & lived in Darby Twp, 1890s.
McMANN, JOHN - bc 1840, OH; mul farm laborer. mother b VA.
m Rebecca (Vines). (Circleville, 1860-1880)
    Rebecca - bc 1856, OH; mul. father b VA; mother b
        OH. (1880)
    Charles F. - b 22 Feb 1881, Circleville.
    George - bc 1864, OH; mul farm laborer. (1880)
    James A. - b 24 Oct 1870, Circleville. mul. (1880)
    Mary Jane - b 1 Aug 1872, Circleville. mul. (1880)
McMANN, JOHN m Mary (Douglas) & lived in Circleville,
1860s. --possibly first spouse of above--
    Charles - b Apr 1866, Circleville; d 11 Oct 1867,
        Circleville of croup.
McMANN (also McMAHON and McMAHON), MARY J. - bc 1837, VA; d
Aug 1878, Circleville of brain tumor. mul. (Circle-
ville, 1870)
    George W. - bc 1846, OH; mul laborer. (1870)
    George - bc 1854, OH; mul. (1870)
    John - bc 1858, OH; mul. (1870)
McMILLEN, CELIA A. - b 1857, Franklin Co; d 7 Feb 1877,
Darby Twp. of typhoid fever.

Ma___, KEZZIAH - bc 1805, VA; bl. parents both b VA.
(Pickaway Twp, 1880)
    Andrew - bc 1848, VA; bl. parents both b VA. (1880)
    Minnie - bc 1877, OH; bl. parents both b VA. (1880)
MADDEN, ELIZA m William Mitchell & lived in Circleville,
1870s.
MADDIE, JOHNSON - b Jan 1842, W VA; bl farmer. parents
both b W VA. m Mary A (____). (Monroe Twp, 1900)
    Mary A. - b Nov 1849, OH. parents both b VA. (1900)
    Jennie - b Nov 1875, OH; bl servant. (1900)
    Robert - b Mar 1873, OH; bl farm laborer. (1900)
MADDY, WILLIAM - b July 1845, OH; bl farm laborer. parents
both b W VA. (Monroe Twp, 1900)
MAINS (also MAYNES), JOHN - bc 1837, NC; bl car man.
parents both b NC. m Jane F. (____). (Circleville,
1880)
    Jane F. - bc 1830, NC; bl. parents both b NC.
        (1880)
    Ada - b 16 July 1871, Circleville. bl. (1880) --
        parents listed as John and Varta (Weaver) Mains--

John - bc 1870, OH; bl. (1880)
Martha - bc 1866, NC; bl. (1880)
Mary - bc 1864, NC; bl. (1880)
MAINS, JOHN - b 1862, OH; d 19 Apr 1868, Circleville of
consumption.
MALONE, SUSAN - b Jan 1829, GA; bl. parents both b GA.
(Circleville, 1860-1900)
    Daniel - bc 1846, GA; bl. (1860)
    Eliza A. - b 1850 or 1852, GA; bl servant. parents
        both b GA. (1860-1880)
    Georgia Anna - b 1856, GA; bl. m Ephraim Hyman &
        lived in Circleville, 1870s. (1860-1870)
    Mary J. - bc 1852, GA; bl. (1860)
    Moses - bc 1848, GA; bl. (1860)
    Peter - b 1858, GA; bl waiter. (1860-1870)
MAME, EDDIE - b 1860, NC; d 19 Apr 1868, Circleville of
pneumonia.
MANCE, MORROW and wife lived in Salt Creek Twp, 1820.
MANIE, MARY m John Redman & lived in Circleville, 1880s.
MANO, JOHN - bc 1839, NC; bl laborer. m Jane (_____).
(Circleville, 1870)
    Jane - bc 1839, NC; bl. (1870)
    Cynthia - bc 1866, NC; bl. (1870)
    John - b 1870, NC; bl. (1870)
    Mary - bc 1861, NC; bl. (1870)
MARCHANT, John - bc 1828, VA; bl laborer. m Sarah (_____).
(Circleville, 1860)
    Sarah - bc 1824, NC; bl. (1860)
    Harriet - bc 1847, OH; bl. (1860)
MARICK, MARY F. - bc 1843, OH; mul. (Deer Creek, 1850)
MARTIN, SAMPSON - b Nov 1878, VA; bl farm laborer. parents
both b VA. (Jackson Twp, 1900)
MASEL, JAMES - bc 1820, DEL; bl farm laborer. m Elisabeth
(_____). (Perry Twp, 1860)
    Elisabeth - bc 1822, DEL; mul. (1860)
    Charles C. - bc 1852, DEL; mul. (1860)
    Cornelia - b 1859, DEL; mul. (1860)
    George W. - bc 1848, DEL; mul. (1860)
    Nathan - bc 1854, DEL; mul. (1860)
    Nehemiah - bc 1856, DEL; mul. (1860)
MASON, GEORGE - bc 1862, OH; bl farm laborer. m Martha
(Jackson). (Scioto Twp, 1880)
    George - b 12 Oct 1885, Circleville.
MASON, MARY - b Mar 1850, OH. parents both b VA. (Circle-
ville, 1900)
    George - b Feb 1876, OH; bl farmhand. parents both b
        OH. (1900)
MASON, MARY m Reuben Stevens & lived in Circleville, 1880s.
--spelled Mayson; may be same as above--

MATHINEAU, ANDREW - bc 1845, OH; mul. (Deer Creek, 1850)
MAXWELL, GEORGE W. m Maggie (Gates) & lived in Circleville, 1880s.
    George W. - b 31 July 1884, Circleville
MAY, ADALINE m Everett Bird & lived in Circleville, 1890s.
MAY, JAMES - b May 1844, VA; mul day laborer and servant. parents both b VA. m Susan (____). (Jackson Twp, 1880; Circleville, 1900)
    Susan - b Jan 1844, VA; mul. parents both b VA. (1880-1900)
    Bylsha - bc 1872, OH; mul. (1880)
    Elizabeth - bc 1869, OH; mul. (1880)
    Noah - b Mar 1881, Jackson Twp; bl day laborer. (1900)
MAY, JOHN C - b Mar 1881, VA; bl day laborer. parents both b VA. (Circleville, 1900)
MAY, MARTHA - bc 1787, VA; mul laborer. parents both b VA. (Jackson Twp, 1880)
    Daniel - bc 1861, OH; mul laborer. (1880)
    Rashel - bc 1863, OH; mul servant. (1880)
    Walter - bc 1856, OH; mul laborer. (1880)
MAYO, ANDREW (also listed as SUDAN) - b Aug 1858, VA; bl farmer. parents both b VA. m Ida and lived in Walnut Twp, 1880s. (Pickaway Twp, 1900)
    Ida (Hanton, Lawson or Woplington) - b Sept 1855, OH; father b VA; mother b TENN. (1900) --various surnames listed in birth records--
    Benjamin E. - b 27 Oct 1888, Williamsport; d Nov 1890, Williamsport of lung fever.
    John Sherman - b 25 Mar 1886, Walnut Twp.
    Mina D. - b Aug 1882, OH; bl houseworker. (1900)
    Nettie E. - b 26 Feb 1891, Deer Creek Twp.
    Susie - b Sept 1884, OH; bl houseworker. (1900)
    William M. - b Dec 1892, OH; bl. (1900)
MAYO, SUSAN lived in Circleville, 1870s.
    Nellie - b 8 June 1870, Circleville.
MEDLAY, WILLIAM - bc 1829, VA; bl farm laborer. (Wayne Twp, 1870)
MEEKS, JESSE M. - bc 1834, VA; bl minister. m Eliza (____). (Circleville, 1870)
    Eliza - bc 1839, OH; bl. (1870)
    Clara - b 2 Apr 1868, Circleville. bl. (1870)
MEREDITH, RICHARD - bc 1831, VA; mul brick maker. m Cordelia (____). (Circleville, 1860)
    Cordelia - bc 1831, PA; mul. (1860)
    Arthur - bc 1854, OH; mul. (1860)
    George - bc 1857, OH; mul. (1860)
    James - b 1860, Circleville. mul. (1860)

MEREDITH, WILLIAM m Martha (Barnes) & lived in Circleville, 1870s.
    Charles - b Sept 1871, Circleville; d Dec 1872, Circleville.
MERIDY, ISAAC - bc 1845, KY; bl laborer. m Elizabeth (_____). (Circleville, 1870)
    Elizabeth - bc 1847, MD; bl. (1870)
    Edward - b 1870, Circleville. bl. (1870)
    Mary J. - bc 1869, Circleville. bl. (1870)
MERRITT, THOMAS - bc 1818, VA; mul laborer. m Mary (_____). with wife, 2 sons and daughter in Circleville, 1840. (Circleville, 1840-1850)
    Mary - bc 1828, PA; mul. (1850)
    Frances E. - bc 1839, Circleville. mul. (1850)
    William - bc 1838, Circleville. mul. (1850)
MILES, CAECELIA - bc 1845, OH; bl. (Circleville, 1860)
MILES, CORDELIA - bc 1847, OH; bl. m George M. Dade & lived in Circleville, 1870s. (Jackson Twp, 1860)
MILES, MARY - bc 1840, OH; bl. (Circleville, 1850)
MILES, MICHAEL and 2 males, 3 females in Circleville, 1840.
MILLER, EDWARD - bc 1836, VA; mul. (Circleville, 1850)
MILLER, FRANCES m Henry Ganaway & lived in Circleville, 1870s and 1880s.
MILLER, HARRY - b 1876, Washington Twp; d 7 Nov 1881, Washington Twp.
MILLER, HESTER E. m Richard Milton Jackson & lived in Darby Twp, 1890s.
MILLER, JOHN - b 1813 or 1815, VA; listed bl & mul laborer. m Lydia (_____). (Circleville, 1850-1860)
    Lydia - bc 1823, VA; mul. (1850)
    Ann - bc 1845, OH; mul. (1850)
    Charles F. - bc 1852, Circleville. bl. (1860)
    James - b 1843, OH; listed bl and mul drayman and laborer. (Circleville, 1850-1880)
    John H. - bc 1854, Circleville. bl. (1860)
    Josephus - b 1846, OH; listed bl & mul barber. (Circleville, 1850-1870) --listed as Joseph in 1870--
    Samuel K. - bc 1847, OH; listed bl & mul. (1850-1860)
MILLER, LUCY lived in Washington Twp. 1870s.
    Noah - b 21 Jan 1875, Washington Twp. Infirmary.
MILLER, MARTHA - bc 1820, Campbell Co, VA. freed by Samuel Miller 3 May 1845 & lived in Pickaway Co, 1846.
MILLER, MARY R. m Thad E. Cromley & lived in Harrison Twp, 1870s.
MILLER, OCTAVIA - b Apr 1833, VA. parents both b VA. (Circleville, 1900)
MILLER, RACHEL - bc 1863, VA; mul. parents both b VA. (Circleville, 1880)

MILTON, ADLINE - bc 1846, OH; bl woman of "easy virtue".
black. (Circleville, 1870)
    Frank - b 1870, Circleville. bl. (1870)
MINOR, WILLIAM - bc 1846, OH; bl farm laborer. (Perry Twp,
1870)
MITCHELL, CATHERINE - b Jan 1843, VA. parents both b VA.
(Circleville, 1900)
MITCHELL, DELILAH - b 13 Mar 1871, Circleville; d 22 June
1874, Circleville of bronchitis.
MITCHELL, ELLIS - b 1845, KY or OH; bl farm laborer.
(South Bloomfield, 1870)
MITCHELL, MARY - bc 1820, NC; bl. parents both b NC.
(Circleville, 1880)
    Daniel - bc 1852, NC; bl barber. parents both b NC.
        (1880)
    Lincoln - bc 1861, OH; bl. parents both b NC.
        (1880)
MITCHELL, SADIE m Richard Redman & lived in Circleville,
1890s.
MITCHELL, SARAH - bc 1803, SC; bl. (Circleville, 1870)
    Ellis - b 1845, KY; bl laborer. (1870) --see sepa-
        rate listing--
    Julia A. - bc 1839, KY; bl laborer. (1870)
    Olander - bc 1846, KY; bl laborer. (1870)
MITCHELL, WILLIAM - b Mar 1832, VA. parents both b VA.
(Circleville, 1900)
    Anna - b July 1857, W VA. parents both b VA. (1900)
MITCHELL, WILLIAM - b 1835, OH; bl farmer. parents both b
SC. m Eliza Jane (_____). (Circleville, 1870-1880)
    Eliza Jane - b 1838, KY; bl. parents both b KY.
        (1870-1880)
    Charles W. - b 15 Jan 1874, Circleville. bl. (1880)
    David - b 4 Jan 1869, Circleville. bl. (1870-1880)
    Emma - bc 1876, Circleville. bl. (1880)
    James M. - b 1859, OH; bl farm laborer. (1870-1880)
    John W. - b 1857, OH; bl butler in hotel. (1870-1880)
    Leona - bc 1866, OH; bl. (1870)
    Martha - b 1863, OH; bl. (1870-1880)
    Mary G. - b 1861, OH; bl domestic servant. (1870-
        1880)
    Sarah - bc 1871, Circleville. bl. (1880)
    William H. - b 1865, OH; bl. (1870-1880)
MOGENS, EDWARD - bc 1800, VA; bl. m Elizabeth (_____).
(Muhlenburg Twp, 1850)
    Elizabeth - bc 1785, VA; bl. (1850)
MONS, ELIZA - b May 1865, VA. parents both b VA, (Darby
Twp, 1900)

MONTGOMERY, PETER - b Feb 1844, KY; bl brick molder and
    laborer. parents both b KY. m Rebecca   (Circleville,
    1880-1900)
        Rebecca (Chavish) or (Johnson). - b Sept 1857, OH;
            bl. father b VA; mother b NC. (1880-1900) --
            birth records list both surnames--
        Flora B. - b 23 June 1874, Circleville. bl. (1880)
        William H. - b 28 Feb 1876, Circleville. bl. (1880)
MOORE, JOHN - b Apr 1872, OH; bl day laborer. parents both
    b OH. (Circleville, 1900)
MOORE, RACHEL - b 1847, NC; d 12 Mar 1891, Circleville of
    consumption. widow.
MOORE, RICHARD and 4 males, 3 females lived in Circleville,
    1840.
MOORE, WESLEY - b Mar 1853, OH; bl farmworker. parents
    both b NC. m 1st, America (____); 2nd, Sarah (____).
    (Walnut Twp, 1880; Circleville, 1900)
        America - bc 1833, OH; bl. parents both b OH.
            (1880)
        Sarah - b May 1853, OH. parents both b NC. (1900)
        Dilsie - bc 1875, OH; bl. (1880)
        Dolly - bc 1866, OH; bl. (1880)
        Henry - b Sept 1844, OH; bl cobler. parents both b
            NC. (1900)
        Lawrence - bc 1876, OH; bl. (1880)
MOORE, WILLIAM - bc 1861, OH; bl laborer. mother b OH.
    (Circleville, 1880)
MORLEY, BOONE - b Dec 1873, OH; bl farm laborer. father b
    NC; mother b VA. m Dolly (____). (Monroe Twp, 1900)
        Dolly - b Oct 1878, OH. father b OH; mother b MICH.
            (1900)
        Edna - b July 1896, OH. (1900)
        Ruphus - b June 1898, OH. (1900)
MORLY, SARAH - bc 1857, OH; bl. parents both b NC.
    (Circleville, 1880)
MORRIS, GEORGE - b Mar 1845, VA; bl laborer. parents both
    b VA. m Martha (____). (Circleville, 1870-1900)
        Martha - b Jan 1849, VA; bl. parents both b VA.
            (1870-1900)
        Levina - b 1867 or 1869, Circleville. bl. (1870-
            1880)
MORRIS, MYRTLE B. - b July 1879, Circleville; d 21 Jan
    1880, Circleville of consumption.
MORRIS, RICHARD H. - bc 1849, OH; bl clergyman. father b
    NC; mother b OH. (Circleville, 1880)
        Thomas E. - bc 1874, OH; bl. (1880)
MOSBY, ELIZABETH - b 22 Dec 1870, Circleville; d 28 Dec
    1870, Circleville.

MOSBY, JAMES - bc 1839, VA; bl plasterer. m Sarah (_____).
    (Circleville, 1870)
        Sarah - b 1843, OH; d 16 Feb 1877, Circleville. bl.
        (1870)
        Alfred - b 1862, OH; d 8 Aug 1876, Circleville of
            consumption. bl. (1870)
        Joseph - b 1865, Circleville; d 14 Apr 1871, Circle-
            ville of consumption.
        Margaret - bc 1859, OH; bl. (1870)
MOSBY, JAMES m Mary (_____) & lived in Circleville, 1860s.
    --this may have been above James with first wife--
        Mary - b 1863, Circleville; d 16 Oct 1867, Circle-
            ville of lung fever.
MOSBY, JENNIE - bc 1868, OH; bl. mother b NC. (Circle-
    ville, 1880)
MOSBY, JOSEPH - b 1842, VA; d 24 Dec 1867, Circleville of
    lung fever. barber.
MOSEBY, WADE - b 1800, 1818 or 1820, Lynchburg, VA; d 27
    Sept 1872, Circleville of consumption. mul carpenter
    and hotel steward. parents both b VA. m Serena
    (_____). (Circleville, 1850-1880)
        Serena - b 1816, VA; mul. parents both b VA. (1850-
            1880)
        George M. - b 1842 or 1844, VA; mul farm laborer.
            (1850-1860)
        James - b 1840, VA; d 28 Jan 1871, Circleville of
            consumption. mul plasterer. (1850-1870)
        Joseph - b 1841, VA; mul farm laborer. (1850-1860)
        Wade - b 1845, VA; mul. (1850-1860)
MOSLEY, W.W. - b 1837, VA; d 2 Jan 1899, Circleville Twp.
    of exposure. laborer.
MOSS, DANIEL T. - bc 1827, PA; mul barber. (Circleville,
    1850)
MOSS, JOHN - bc 1849, VA; d 25 Apr 1868, Circleville of
    accident.
MOTTER, MARY - b 1802; d 23 Dec 1867, Circleville of
    consumption.
MOULTON, MARIAH - bc 1834, VA; bl. (Circleville, 1870)
        Amelia - bc 1858, VA; bl. (1870)
        George - b 1869, Circleville. bl. (1870)
        William - bc 1854, VA; bl laborer. (1870)
MOYER, ELLA m James W. Wolf & lived in Salt Creek Twp,
    1890s.
MULLEY, SMITH - bc 1825, VA; bl laborer. (Circleville,
    1870)
MUNCIE, SARAH J. m Derius McAtee & lived in Wayne Twp,
    1880s.

MURRAY, JAMES W. - b 1824, VA; bl gardener. parents both b
VA. m Hannah (_____). (Circleville, 1860-1880)
    Hannah - b 1817 or 1821, VA; bl. parents both b VA.
    (1860-1880)
MYERS, CHARLES - bc 1857, OH; bl farm laborer. parents
both b VA. (Muhlenburg Twp, 1880)
MYERS, MARY m John Redman & lived in Circleville, 1880s.
MYERS, SAMUEL - bc 1848, ALAB; bl farm laborer. (Jackson
Twp, 1870)
MYERS, SAMUEL - bc 1856, OH; bl farm laborer. (Jackson
Twp, 1870)
MYERS, THOMAS - bc 1845, VA; bl laborer. m Maria (_____).
(Circleville, 1870)
    Maria - bc 1839, VA; bl. (1870)
    Carrington - bc 1861, VA; bl. (1870)

NAPIER, RICHARD - bc 1820, OH; mul. m Mary J. (_____).
(Jackson Twp, 1860)
    Mary J. - bc 1825, OH; mul. (1860)
    Jane - bc 1848, OH; mul. (1860)
NAPPER, MARY - bc 1847, OH; mul. (Circleville, 1860)
NAPPER, REBECCA JANE m Frank Fox & lived in Wayne Twp,
1870s.
NAPPY, REACY m John P. Lucas & lived in Wayne Twp, 1860s.
NASH, WILLIAM - bc 1847, VA; mul clergyman. parents both b
VA. m Fannie (_____). (Circleville, 1880)
    Fannie - bc 1852, OH; mul. parents both b VA. (1880)
    Cornelia - bc 1874, OH; mul. (1880)
    Edward - bc 1877, OH; mul. (1880)
    Joseph A. - bc 1872, OH; mul. (1880)
NEGRESS, EMILY m Johnson Bartlett & lived in Circleville,
1850s.
NEGRO, PARIS m Jane (Heim) & lived in Circleville, 1860s.
    daughter - b 4 Nov 1868, Circleville.
NEWGATE, MARY JANE m George Perry & lived in Circleville,
1870s.
NEWTON, ELIZABETH - b 17 Mar 1875, Darby Twp; d 31 May
1876, Darby Twp.
NICHOLS, ELISABETH - b Aug 1817, OH. parents both b OH.
(Circleville, 1900)
    Florence - b Oct 1887, OH. (1900)
    James - b Jan 1892, OH. (1900)
NICKELS (also NICHOLS, NICHOLAS) --all interchangeable in
various citations--
NICKELS, ABRAHAM - b 1853, OH; bl farmhand. parents both
b OH. m. Malinda or Mary M. (Hargo). (Deer Creek,
1880)

Mary M. (or Malinda) - bc 1858, OH; bl. parents both
   b OH. (1880) -Malinda may have been second name-
Abraham - b 1878, Deer Creek; d. 21 Dec 1879, Deer
   Creek.
George Harness - b 22 Dec 1884, Deer Creek.
Mary F. - bc 1874, OH; bl. (1880)
Roseann - bc 1878, OH; bl. (1880)
NICHOLAS, AGNES m John Harris & lived in Deer Creek, 1880s.
NICHOLS, EDWARD - b 24 Jan 1876, Circleville.
NICKELS, GEORGE HARRIS - b 1821 or 1823, OH; bl farmer and
   laborer. father b KY; mother b OH. m 1st, Sarah
   (_____).; 2nd, Elizabeth (Vargo). (Jackson Twp, 1850;
   Muhlenburg Twp, 1860-1870; Williamsport, 1880) --listed
   as Harris in 1850 census, George in all others--
   Sarah - b 1825 or 1827, OH; bl. (1850-1860)
   Elizabeth (Vargo) - bc 1836, OH; bl. parents both b
      VA. (1880)
   Abraham - b 1853, OH; bl. (1860) --see separate
      listing--
   Allen - bc 1864, OH; bl. (1880)
   Gustavus - b 1858, OH; d 10 July 1869, Circleville of
      consumption.
   Hannah - bc 1861, OH; bl. had daughter Elizabeth by
      John Nickels in 1877. (1880)
   Harney or Harvey - bc 1858, OH; bl. (1860)
   Harvey - bc 1876, OH; bl. (1880)
   Henry C. - b 1847, OH; bl. (1850-1860)
   James - bc 1865, OH; bl. (1880)
   John - bc 1856, OH; bl. (1860)
   John - bc 1872, OH; bl. (1880)
   Mary F. - b 1845, OH; bl. (1850-1860)
   Reason W. - bc 1851, OH; bl. (1860)
   Sarah A. or H. - b 1850, Jackson Twp. bl. (1850-
      1860)
NICHOLS, GEORGE H. - bc 1835, OH; mul farm laborer. m
   Nancy. (Muhlenburg, 1870)
   Nancy (Smith) (or Criger) - bc 1848, OH; mul. (1870)
   Edward - b 1 Jan 1872, Deer Creek. --listed in
      Washington Twp, 1880 census.
   George H. - b 8 Apr 1869; mul. (1870)
   Mary E. - b 8 Apr 1869; mul. (1870)
NICKELS, MARY m Everet Jackson & lived in Muhlenburg Twp,
   1880s.
NICKELS, WILLIAM - b 1772 or 1780, VA; d 6 Nov 1875,
   Pickaway Co. of old age. with 3 males and 1 female in
   Jackson Twp, 1840. --also spelled Nichols-- --may be
   same as below--

NICKELS, WILLIAM - b 1775, KY; bl farm laborer. m Percilla
   (_____). (Jackson Twp, 1850, 1870; Muhlenburg Twp,
   1860) --also spelled Nicholas and Nichols--
      Percilla - b 1800 or 1810, VA; bl. (1850-1870)
      Louisa - b 1846, Jackson Twp; bl housemaid. m
      Dempsey Keys and lived in Circleville.
NICKENS, DAVID and 1 son, 4 females lived in Washington
   Twp, 1820.
NICKENS, EMMA - bc 1859, OH; bl nurse. (Circleville, 1870)
NICKENS, HENRY - b 1831, OH; bl cartman. m 1st, Harriet
   (_____); 2nd, Mary (_____). (Circleville, 1860-1870)
      Harriet - bc 1831, NC; bl. (1860)
      Mary - bc 1843, OH; bl. (1860)
      Andrew - bc 1855, OH; bl. (1860)
      Ardella - bc 1847, OH; bl. m James Burney & lived in
         Circleville, 1870s and 1880s. (1860)
      Edson B. - b 1855, OH; bl laborer. (1860-1880)
      Elizabeth - bc 1867, OH; bl. (1870)
      Irwin - b 1859, Circleville. bl laborer. (1860-
         1880)
      Leah A. - bc 1856, OH; bl. (1860)
      Leurett - bc 1858, OH; bl. (1870)
      Lydia - bc 1864, OH; bl. (1870)
NICKENS, LEWIS and 2 females lived in Jackson Twp, 1830.
NOOKS, NOAH - bc 1858, OH; bl barber. mother b VA. m
   Laverta (_____). (Circleville, 1880)
      Laverta - bc 1860, OH; bl. father b OH; mother b NC.
         (1880)
NOON, WILSON J. - bc 1820, VA; mul. m Narissa (_____).
   (Circleville, 1850)
      Narissa - bc 1820, OH; mul. (1850)
      James - bc 1848, Circleville. mul. (1850)
      Joseph - bc 1848, Circleville. mul. (1850)
      Matilda - bc 1846, Circleville. mul. (1850)
      Samuel - b 1850, Circleville. mul. (1850)
NORMAN, CORDELIA - b Mar 1836, VA. parents both b VA.
   (Circleville, 1900)
NORMAN, FANNIE - bc 1850, W VA; d 6 Mar 1885, Circleville
   in childbirth. married.
NORMAN, FRANCIS - bc 1855, OH; mul. parents both b VA.
   (Circleville, 1880)
NORMAN, J. R. m F. C. (Dickerson) & lived in Circleville,
   1880s.
      Esther E. - b 23 Jan 1881, Circleville.
NORMAN, LOUISA m James Wright & lived in Circleville,
   1870s.
NORMAN, WILLIAM - b 1814, 1816 or 1818, VA; listed bl & mul
   Baptist clergyman. mother b VA. m Catherine (Redman).
   (Circleville, 1860-1880)

Catherine - b 1816, W VA; d 2 June 1885, Pickaway Co.
    mul. parents both b VA. (1860-1880)
Harriet - bc 1844, OH; bl. (1860)
Joseph - b 26 June 1857, Circleville. listed bl &
    mul ice dealer. (1860-1880)
Laura - bc 1852, OH; mul. (1860)
William H. - b 1837, OH; d 13 Aug 1879, Chillicothe
    of consumption. listed bl & mul barber. married.
    (1860-1870)

OGAL, DANIEL - bc 1819, NC; bl laborer. m Lucy (_____).
    (Circleville, 1870)
    Lucy - bc 1822, NC; bl. (1870)
    Benjamin - bc 1849, NC; bl. (1870)
    Clemons - bc 1859, NC; bl. (1870)
    David - bc 1862, NC; bl. (1870)
    Jonathan - bc 1857, NC; bl. (1870)
    Rosa - bc 1855, NC; bl. (1870)
    Susan - bc 1852, NC; bl. (1870)
OLDS, MARTHA - bc 1820, VA; mul. (Circleville, 1850)
OTER, LUCY - bc 1860, VA; bl. (Muhlenburg Twp, 1870)
OTEY, GEORGE lived in Darby Twp, 1870s.
    Carrie B. - b 24 Dec 1876, Darby Twp.
OUTLAND, ROSANNA - b 1836, Wayne Co, IND; d 27 Nov 1876,
    Circleville of heart disease. married.

PALM, ELIZABETH - bc 1857, OH; bl. (Circleville, 1860)
PARKER, FERDINAND - b Mar 1845, VA; mul plasterer. parents
    both b VA. m Ellen V. (Walker) (Circleville, 1880-
    1900)
    Ellen V. - bc 1849, OH; mul hairdresser. parents
        both b VA. (1880)
    Clara E. - b 27 Jan 1879, Circleville. mul. (1880)
    Harry B. - b Sept 1873, OH; mul. (1880-1900)
    Martha V. - b 20 Dec 1876, Circleville. mul. (1880)
    Samuel - b 2 June 1874, Circleville. mul. (1880)
PARSLEY, SAMUEL - bc 1855, VA; mul. parents both b VA.
    (Muhlenburg Twp, 1880)
PASTORIA, _____ m Edward Scott & lived in Muhlenburg Twp,
    1870s.
PATRICK, NELLIE - bc 1884, Circleville; d 20 Sept 1890,
    Circleville of consumption.
PATTEN (also spelled PATTENT and PATTON)
PATTEN, ALEXANDER - b July 1832, KY; bl laborer. parents
    both b TENN. m Caroline (Durham). (Circleville, 1870-
    1900)
    Caroline - b Nov 1838, ALAB; bl. parents both b VA.
        (1870-1900)

Alexander - b 1860 or 1862, ALAB; d 12 July 1892,
    Circleville of consumption. bl barber. married.
    (1870)
Amanda - bc 1868, Circleville. bl. (1870)
Cardwell - bc 1851, VA; bl housemaid. (1870)
Dolly - bc 1853, ALAB; bl cook. (1870)
Edward - b May 1894, OH. (1900)
Emma - bc 1861, ALAB; bl. (1870)
Florence - b Dec 1893, OH. (1900)
Maggie - b 1863, ALAB; listed bl & mul. had daughter
    in 1893 or 1894, Circleville. (Circleville, 1870-
    1880)
Mary - b July 1891, OH. (1900)
Midas - b 1870, Circleville. bl. (1870)
Porter - bc 1854, ALAB; bl laborer. (1870)
William A. - b 5 Apr 1871, Circleville.
PATTEN, ALEXANDER m Cinderella (White) & lived in Circle-
    ville, 1870s.
    Cinderella - b 1853, Mobile, ALAB; d 1 July 1889,
        Circleville of consumption.
    Alexander - b 10 Jan 1870, Circleville.
    Charles - b 6 Dec 1872, Circleville
    Dolphus - b 5 Dec 1872, Harrison Twp.
    James Mader - b 1 Aug 1876, Circleville
    Louisa - b 5 Dec 1877, Circleville.
    Sydney - b July 1871, Circleville; d 1 Dec 1877,
        Circleville.
PATTEN, ALEXANDER - b 1873, Circleville; d 29 Apr 1878,
    Circleville.
PATTEN, ANNA m Samuel Smith & lived in Circleville, 1890s.
PATTEN, DRUSILLA m Noah Hudson & lived in Circleville,
    1870s-1900s.
PATTEN, ELIOTT - bc 1831, TENN; bl gardener. mother b
    TENN. m Caroline (____). (Circleville, 1880)
    Caroline - bc 1835, ALAB. bl. mother b VA. (1880)
    Eliott - bc 1862, ALAB; bl laborer. (1880)
    Ella - bc 1854, ALAB; bl cook. (1880)
    Emery - bc 1860, ALAB; bl domestic laborer. (1880)
    James - bc 1876, ALAB; bl. (1880)
    Louisa - bc 1871, ALAB; bl. (1880)
PATTEN, EMILY - bc 1861, VA; bl servant. mother b ALAB.
    (Circleville, 1880)
PATTEN, ISAAC - bc 1854, GA; bl farm laborer. (Wayne Twp,
    1870)
PATTEN, MAUD - b 1868, Circleville; d Sept 1874, Circle-
    ville of consumption.
PATTERSON, HANNAH - bc 1787; d 9 July 1880, Deer Creek of
    old age. widow.

PATTON, ELISABETH - b Aug 1870, OH. father b OH; mother b
    NC. (Circleville, 1900)
        Josephine - b Jan 1891, OH. father b MISS; mother b
            VA. (1900)
PAYNE, ADDIE - b June 1876, OH; bl servant. parents both b
    OH. (Washington Twp, 1900)
PAYNE, CLARENCE - b Apr 1876, IND; bl hosler. (Circle-
    ville, 1900)
PAYNE, EDWARD - bc 1853, OH; mul express wagon driver.
    father b OH; mother b VA. m Fanny (_____). (Circle-
    ville, 1880)
        Fanny - bc 1854, VA; mul. parents both b VA. (1880)
PAYNE, FRANK - bc 1885, Fayette Co; d Feb 1890, New Holland
    of diptheria.
PAYNE, GILBERT - bc 1856, OH; bl reverend. parents both b
    KY. (Scioto Twp, 1880)
PAYNE, JOHN T. - bc 1846, Bloomfield; d 1 Feb 1891, Circle-
    ville of hemorrhage. laborer.
PAYNE, LAWRENCE m Emily (Logan) & lived in Perry Twp,
    1890s.
        Mack - b 20 Oct 1886, Fayette Co.
        Ruth - b 16 Mar 1892, Perry Twp.
PEAL, JEANETTE m Theodore Adams & lived in Darby Twp,
    1870s.
PERKINS, ANDREW - bc 1843, VA; bl farm laborer. (Wayne
    Twp, 1870)
PERKINS, WARNER - bc 1834, DEL; bl. m Nancy (_____).
    (Wayne Twp, 1860)
        Nancy - bc 1835, DEL; bl. (1860)
        George - bc 1857, OH; bl. (1860)
        John - bc 1859, OH; bl. (1860)
PERLS, FREDERICK - b 1822 or 1825, NC; bl farm laborer and
    slaughter house laborer. parents both b VA. m Anna or
    Almira (_____). (Circleville, 1850-1880)
        Anna or Almira - b 1826, OH; mul. (1850-1860)
        John - bc 1844, OH; mul. (1850)
PERRY, EDWARD - b Mar 1875, OH; bl farm laborer. parents
    both b OH. (Jackson Twp, 1900)
PERRY, JAMES - b 1810, MD or SC or 1818, VA; d 24 June
    1898, Washington Twp. Infirmary of old age. mul farmer.
    at death listed as pauper. m Marion or Mary (Reicher-
    son). (Pickaway Twp, 1850-1860) --census and death
    records list different states of birth--
        Mary or Marion - b 1817 or 1819, VA; mul. (1850-
            1860)
        George M. - b 1844, VA; mul. (1850-1860)
        Margaret - bc 1845, VA; mul. (1850)

Mary Jane - b 17 Nov 1839, VA; d 27 Feb 1877, Picka-
way Twp. of bronchitis. mul. (1850-1860)
William R. - b 1851, Pickaway Twp. mul. (1860)
PERRY, MARY JANE - b 1849, Hocking Co; d 18 Sept 1879,
Pickaway Co. of consumption.
PERRY, SARAH C. - bc 1847, WISC; mul. parents both b NY.
(Pickaway Twp, 1880) --m. to Robert Perry listed as
Indian--
PERRY, THERESA - b 1870, Pickaway Co; d 20 Nov 1886, Picka-
way Co. of lung disease.
PETERS, JOHN - bc 1828, VA; bl commercial laborer. (Perry
Twp, 1860)
PETERS, THOMAS - bc 1851, OH; mul laborer. parents both b
OH. m Emma L. (_____). (Darby Twp, 1880)
    Emma L. - bc 1860, VA; mul. parents both b VA.
    (1880)
    William M. - b 1880, OH; mul. (1880)
PETERS, THOMAS C. - bc 1849, OH; mul school teacher.
parents both b VA. m Emma (Stepter). (Muhlenburg Twp,
1880) --data is similar to above Thomas and family and
is probably the same family--
    Emma - bc 1860, OH; bl. parents both b VA. (1880)
    Ann - b 1 May 1882, Muhlenburg Twp.
    William - b 7 Jan 1880, OH; black. (1880)
PETERSON, ANTHONY - b Feb 1894, OH. parents both b OH.
(Circleville, 1900)
    Sadie - b Oct 1899, OH. father b VA; mother b OH.
    (1900)
PETERSON, JOHN - bc 1852, TENN; bl house servant. (Circle-
ville, 1870)
PETERSON, KATE m David Dayton & lived in Circleville,
1860s.
PETERSON, MAGGIE - bc 1856, OH; bl. (Circleville, 1870) --
may be d/o Mary Peterson--
PETERSON, MARY - bc 1832, OH; bl. (Circleville, 1860)
    Margaret - bc 1858, OH; bl. (1860)
    Priscilla - bc 1856, OH; bl. (1860)
    Susanna - b 1860, Circleville. bl. (1860)
PETERSON, MARY - b Mar 1843, VA; parents both b VA.
(Circleville, 1900)
    Ida - b June 1877, OH. parents both b NC. (1900)
PETERSON, MINDORA - b June 1875, Circleville; d 4 Sept
1876, Circleville of brain fever.
PETERSON, REUBEN B. - b 1835 or 1838, VA; bl laborer.
mother b VA. m Mary C. (Holmes). (Circleville, 1860-
1880)
    Mary C. - bc 1839, VA; d 1882, Circleville of con-
    sumption. bl. (1870-1880)

90

Isabel - bc 1877, Circleville. bl. (1880)
Lucy Ann - b 1867, Circleville. bl. (1870-1880)
Mary - bc 1868, Circleville. bl. (1870)
Reuben, Jr. - b. 1869, Circleville. black. (1880)
    -see separate listing--
Robert Lewis - b 4 Oct 1872, Circleville
Rose - bc 1859, OH; bl. (1870)
PETERSON, ROSE - bc 1863, OH; bl domestic servant. father
b OH; mother b VA. (Circleville, 1880) --may be d/o
Reuben and Mary C. Peterson--
PETERSON, RUBIN - b Sept 1869, OH; bl day laborer. father
b OH; mother b VA. m. Jennie (_____). (Circleville,
1900)
    Jennie - b July 1876, OH. father b OH; mother b VA.
        (1900)
    Netty - b Feb 1897, Circleville. (1900)
PETERSON, WILLIAM - bc 1836, VA; d 26 Feb 1896, Washington
Twp. of brain fever. bl laborer. m Mary (_____).
(Circleville, 1860)
    Mary - bc 1827, PA; bl. (1860)
    Ephraim W. - bc 1859, Circleville. bl. (1860)
    William E. - bc 1857, OH; bl. (1860)
PETTYFORD, ROSWELL - b 1852, NC; d 7 Sept 1885, Circle-
ville. bl laborer and saloon keeper. mother b NC. m
Susan (_____). (Circleville, 1870-1880)
    Susan - bc 1859, OH; bl. father b OH; mother b NC.
        (1880)
PHILLIPS, ARTHUR - b 1890, Circleville; d 1 May 1891,
Circleville.
PHILLIPS, BAZIL lived in Circleville, 1860s.
    son - b 4 Jan 1869, Circleville.
PHILLIPS, GIBSON - bc 1844, OH; bl farm laborer. father b
MISS; mother b OH. m 1st, Jane (_____); 2nd, Mary A.
(Brown). (Jackson Twp, 1860; Circleville Twp, 1870;
Circleville, 1880)
    Jane - b 1 Apr 1834, VA; d 6 July 1875, Circleville
        Twp. of inflamation of bowels. bl. (1870)
    Anna - b 1866, OH; bl. (1870-1880)
    Christopher - b 1860 or 1868, OH; bl worker in brick-
        yard. (1870-1880)
    Jane - bc 1871, OH; bl. (1880)
    John - b 18 July 1878, Circleville; d 20 Mar 1879,
        Circleville of internal fever.
    Martha J. - b 21 Aug 1870, Circleville.
    Mary - b 1863 or 1865, OH; bl. (1870-1880)
    William - bc 1858, VA; bl day laborer. (1880)
    MARIA - bc 1810, OH; bl. father b OH; mother b VA.
        (1880)

PHILLIPS, HARRIET - b Aug 1858, OH; bl housekeeper. father
  b VA; mother b NC. (Circleville, 1900)
    Gibson - b Feb 1881, OH; bl day laborer. parents
      both b OH. (1900)
    Hannah - b Feb 1885, OH. parents both b OH. (1900)
PHILLIPS, JOHN and 2 males, 5 females lived in Jackson Twp,
  1840.
PHILLIPS, MARY m James Rollins & lived in Circleville,
  1870s.
PIERCE, ANNA m James Randolph & lived in Circleville,
  1870s.
PITMAN, DANIEL - b Mar 1831, VA; bl laborer. parents both
  b VA. m Sarah (____). (Circleville, 1880-1900)
    Sarah - b Jan 1843, OH; bl. father b VA; mother b
      NC. (1880-1900)
    Naoma - bc 1866, OH; bl. (1880)
PITTS, HAMPSHIRE - bc 1779. freed by Arthur Pitts in
  Robertson Co, TENN, Aug 1819. lived in Circleville,
  1820.
POINDEXTER, ABRAHAM - b 1850, VA; mul farmer. parents both
  b VA. m Margaret (____). (same listings for both
  Darby and Muhlenburg Twps, 1880)
    Margaret - bc 1860, NC; mul. parents both b NC.
      (1880)
    Harley - bc 1878, OH; mul. (1880)
POINDEXTER, ELIZABETH - b 1834, Circleville; d 30 June
  1887, Circleville of lung disease.
POINDEXTER, JOSEPH - b 1817, 1820 or 1822, Richmond, VA; d
  22 Feb 1891, Circleville of old age. mul blacksmith and
  laborer. m Evaline (____). (Circleville, 1850-1880)
    Evaline - b 1820 or 1823, VA; mul. (1850-1880)
    Catherine - bc 1836, OH; mul. (1850)
POINDEXTER, MATTIE - b 1870, Circleville; d 30 Nov 1887,
  Circleville of lung disease.
POINDEXTER, THOMAS - bc 1853, VA; bl farm laborer. parents
  both b VA. m Hannah (____). (Monroe Twp, 1880)
    Hannah - bc 1854, OH; bl. parents both b OH. (1880)
    Mary A. - bc 1878, OH; bl. (1880)
    Samuel - b 29 Feb 1880, Monroe Twp. bl. (1880)
    William - bc 1877, OH; bl. (1880)
    MARY - bc 1830, VA; bl. parents both b VA. (1880)
POINDEXTER, WILLIAM - bc 1861, OH; bl farm laborer.
  parents both b VA. (1880)
POINTER, HARRISON - bc 1836, OH; mul. (Circleville, 1850)
POINTER, JAMES S. - bc 1833, OH; mul. (Circleville, 1850)
POPE, WILLIAM - b Dec 1855, KY; bl day laborer. parents
  both b KY. m Minnie (____). (Circleville, 1900)

92

Minnie - b Sept 1859, OH; bl cook. parents both b
   OH. (1900)
   Ada - b Sept 1895, OH. (1900)
POULSON, CORDELIA - bc 28 Aug 1838; d 20 June 1876, Darby
   Twp. married.
PRATT, JENNIE - bc 1808, OH; bl servant. (Madison Twp,
   1860)
PRATT, MARY - b 4 Apr 1824, PA; d 12 Feb 1877, Darby Twp.
   married.
PRICE, ELLEN m James Commander & lived in Circleville,
   1870s.
PRITCHARD, JAMES - bc 1772, VA; bl. m Hannah (_____).
   (Monroe Twp, 1850)
   Hannah - bc 1774, VA; bl. (1850)
PRITCHARD, JAMES - bc 1851, VA; mul. (Muhlenburg Twp,
   1860)
   Matilda - bc 1857, OH; mul. (1860)
PRITCHARD, MARY VIRGINIA - b 2 Aug 1848, Hardy Co, W VA; d
   20 July 1873, Harrison Twp. of brain inflamation.
PUTNAM, JOHN - bc 1825, VA; mul shoemaker. (Circleville,
   1870)
   Martha - bc 1844, VA; mul. (1870)

QARLES, CHARLES- bc 1844, OH; bl servant. (Wayne Twp,
   1860)

RAGLAND, CHARLES R. m R. (Bouderand) & lived in Muhlenburg
   Twp, 1870s.
   Robert F. - b 23 Jan 1872, Jefferson Twp, Ross Co.
RAGLIN, PATRICK m Sallie or Sarah (Stepter) & lived in
   Darby Twp, 1870s.
   Clara - b 14 Aug 1878, Muhlenburg Twp.
   Fletcher - b 4 Sept 1873, Darby Twp.
RAMEY, HARRISON - bc 1820, KY; bl farmer. m Frances
   (_____). (Circleville, 1850)
   Frances - bc 1822, VA; bl. (1850)
RAMSIE, DAISY ALMEDA - b 1880, Nelson Co, VA; d 26 Feb
   1881, Wayne Twp.
RANDALL, CLEMENTINE m Ballard T. Steward & lived in Wayne
   Twp.
RANDOLPH, JAMES m Anna (Pierce) & lived in Circleville,
   1870s.
   William - b 8 Dec 1871, Circleville.
RANDOLPH, ROBERT R. - b 1824 or 1827, VA; mul barber. m
   Eliza (_____). (Circleville, 1850-1860)
   Eliza - bc 1831, OH; mul. (1860)
   Cornelia Jane - b 1845, OH; bl. (1850-1860)

93

RANSOM, HARLEY - bc 1878, OH; bl. parents both b VA.
(Scioto Twp, 1880)
RANSOM, SAMUEL - bc Dec 1875, Bridgeport, OH; d 28 Apr
1877, Circleville of consumption.
RANSOM, THOMAS - bc 1859, VA; mul farm laborer. parents
both b VA. m Eliza (Dans). (Harrison Twp, 1880)
    Harvey L. - b 1 Jan 1878, Harrison Twp.
RATTEN, AMANDA - b 1867, Circleville; d June 1870, Circle-
ville of lung fever.
RAY, DANIEL - bc 1847, OH; bl. (Circleville, 1860)
REDDIX (also REDDICKS), JAMES - bc 1860, VA; bl. parents
both b VA. m Sallie (Jackson). (Muhlenburg Twp, 1880)
    James, Jr. - b 21 Nov 1883, Circleville; d 3 Dec
        1883, Circleville.
    James - b 20 Oct 1885, Circleville
    Kate - b 14 May 1890, Circleville
    Shirley - b 23 Oct 1883, Circleville
    Thomas - b 22 Oct 1887, Circleville
REDMAN, ADAM - bc 1834 or 1839, VA; listed bl & mul farm
laborer. parents both b VA. m Lucy Lee (Allen). (Walnut Twp, 1870; Darby Twp, 1880)
    Lucy (also Elizabeth) - b 1842 or 1844, VA; listed bl
        & mul. parents both b VA. (1870-1880)
    Charles L. - b 1869, OH; listed bl & mul. (1870-
        1880)
    Florence Mary - bc 1874, OH; mul. (1880)
    Margaret E. - b 1866, OH; listed bl & mul. (1870-
        1880)
    Mary Ellen - bc 1872, OH; mul. (1880)
    Milton E. - b 1864, VA; listed bl & mul farm laborer.
        (1870-1880)
    Mortimer - b 22 Aug 1879, Darby Twp; mul. (1880)
    Noly Ann - bc 1878, OH; mul. (1880)
    Vera - b 21 May 1885, Williamsport.
REDMAN, ALVA - bc 1890, Circleville; d 25 Feb 1891,
Circleville.
REDMAN, ANDERSON - bc 1875, OH; bl. father b KY; mother b
VA. (Scioto Twp, 1880)
REDMAN, CHARLES - bc 1875, OH; mul. mother b OH. (Circle-
ville, 1880)
REDMAN, CLINT - bc 1858, VA; mul laborer. parents both b
VA. (Jackson Twp, 1880)
REDMAN, DANIEL - b Apr 1845, VA; mul farm laborer. parents
both b VA. m Eliza (____). (Circleville, 1880-1900)
    Eliza - b Oct 1849, OH; bl. parents both b VA.
        (1880-1900)
    Zachariah - b Mar 1874, Circleville. bl. (1880-
        1900)

REDMAN, DAVID - bc 1847, VA; mul farm laborer. (Scioto
  Twp, 1870)
      Ellen - bc 1851, MD; mul. (1870)
      Jacob - bc 1852, VA; mul farm laborer. (1870)
      Martha - bc 1864, OH; mul. (1870)
REDMAN, DOLLIE m Hutson Jones and lived in Darby Twp.
REDMAN, E. - bc 1856, VA; bl farmer. parents both b VA. m
  Mary A. (____). (Pickaway Twp, 1880)
      Mary A. - bc 1857, OH; bl. parents both b VA.
        (1880)
      Ada - bc 1879, Jackson Twp; d 30 Mar 1885, Circle-
        ville of consumption. bl. (1880)
      Francis - bc 1875, OH; mul. (1880)
REDMAN, E. WILLIAM - b Feb 1875, OH; bl farmer. father b
  VA; mother b OH. m. Jennie (____). (Jackson Twp,
  1900)
      Jennie - b Oct 1871, OH. father b VA; mother b NC.
        (1900)
      H. John - b June 1898, OH. (1900)
REDMAN, EDWARD - bc 1805, VA; bl farmer. m Margaret
  (____). (South Bloomfield, 1870)
      Margaret - bc 1805, VA; bl. (1870)
      Elizabeth - bc 1846, VA; bl. (1870)
      Hanee - bc 1843, VA; bl farm laborer. (1870)
      Joseph - bc 1853, VA; bl farm laborer. (1870)
      Martha - bc 1857, VA; bl. (1870)
      Rinick - bc 1852, VA; bl farm laborer. (1870)
      William - bc 1844, VA; bl farm laborer. (1870)
REDMAN, EDWARD JACOB - bc 1857, Chillicothe; d 17 Feb 1885,
  Circleville of consumption. married.
REDMAN, EDWARD m Jane (Thomas) & lived in Williamsport,
  1890s.
      John Hanson - b 15 June 1898, Williamsport.
REDMAN, ELIZA - bc 1812, VA; bl. both parents b VA.
  (Jackson Twp, 1880)
REDMAN, FLORENCE MAY m Mike Reed & lived in Deer Creek Twp,
  1890s.
REDMAN, GEORGE - b 1785, Culpeper Co, VA. freed by John
  Strother, 24 Feb 1808. lived with 1 male, 3 females in
  Washington Twp, 1820.
REDMAN, GEORGE - b 1867, Circleville; d 27 Mar 1897, Wash-
  ington Twp. Infirmary of pneumonia.
REDMAN, HANSON m Annie (Rucy) & lived in Circleville,
  1880s.
      Harley - b 10 May 1879, Monroe Twp.
      William Edward - b 16 Jan 1874, Circleville.
REDMAN, HARRIET m. Joseph Thomas & lived in Circleville,
  1880s.

95

REDMAN, HARRISON - b 1842 or Apr 1848, VA; mul farmer.
parents both b VA. m Resa (_____). (Monroe Twp, 1880;
Williamsport, 1900)
    Resa - b Oct 1853, OH; mul. parents both b NC.
      (1880-1900)
    Alice G. - b Nov 1872, OH; d 15 Nov 1888, Wayne Twp.
      killed on railroad tracks. mul. (1880)
    Anna K. - b Aug 1875, OH; mul. (1880-1900)
    Edward - bc 1874, OH; mul. (1880)
    Harley - b May 1879, OH; mul. (1880-1900)
    Hattie M.- bc 1877, OH; mul. (1880)
    John - bc 1870, OH; mul. (1880)
REDMAN, HATTIE - bc 1875, OH; mul. parents both b OH.
(Washington Twp, 1880)
REDMAN, HESTER (also listed as Ellen) m Solomon Lynch &
lived in Circleville.
REDMAN, ISAAC - bc 1813, VA; bl farm laborer. m Elizabeth
(_____). (Scioto Twp, 1870)
    Elizabeth - bc 1813, VA; bl. (1870)
    Charles - bc 1851, VA; bl. (1870)
    Isaac - bc 1858, VA; bl. (1870)
REDMAN, ISAIAH - bc 1828, VA; bl farmer. m Elizabeth
(_____). (Jackson Twp, 1870)
    Elizabeth - bc 1829, OH; bl. (1870)
    Edward - bc 1857, VA; bl farm laborer. (1870)
    George - bc 1861, VA; bl. (1870)
    John R. - bc 1869, VA; bl farm laborer. (1870)
    Lucy - bc 1864, VA; bl. (1870)
    Mary - bc 1849, VA; bl housemaid. (1870)
    Richard - bc 1876, OH; bl. (1870)
    Sarah - bc 1869, OH; bl. (1870)
REDMAN, JACKSON - bc 1835, VA; mul farm laborer. parents
both b VA. m Nancy A. (Kemper) (Muhlenburg Twp, 1880)
    Nancy A. - bc 1848, OH; mul. father b VA; mother b
      NC. (1880)
    Charles A. - bc 1868, OH; mul. (1880)
    Elizabeth - bc 1871, OH; mul. (1880)
    Jackson - b 29 Nov 1882, Circleville.
    Jesse C. - bc 1872, OH; mul. (1880)
    Josiah - b Nov 1876, OH; mul. (1880)
    William H. - bc 1866, OH; mul. (1880)
    daughter - b 22 Dec 1880; d 23 Dec 1880 of strangu-
      lation.
REDMAN, JACOB - bc 1839, VA; bl farmer. (Jackson Twp,
1870)
REDMAN, JACOB - b Mar 1853, VA; mul farm laborer. parents
both b VA. m Matilda (Jackson). (Circleville, 1880-
1900)

Matilda - b Aug 1853, OH; mul.   parents both b VA.
   (1880-1900)
Jacob - b 1 Sept 1877, Circleville.
R. James - b July 1876, Circleville. mul. (1880-
   1900)
REDMAN, JACOB m Mary (Davis) & lived in Circleville, 1880s.
   Maud - b 23 June 1883, Circleville.
REDMAN, JAMES - bc 1855, OH; bl farm laborer. parents both
   b VA. m Mary (___). (Circleville, 1880)
   Mary - bc 1850, OH; bl cook. (1880)
   John - bc 1878, Circleville. bl. (1880)
   SALLY - bc 1821, VA; bl. parents both b VA.
REDMAN, JAMES A. - bc 1837, VA; bl. (Scioto Twp, 1870)
REDMAN, JAMES (also listed as Joseph) m Eliza (Davis) &
   lived in Pickaway Co., 1870s.
   Davis Anderson - b 30 Oct 1874, Harrison Twp.
   Mamie - b 8 May 1875, Circleville.
REDMAN, JAMES m Mollie (Garnes) & lived in Circleville,
   1880s.
   J.A. - b 16 June 1885, Circleville.
REDMAN, JOHN - bc 1840, OH;bl farm laborer. m Nancy
   (____). (Wayne Twp, 1870)
   Nancy - bc 1848, OH; bl. (1870)
   Charles - b 7 Jan 1868, OH; bl. (1870)
   Elizabeth - b 1870, OH; bl. (1870)
   William - bc 1866, OH; bl. (1870)
REDMAN, JOHN m Mary (Myers) & lived in Circleville, 1880s.
   Elliott - b 2 Sept 1884, Circleville.
   Michael - b 11 Mar 1883, Circleville.
REDMAN, JOHN P. m Dollie (Cox) & lived in Washington Twp,
   1890s.
   Dorothy Iona - b 20 May 1899, Washington Twp.
   Richard A. - b 5 June 1898, Washington Twp.
REDMAN, JOSEPH - bc 1843, W VA; mul farm laborer. parents
   both b W VA. m Mary V. (___). (Circleville, 1880)
   Mary V. - bc 1855, MO; mul. parents both b MO.
   (1880)
REDMAN, JOSEPHINE - b Apr 1879, OH. parents both b VA.
   (Circleville, 1900)
REDMAN, JOSIAH - bc 1827, VA; bl. parents both b VA. m
   Mary E. (____). (Pickaway Twp, 1880)
   Mary E. - bc 1828, VA; bl. father b VA; mother b MD.
   (1880)
   George W. - bc 1860, VA; bl. (1880)
   John R. - bc 1859, VA; bl farmer. (1880)
   Lucy C. - bc 1861, VA; bl. (1880)
   Margaret E. - b July 1873, OH; bl servant. (1880;
   Darby Twp, 1900)

Richard U. - bc 1866, OH; bl. (1880)
        Sarah C. - bc 1868, OH; bl. (1880)
REDMAN, KATE - b 1873; d 15 Oct 1886 of rheumatism.
REDMAN, LOUISA and 4 males, 3 females in Madison Twp, 1830.
REDMAN, MAMIE - b Aug 1871; d 10 Sept 1875, Circleville of
    fever.
REDMAN, MARY - bc 1858, Circleville; d 22 June 1884, Cir-
    cleville of consumption.
REDMAN, MARY - bc 1877, Circleville; d 1892, Circleville of
    consumption.
REDMAN, MARY E. m William Stonup & lived in Circleville,
    1880s.
REDMAN, MAUDE - b Dec 1883, Circleville; d 5 June 1884,
    Circleville of lung fever.
REDMAN, NARCIS m Henry Hudson & lived in Circleville.
REDMAN, NUTT (possibly Knute) - bc 1849, OH; bl laborer.
    (Circleville, 1870)
REDMAN, ORDELIA - bc 1851, VA; bl. (Muhlenburg Twp, 1870)
        Elizabeth - bc 1868, OH; bl. (1870)
REDMAN, RICHARD - b 1839 or 1841, VA; mul farm laborer.
    parents both b VA. m Mary (Davis). (Circleville, 1880)
        Mary - b 1848 or 1852, VA; mul. parents both b VA.
        (1880)
        Alice - b 15 Feb 1874, Circleville. mul. (1880)
        Bertha - bc 1876, Circleville. mul. (1880)
        Emma - b 1870, Circleville. mul. (1880)
        Grace - bc 1878, Circleville. mul. (1880)
        John - bc 1866, Circleville. mul. (1870)
        Josie - b 1880, Circleville. mul. (1880)
        Mary E. - b 26 Jan 1872, Circleville. mul. (1880)
REDMAN, RICHARD - b 1842, OH; mul farm laborer. parents
    both b VA. m Julia (Wyatt). (South Bloomfield, 1870;
    Jackson Twp, 1880)
        Julia - b 1849, OH; mul. parents both b NC. (1870-
        1880)
        Annie - bc 1872, OH; mul. (1880)
        Becky - bc 1873, OH; mul. (1880)
        Dora - b 1869, Circleville. mul. (1870-1880)
        Georgia - bc 1875, OH; mul. (1880)
        Harly - b 17 Jan 1879, Circleville. mul. (1880)
        Harvey - b 17 Jan 1878, Muhlenburg Twp.
        John - b 1880, Jackson Twp. mul. (1880)
        Mary - b 6 Dec 1867, Circleville. mul. (1870-1880)
        Sarah - b 8 Sept 1871, Circleville.
REDMAN, RICHARD m Sadie (Mitchell) & lived in Circleville,
    1890s.
        Fannie - b 9 Dec 1890, Circleville.

REDMAN, SARAH - b 1819; d 30 Mar 1895, Circleville. bl
   domestic servant. (South Bloomfield, 1870)
      Thornton - bc 1850, VA; bl. (1870)
      James - bc 1851, VA; bl. (1870)
REDMAN, SARAH lived in Circleville, 1870s.
      Sarah - b 1 Nov 1873, Circleville.
REDMAN, SARAH - b Nov 1865, OH. father b NC; mother b OH.
   (Circleville, 1900)
      Lena - b June 1871, OH. parents both b OH. (1900)
      Richard - b June 1887, OH; bl barber. parents both b
         VA. (1900)
REDMAN, SCOTT M. - bc 1859, W VA; mul. parents both b W
   VA. (Circleville, 1880)
      Henrietta - bc 1869, OH; mul. (1880)
      Mary E. - bc 1866, OH; mul. (1880)
REDMAN, WILLIAM - bc 1825, VA; mul laborer. m Eliza
   (___). (Circleville Twp, 1860)
      Eliza - bc 1828, VA; mul. (1860)
      Ann - bc 1853, OH; mul. (1870)
REDMAN, WILLIAM - b Feb 1840, VA; mul farm laborer.
   parents both b VA. m Margaret (Jackson). (Circleville,
   1870-1900)
      Margaret - b Apr 1845, VA; mul. parents both b VA.
         (1870-1900)
      Bell - b 1866 or 1869, OH; mul. (1870-1880)
      Daniel - bc 1876, Circleville. mul. (1880)
      George - b 1 Oct 1889, Circleville Twp.
      Hanby - b 24 Dec 1875, Jackson Twp.
      Harry - b Apr 1881, OH; mul farm laborer. (1900)
      Harvey - b 30 Nov 1877, Wayne Twp. mul. (1880)
      Jackson - b Mar 1883, OH; mul farm laborer. (1900)
      Maggie - b 1880, Circleville. mul. (1880)
      Mary - b 4 Dec 1886, Circleville.
      Minnie - b Aug 1886, OH. (1900)
      William - bc 1871, OH; mul. (1880)
REDMAN, WILLIAM - b 6 Oct 1865, Circleville; d 24 Apr 1876,
   Circleville of abcess of liver.
REED, ELIZABETH - bc 1862, OH; mul. father b VA; mother b
   OH. (Muhlenburg Twp, 1880)
REED, GEORGE - bc 1845, VA; mul laborer. (Circleville,
   1860)
REED, MICHAEL - b Mar 1873, OH; bl farmer. parents both b
   OH. m Florence May (Redman) & lived in Deer Creek Twp,
   1890s. (Deer Creek Twp, 1900)
      Florence May- b July 1873, OH. parents both b VA.
         (1900)
      Carmel - b July 1895, Deer Creek Twp. (1900)
      Edith G. - b 11 Apr 1897, Deer Creek Twp.
      Shirley M. - b 15 Dec 1898, Deer Creek Twp.

REID, JESSE - bc 1810, VA; bl farm laborer. m Ellen
   (____). (Walnut Twp, 1870)
     Ellen - bc 1827, VA; bl. (1870)
     Hanee - bc 1867, OH; bl. (1870)
     Mary - bc 1853, OH; bl. (1870)
     Nancy - bc 1855, OH; bl. (1870)
     Nomro (?) - bc 1861, OH; bl. (1870)
REVELS, GEORGE - b Mar 1856, OH; bl barber. father b NC;
   mother b OH. m Maggie (____). (Scioto Twp, 1900)
     Maggie - b Apr 1878, OH. parents both b OH. (1900)
REYNOLDS, DOCTOR - b 1802, 1805, 1807 or 1808, VA; d 16 Nov
   1898, Circleville of pneumonia. bl laborer. parents
   both b VA. m Julia (____). (Circleville, 1860-1880)
   --also listed as Rennels and Runnels-- --second death
   listing as same date but 88 years and death in Washington Twp. Infirmary--
     Julia - b 1804 or 1809, VA; bl. (1860-1880)
     Charles - bc 1850, OH; bl. (1860)
     Doctor - bc 1826, OH; bl hostler. (1870)
     George - bc 1859, OH; bl. (1870)
     Harry - bc 1837, VA; mul plasterer. (1860)
     Seavitee (?) - bc 1842, OH; mul. (1860)
REYNOLDS, FRANK - bc 1846, VA; mul laborer. (Circleville,
   1870)
     Laura - bc 1851, OH; bl. (1870) --possibly spouse--
REYNOLDS, HENRY m Rose (____) & lived in Muhlenburg Twp,
   1870s.
     Persilla - b 6 Dec 1877, Columbus.
REYNOLDS, MARY - bc 1854, OH; bl. (Wayne Twp, 1860)
RENELS, MARGUS lived in Circleville, 1860s.
     child - bc 1 Jan 1868, Circleville; d 8 Oct 1868,
        Circleville of "something eaten."
REYNOLDS, WILLIAM - bc 1850, OH; bl farm laborer. parents
   both b VA. m Martha (____). (Monroe Twp, 1880)
     Martha - bc 1854, OH; bl. parents both b VA. (1880)
RICE, ALEXANDER m Eliza (Combs) & lived in Circleville,
   1870s.
     child - b 9 Sept 1876, Circleville; d 12 Sept 1876,
        Circleville.
RICHARDSON, SUSAN - b 1800, VA; d 2 July 1891, Washington
   Twp. of old age. mul. m to white Scotsman. (Circle-
   ville Twp, 1850; Washington Twp, 1860-1880)
     Ann - b 1823 or 1828, VA; mul housemaid. (1850-1880)
     Eleanor - bc 1878, Washington Twp. mul. (1880) --
        probably child of Ellen--
     Ellen M. - bc 1856 or 1858, OH; mul. (1870-1880)
     George - bc 1857, OH; mul farmer. (1880)
     Jane - bc 1827, VA; mul. (1850)

100

Margaret - b 1823 or 1831, VA; mul housemaid. (1850)
Susan B. - bc 1824, VA; mul farmer. (1860)
Thomas - bc 1831, VA; mul farmer. (1850)
William P. - b 1825, Lynchburg, VA; d 24 Dec 1885,
    Circleville of pleurisy. mul farmer. (1850-1880)
RICKART, WILLIAM - bc 1843, Ireland; mul farm laborer.
  (Wayne Twp, 1860)
RICKEY, PHILLIP - bc 1796, VA; bl farmer. m Julia A.
  (_____). (Monroe Twp, 1860)
    Julia A. - bc 1806, VA; bl. (1860)
    Caroline - bc 1839, VA; bl. (1860)
    Daniel - bc 1832, VA; bl farmhand. (1860)
    Elnora - bc 1848, OH; bl. (1880)
    Henry - bc 1835, VA; bl farmhand. (1860)
    Lucinda - bc 1845, OH; bl. (1860)
    Mary F. - bc 1854, OH; bl. (1860)
RIGHT, SAM lived in Washington Twp, 1820.
RING, JOHN - bc 1842, Ireland. bl. (Circleville, 1860)
RINGLE, DAFNEY - bc 1755, MD; bl. (Jackson Twp, 1850)
ROBERTS, A HARRIET - b May 1888, OH; bl domestic.
  (Circleville, 1900)
ROBERTS, ANDREW and 1 male, 2 females lived in Jackson Twp,
  1830.
ROBERTS, JOHN - bc 1800, VA; bl . (Muhlenburg Twp, 1870)
    Eliza - bc 1820, NC; bl. (1870) --possibly spouse--
ROBERTS, MARGARET A. m Jeremiah Hargo & lived in Muhlenburg
  Twp.
ROBERTSON, ROBERT - b 1838, VA; bl engineer. m Martha
  (Jackson). --also listed as Robinson--
    Ada - b 11 May 1876, Circleville.
    James W. - b 3 Dec 1873, Circleville.
ROBINSON, JAMES - b Apr 1874, ARK; bl day laborer. father
  b ARK; mother b KY. m Mary (_____). (Circleville,
  1900)
    Mary - b Mar 1871, OH. parents both b OH. (1900)
    Fawncion (?) - b Sept 1898, OH. (1900)
    Turney - b Aug 1896, OH. (1900)
ROLLINS, JAMES - bc 1845, KY; bl laborer. m Maria (_____).
  (Circleville, 1870)
    Maria - bc 1856, KY; bl. (1870)
    Annie - bc 1864, OH; bl. (1870)
    David - bc 1868, OH; bl. (1870)
    Lucy - bc 1866, OH; bl. (1870)
    son - b 19 Feb 1869, Circleville.
ROMAN, GEORGE - b Mar 1855, VA; bl day laborer. parents
  both b VA. m Mary (_____). (Circleville, 1900)
    Mary - b Dec 1845, KY; bl restaurant worker.
      parents both b KY. (1900)

ROSE, MARY B. - bc 1877, OH; mul. parents both b OH.
(Washington Twp, 1880)
ROSS, ALVINA - bc 1829, VA; bl. (Circleville, 1860)
Harriet E. - bc 1858, OH; bl. (1860)
ROWEN, HENRY - bc 1815, VA; bl carpenter. m Ellen (____).
(Circleville, 1850)
Ellen - bc 1816, VA; bl. (1850)
Addison - bc 1848, OH; bl. (1850)
Ambos - bc 1844, OH; bl. (1850)
Ann E. - bc 1839, VA; bl. (1850)
Charles - bc 1840, VA; bl. (1850)
Charlotte - bc 1853, VA; bl. (1850)
James - b 1837, VA; bl. (Circleville, 1850-1860)
RUGER, WILLIAM - b 10 Sept 1894, Washington Twp. Infirmary
to Lizzie Camp.
RUNNELS, AMERICA - bc 1834, OH; bl. (Circleville, 1860)
Mary - bc 1853, OH; bl. (1860)
RUNNELS, GEORGE m ____ (Wyatt) & lived in Circleville,
1870s.
James - b 6 Dec 1876, Circleville.
RUPEL, JOSEPH - bc 1841, OH; mul farmhand. (Monroe Twp,
1860)
RUSH, JULIA m John Bizzel & lived in Circleville.
RUSSELL, DELL (or Mozell) m James Thacker & lived in Wayne
Twp.
RUSSELL, JOSHUA - bc 1812, VA; bl shoemaker. m Martha
(____). (Circleville, 1870)
Martha - bc 1825, VA; bl. (1870)
James - bc 1866, OH; bl. (1870-1880)
William - b 1864, OH; bl barber. father b NC; mother
b VA. (Circleville, 1870-1880)
RUSSELL, MARY - bc 1832, VA; bl cook. (Circleville, 1870)
RUSSELL, MARY S. - bc 1882, Circleville; d 20 Dec 1885,
Circleville of Bright's Disease.
RUSSELL, SUSAN m Lewis Green & lived in Circleville.
RUSSELL, WILLIAM - bc 1849, VA; bl farm laborer. (Deer
Creek, 1870)

SACKET, ELIZABETH - bc 1857, OH; bl housemaid. (Circle-
ville, 1870)
SAINS, GEORGE - bc 1855, OH; bl. (Circleville Twp, 1860)
SAMPLE, JAMES m Mattie (Franklin) & lived in Circleville,
1870s.
Lizzie - b 7 Sept 1878, Circleville
SAMPSON, SALLIE m. Edson Jackson & lived in Circleville.
SANDERS, CALVIN - bc 1835, VA; bl farm laborer. parents
both b VA. m Ann (____). (Muhlenburg Twp, 1880)
Ann - bc 1845, VA; bl. parents both b VA. (1880)

Charles - bc 1858, VA; bl farm laborer. (1880)
Susan - bc 1863, VA; d 12 June 1884, Circleville of
    consumption. (1880)
SANDERS, EILEEN - b 1869, Circleville; d Mar 1870, Circle-
ville of consumption.
SANDERS, JOHN - bc 1879, Circleville; d 17 Feb 1881,
Circleville.
SANDERS, JONATHAN H. - bc 1837, VA; bl farmer. (Harrison
Twp, 1870)
SANDERS, SARAH m William Haley & lived in Wayne Twp.
SANFORD, NOAH - b May 1866, OH; bl day laborer. parents
both b OH. (Circleville, 1900)
    Allen - b Nov 1884, OH. (1900)
    Edith - b Dec 1886, OH. (1900)
    Eva M. - b Aug 188, OH. (1900)
SANFOIRD, TIS___ - b Feb 1860, OH. parents both b VA.
(Circleville, 1900)
SANFORD, WILLIAM - b 1845; d 19 July 1867, Circleville of
consumption.
SATCHELL or SHATSELL, DOROTHEA - b June 1877, Circleville;
d 6 May 1878, Circleville of consumption.
SATCHELL OR SHATSELL, WILLIAM - bc 1816, OH; bl blacksmith.
m Ann C. (Freeman). (Circleville, 1860)
    Ann C. - b Dec 1828, OH; bl. father b VA; mother b
        OH. (1860-1900)
    Dorothy - bc 1859, OH; bl. (1870)
    Elizabeth - b 1857, VA; bl. had son Charles W. by
        Henry Johnson, 3 Oct 1877. (1860)
    Mary Magdalena - b June 1857, Pickaway Twp; bl ser-
        vant. (1860-1880)
SAVAL, SUSAN - bc 1851, OH; mul. (Jackson Twp, 1860)
SAXTEN, WILLIAM - bc 1835, VA; bl blacksmith. (Perry Twp,
1860)
SCOTT, ALEXANDER - b July 1825, OH. parents both b OH.
(Circleville, 1900)
SCOTT, ANN - bc 1831, OH; bl. (Cirlceville, 1850)
SCOTT, ANNE - b Aug 1846, NC; bl laundress. parents both b
NC. (Circleville, 1900)
    Otis - b July 1872, OH. father b OH; mother b NC.
        (1900)
SCOTT, CLAYBORNE - b 1838, VA; bl cooper. parents both b
VA. m Mary (____). (Muhlenburg Twp, 1870-1880)
    Mary - bc 1835, VA; bl. parents both b VA. (1870)
    William J. - bc 1860, VA; bl. (1880)
SCOTT, DOLLY m W. S. Whitaker & lived in Circleville.
SCOTT, EARL - bc 1790, NC; bl. m Rebecca (____). (Monroe
Twp, 1860)
    Rebecca - bc 1815, NC; bl. (1860)

103

Abraham - bc 1837, NC; bl farmhand. (1860)
Berry - bc 1831, NC; bl farmhand. (1860)
Hardy - bc 1853, OH; bl. (1860)
Mary - bc 1845, NC; bl. (1860)
Sarah - bc 1853, NC; bl. (1860)
SCOTT, EDWARD - bc 1837, VA; bl farmer. parents both b VA.
   m Fostoria (_____). (Darby Twp, 1880)
      Fostoria - bc 1850, VA; bl. parents both b VA.
         (1880)
      Estell - b 17 Aug 1871, Ross Co.
      U. Scott - bc 1868, OH; bl. (1880)
SCOTT, HARLAND - bc 1785, NC; bl day laborer. m Kate
   (_____). (Muhlenburg Twp, 1860)
      Kate - bc 1795, NC; bl. (1860)
      Berry - bc 1810, NC; bl day laborer. (1860)
      Cage - bc 1820, NC; bl day laborer. (1860)
      Hardy - bc 1849, OH; bl. (1860)
      Harrod - bc 1795, NC; bl day laborer. (1860)
      Pricilla - bc 1825, NC; bl. (1860)
      Sherod - bc 1851, OH; bl. (1860)
SCOTT, HENRY - bc 1825, NC; bl day laborer. m Charlotte
   (_____). (Monroe Twp, 1860)
      Charlotte - bc 1825, NC; bl. (1860)
      Elisabeth - bc 1847, NC; bl. (1860)
      Jason - bc 1858, OH; bl. (1860)
      Joseph - bc 1850, NC; bl. (1860)
      Lavinia - bc 1846, NC; bl. (1860)
      Mary - bc 1846, NC; bl. (1860)
      Minerva - bc 1856, OH; bl. (1860)
      Randal - bc 1855, IND; bl. (1860)
      Rebecca - bc 1852, IND; bl. (1860)
      Ruth - bc 1854, IND; bl. (1860)
SCOTT, JAMES - bc 1855, OH; mul. (Wayne Twp, 1880)
SCOTT, LIZZIE m Julian Thomas & lived in Circleville,
   1880s.
SCOTT, LORENZO - b Sept 1843, NC; listed bl & mul laborer.
   parents both b NC. m Susan (_____). (Circleville, 1870-
   1900)
      Susan (also Susanna) - b 1847, OH; listed bl & mul.
         father b OH; mother b NC. (1870-1880)
      Albert W. - bc 1857, Circleville. bl. (1870)
      Corneila - b 1859, Circleville. listed bl & mul.
         (1870-1880)
      Frederick - b Sept 1882, OH. parents both b OH.
         (1900)
      Julia A. - b 30 Aug 1873, Circleville. mul. m
         Lorenzo Bradley. (1880)

Lorenzo - b 1869, Circleville; d 23 July 1885, Circleville of spinal problem.
Mary - b Sept 1856, OH. parents both b VA. (1900)
Odus - bc 1872, Circleville. mul. (1880)
William A. - bc 1867, Circleville. mul. (1880)
MARY - b Feb 1823, VA. parents both b VA. (1900)
SCOTT, LYDIA - b May 1850, NC. parents both b NC. (Circleville, 1900)
SCOTT, MARY - b Sept 1835, VA; bl house servant. parents both b VA. (Pickaway Twp, 1900)
SCOTT, MATTIE - bc 1858, Circleville; d 20 Apr 1895, Circleville of consumption.
SCOTT, PASTORA - b 1832, VA; d 18 Nov 1894, Darby Twp. of heart disease. married.
SCOTT, RANDOLPH (or RANDAL) - bc 1796, VA. freed by Peter Scott in Dinwiddie Co, VA. lived with 2 males, 3 females in Circleville, 1830-1840.
SCOTT, R. L. - bc 1856, Pickaway Co; d 10 Mar 1890, Pickaway Twp. of lung disease. laborer. --probably Reaves Scott--
SCOTT, WILLIAM - b 1816, 1818, 1820 or 1823, VA; d 2 Nov 1895, Circleville of heart disease. listed bl & mul cooper and gardener. m Mary (____). (Circleville, 1850-1880)
    Mary - b 1824, VA; listed bl & mul nurse. (1850-1880)
    Benjamin - b 1850, Circleville; mul.. (1850)
    Elizabeth - b 1858, Circleville; listed bl & mul. (1860-1880)
    Lorenzo - b 1844, Circleville; mul. (1850-1860) -- see separate listing--
    Martha - bc 1866, Circleville. listed bl & mul. (1870-1880)
    Mary - b 1849, Circleville; mul. (1860-1880)
    Reaves - b 1856, Circleville; listed bl & mul barber. (1860-1880)
    Samuel - bc 1846, Circleville; mul. (1850)
    Timothy - b 1859, Circleville; listed bl & mul barber. (1870-1880)
    Virginia - b 1848, Circleville; mul. m Henry Lucas. (1850-1860)
SEA, GEORGE - b Dec 180, W VA; bl laborer. parents both b W VA. m Mary (____). (Circleville, 1900)
    Mary - b June 1855, NC. parents both b NC. (1900)
SEA, GEORGE - b June 1889, OH. parents both b OH. (Circleville, 1900)
SEWARD, EDWARD - bc 1854, OH; bl farm laborer. father b OH; mother b VA. (Scioto Twp, 1880)

SEWARD, EDWARD - b July 1868, OH; bl farmer. parents both
    b VA. m Jennie (_____). (Darby Twp, 1900)
        Jennie - b Aug 1873, OH. father b OH; mother b VA.
            (1900)
        Edna - b Sept 1895, OH. (1900)
        Ellen - b Oct 1893, OH. (1900)
        James W. - b Dec 1899, OH. (1900)
        Margaret - b Sept 1897, OH. (1900)
        Maynard - b July 1887, OH. (1900)
        Rebecca - b July 1891, OH. (1900)
        Stanley - b June 1889, OH. (1900)
SEWARD, HENRY - b Dec 1849, VA; bl farmer. parents both b
    VA. (Darby Twp, 1900)
        Alma - b Oct 1888, OH. mother b OH. (1900)
        Joseph - b Apr 1890, OH. mother b OH. (1900)
SEWARD, HORACE - b Oct 1826, VA; bl gardener. parents both
    b VA. m Martha A. (_____). (Scioto Twp, 1900)
        Martha A. - b Oct 1834, VA. parents both b VA.
            (1900)
SEWARD, ISAAC m Rosie (Tanner) & lived in Darby Twp, 1880s.
        Cynthia - b 22 Mar 1885, Darby Twp.
        Kesa Belle - b 15 Feb 1887, Harrisburg.
SEWARD, MARY - b July 1837, VA; bl. parents both b VA.
    (Darby Twp, 1880-1900)
SEWARD, SAMUEL m Sarah Ann (Jackson) & lived in Darbyville,
    1890s.
        Nathan - b 13 Jan 1890, Muhlenburg Twp.
SEWARD, SAMUEL - bc 1879, Wayne Twp; d 13 June 1891, Wayne
    Twp. of consumption.
SEWARD, SARAH - bc 1850, Jackson Co; d 10 May 1877, Darby
    Twp. of gangrene. married.
SEWARD, THOMAS - bc 1827, VA; bl farm laborer. parents
    both b VA. m Martha (_____). (Darby Twp, 1880)
        Martha - bc 1827, VA; bl. parents both b VA. (1880)
SEWARD, WILLIAM - bc 1851, VA; bl farmer. father b VA;
    mother b OH. m Maria (Brinn). (Darby Twp, 1880)
        Maria - bc 1859, OH; bl. parents both b OH. (1880)
        Henrietta - b 1880, Darby Twp; bl. (1880)
        Joseph T. - bc 1878, OH; bl. (1880)
        Larry - b 25 Nov 1879, Darby Twp.
        R. Hays - bc 1877, OH; bl. (1880)
SEWELL, ALLISON - bc 1820, NC; mul farmer. m Aranetta
    (_____). (Circleville, 1850)
        Aranetta - bc 1822, NC; bl. (1850)
        Susan - b 1850, Circleville. bl. (1850)
SHAFER (also SHAFFER), BARTLETT - bc 1775, NC; bl laborer.
    (Darby Twp, 1850)

SHAFER, BARDETT m Louisa (_____) & lived in Circleville, 1870s and 1880s.
    Lilly - b 20 Apr 1871, Circleville. bl. (1880)
    Peter - bc 1873, Circleville. bl. parents both b
        OH. (1880)
SHAFER, BIRD m Laura (Decker) & lived in Circleville, 1870s.
    Samuel - b 17 Dec 1871, Circleville
SHAFER, JOHN - bc 1846, OH; mul. (Jackson Twp, 1860)
SHAFTSBY, WILLIAM - bc 1829, OH; mul blacksmith. (Circleville, 1850)
SHANK, ELLEN m Jerry Wyatt & lived in Circleville, 1880s.
SHEPARD, CLAYBORN - b 1840 or 1843, NC; bl laborer. (Circleville, 1860)
    Mary E. - bc 1842, NC; bl. (1860) --possibly spouse--
SHEPHERD, ROSA - bc 1845, NC; bl housemaid. (Circleville, 1870)
SHEPHERD, ROXANNA (or Roxey Anna) m Horace Harvey & lived in Circleville.
SHERIDAN, JAMES - bc 1867, OH; bl servant. parents both b OH. (Harrison Twp, 1870)
SHERIDAN, JANE - bc 1860, Bloomfield; d 15 Mar 1880, Deer Creek Twp. of dropsey. married.
SHERIDAN, JOHN - bc 1829, KY; bl farm laborer. m Isabella (Johnson). (Jackson Twp, 1870)
    Isabella - bc 1837, KY; bl. (1870)
    Henry - bc 1859, OH; bl farm laborer. (1870)
    James - bc 1862, OH; bl. (1870)
    Orany - bc 1861, OH; bl. (1870)
    Sarah - bc 1857, OH; bl housemaid. (1870)
    Thomas - b 4 Apr 1883, Circleville.
    Turney - b 4 Jan 1872, Circleville.
SHERIDAN, JOHN R. - bc 1850, OH; bl laborer. father b KY; mother b NC. (Circleville, 1880)
    James - bc 1864, OH; bl errand boy. father b NC; mother b OH. (1880)
SHERIDAN, REBECCA - b 1832, NC or OH; bl house servant. parents both b NC. (Circleville, 1870-1880)
SHERIDAN, SARAH - bc 1860, OH; bl servant. parents both b VA. (Circleville, 1880)
SHERIDAN, SILAS - bc 1821, VA; bl farm laborer. father b Africa; mother b MD. m Jane (_____). (South Bloomfield, 1870; Harrison Twp, 1880)
    Jane - bc 1843, OH; bl. (1870)
    Elizabeth - b 1867, South Bloomfield. bl. (1870-1880)

Harriett - b 17 May 1873, South Bloomfield. bl.
(1880)
John - b 1869, South Bloomfield. bl. (1870-1880)
Taylor - bc 1875, South Bloomfield. bl. (1880)
Tecumseh - bc 1879, South Bloomfield. bl. (1880)
SHORT, ELIZABETH m Harry Hill & lived in Darby Twp.
SIDERS, WILLIAM H. - b 17 June 1876, Darby Twp; d 15 Oct
1876, Darby Twp. of diptheria.
SIMMONS, REBECCA m James Tibbs & lived in Circleville.
SMITH, ALBERT m Frances (Dade) & lived in Pickaway Co,
1870s.
    Mary J. - b 10 Oct 1875, Jackson Twp.
    Robert - b 30 Nov 1871, Circleville.
SMITH, ALFRED - bc 1841, OH; bl farm laborer. m Tampa
(Thornton). (Walnut Twp, 1870)
    Bertha - b 6 Apr 1875, Walnut Twp.
    Maggie - b 26 Feb 1877, Walnut Twp.
SMITH, ALICE - b July 1865, OH. parents both b VA. (Cir-
cleville, 1900)
    _____ - b Aug 1860, OH; bl barber. parents both b
    VA. (1900)
SMITH, AMY J. - b 1874, Jackson Twp; d 10 Feb 1876, Jackson
Twp.
SMITH, CAROLINE - bc 1842, VA; bl housemaid. (Circleville,
1870)
SMITH, CHARLEY - bc 1834, Circleville; d 8 Feb 1890, Cir-
cleville.
SMITH, DELILA m Benjamin Hudson & lived in Circleville.
SMITH, ELLA - b 1872, Circleville; d 28 Feb 1876, Circle-
ville of cholera.
SMITH, GARNET - b Sept 1883, OH. parents both b OH.
(Circleville, 1900)
SMITH, GEORGE and 1 male, 3 females in Circleville, 1840.
SMITH, GEORGE - bc 1833, LA; bl barber. (Deer Creek Twp,
1860)
SMITH, GEORGE - bc 1846, OH; mul farmhand. parents both b
OH. m Roxy (_____). (Deer Creek, 1880)
    Roxy - bc 1860, OH; mul. parents both b OH. (1880)
    George E. - bc 1878, OH; mul. (1880)
SMITH, GEORGE m Sarah (_____) & lived in Circleville,
1880s.
    Charles - b 19 Feb 1889, Circleville.
SMITH, GEORGE - b Oct 1860, OH; bl laborer. parents both b
OH. m. Eva (Turner). (Circleville, 1900)
    Eva - b Mar 1862, OH. parents both b OH. (1900)
    Bessie - b Oct 1881, OH; bl cook. (1900)
    Jane - b May 1894, Circleville. (1900)
    Leoto - b 8 Feb 1892, Circleville. (1900)

108

Leroy - b Aug 1899, Circleville. (1900)
Myrtle - b Mar 1896, Circleville. (1900)
SMITH, HENRY - bc 1868, Pike Co; d 7 Feb 1888, Circleville
of consumption. laborer.
SMITH, JAMES and 4 males, 8 females in Jackson Twp, 1820.
SMITH, JAMES - b Sept 1835, OH; bl farm laborer. parents
both b OH. m Catherine (_____). (Circleville, 1880-
1900)
Catherine - b Feb 1836, VA; mul. parents both b VA.
(1880)
Clifford - bc 1864, OH; mul drayman. (1880)
Effy - bc 1876, OH; mul. (1880)
Ellen - bc 1869, OH; mul. (1880)
George - bc 1861, OH; mul farm laborer. (1880)
Henry - bc 1866, OH; mul farm laborer. (1880)
John - bc 1860, OH; mul farm laborer. (1880)
Samuel - b Sept 1874, OH; mul. (1880-1900)
Viola - b 1880, Circeville. mul. (1880)
SMITH, JOHN and 4 females lived in Washington Twp, 1820.
SMITH, JONATHAN - bc 1805, VA; mul laborer. m Nancy
(_____). (Darby Twp., 1840-1850)
Nancy - bc 1821, OH; mul. (1840-1850)
Elizabeth - bc 1834, OH; mul. (1850)
George - bc 1849, Darby Twp. mul. (1850)
Hiram - bc 1844, Darby Twp. mul. (1850)
James - bc 1840, Darby Twp; mul. (1850)
Nancy - bc 1847, Darby Twp. mul. m George H.
Nichols. (1850)
Sarah A. - bc 1836, OH; mul. (1850)
SMITH, JOHN - b 1829 or 1832, VA; listed bl & mul laborer.
m Amicia (_____). (Circleville, 1860-1870)
Amicia ("Meese") - b 1836 or 1839, NC or VA; listed
bl & mul. (1860-1870)
Daniel - b 1880, Circleville. mul. (1880)
Dolly - b 1869, Circleville. mul. (1870-1880)
James - b 1865, Circleville; mul barber. (1870-1880)
Jonathan - bc 1859, OH; mul. (1870)
Mary - b 1867, Circleville. mul. (1870-1880)
son - b 6 Feb 1871, Circleville.
TOBIAS - bc 1787, VA; mul farm laborer. parents both
b VA. (1880)
SMITH, L. MARY - b June 1897, OH. father b IND; mother b
OH. (Circleville, 1900)
SMITH, LEVIN - bc 1790, MD; bl laborer. m Lydia (_____).
with and 2 females in Washington Twp, 1820; with 2 males
and 5 females in Circleville, 1830; with 2 males and 1
female in Circleville, 1840. (Washington Twp, 1820;
Circleville, 1830-1850)

109

Lydia - b 1779, 1789 or 1791, DEL, MD or VA; d 13 Mar
    1875, Circleville of old age. bl. (1820-1870)
Levin - bc 1835, Circleville. bl. (1840-1850)
Trussio - bc 1839, VA; bl laborer. (1870)
SMITH, LEWIS m Martha (Becker) & lived in Deer Creek,
    1880s.
    Von - b 9 July 1889, Deer Creek.
SMITH, LOUISE m James Collins & lived in Circleville.
SMITH, MARFIELD - b 1871, Circleville; d Sept 1878, Circle-
    ville.
SMITH, MARY - bc 1833, OH; bl domestic. (Jackson Twp,
    1860)
SMITH, MARY m Harrison Weaver & lived in Circleville.
SMITH, NATHAN - b 1847, VA; bl farm laborer. m Alice
    (_____). (Wayne Twp, 1880) --2nd listing in Jackson
    Twp.--
    Alice - bc 1849, VA; bl. (1870)
    Jane - bc 1858, OH; bl. (1870)
SMITH, SALLY (or Sarah) - b 1800, VA; bl washerwoman.
    parents both b VA. (Circleville, 1850-1880)
SMITH, SARAH - bc 1841, OH; bl. (Circleville, 1850) --
    also listed in Muhlenburg Twp, 1850--
    Nancy - bc 1859, OH; bl. (Muhlenburg Twp, 1850)
SMITH, SUSAN - b Apr 1880, Circleville; d 15 Sept 1880,
    Circleville of fever.
SMITH, WILLIAM H. m Mary C. (Wright) & lived in Circle-
    ville, 1880s-1890s.
    Francis L. - b 1 Nov 1887, Circleville.
    Kathleen - b 28 Dec 1892, Circleville.
SMITH, ZACHARIA - b 1821 or 1830, OH; mul farmer. m Char-
    lotte (_____). (Jackson Twp, 1850-1860)
    Charlotte - bc 1825, OH; mul. (1860)
    Mary - bc 1857, Jackson Twp. mul. (1860)
    Winfield - bc 1859, Jackson Twp. mul. (1860)
    infant - b 1860, Jackson Twp. mul. (1860)
SMITHEN, FRANCES M. G. - b 1846, OH; mul farm laborer. m
    Mary (_____). (Monroe Twp, 1870)
    Mary - bc 1848, OH; mul. (1870)
    Lucinda - bc 1868, OH; mul. (1870)
SMITHEN, FRANK - b Jan 1838, OH; bl farm laborer. parents
    both b OH. (Walnut Twp, 1900)
    Martin - b Sept 1882, OH; bl farm laborer. (1900)
SMITHEN, FRANK m Rose (Winters) & lived in Circleville,
    1880s. --may be same as above--
    Mary E. - b 4 June 1886, Circleville; d 6 June 1886,
        Circleville.
SMITHEN, JOSIE - b July 1892, OH. parents both b OH.
    (Williamsport, 1900)

SMITHEN, MARY E. lived in Circleville, 1870s.
 Marion - b 9 Apr 1877, Circleville to Mary E. Smithen
  and Henry Johnson.
SMITHEN, THOMAS - b 1809 or 1811, VA; mul day laborer and
 shoemaker. parents both b VA. m Lucinda R. (Gregory).
 (Monroe Twp, 1860-1880)
  Lucinda R. - b 1818, VA; mul. parents both b VA.
   (1860-1880)
  Cynthia Olive - b 1860, Monroe Twp. mul. m Thornton
   McClair. (1860-1880)
  Elvira Catherine - b 1854, OH; d 20 Jan 1877, Circle-
   ville of consumption. mul. (1860-1870)
  Frances M. G. - b 1846, OH; mul. (1860) --see sepa-
   rate listing--
  George W. - b 5 Dec 1857, Monroe Twp. mul. (1870)
  Martha A - bc 1850, OH; mul. (1860)
  Mary E. - b 1847, OH; mul. (1860-1880) --see sepa-
   rate listing--
  Sarah J. - bc 1855, OH; mul. (1870)
  William - b 1852, OH; mul farm laborer. (1860-1870)
SOUERS, H. L. - bc 1857, VA; bl farmer. parents both b VA.
 (Darby Twp, 1880)
  Porter Leo - bc 1867, OH; bl farmer. parents both b
   VA. (1880)
SOUERS, ISAAC - bc 1847, VA; bl farmer. parents both b VA.
 m. Rose Ann (Harris). (Darby Twp, 1880)
  Rose Ann - bc 1850, OH; bl. father b VA; mother b
   NC. (1880)
  Abraham - bc 1868, OH; bl laborer. (1880)
  Isaac W. - bc 1870, OH; bl laborer. (1880)
  Philip F. - bc 1873, OH; bl. (1880)
  Pleasant - bc 1877, OH; bl. (1880)
  Samuel - bc 1867, OH; bl laborer. (1880)
  Virginia - bc 1875, OH; bl. (1880)
  William H. - b 20 Oct 1878, Muhlenburg Twp. mul.
   (1880)
SOUERS, MARY J. - bc 1843, OH; mul. parents both b OH.
 (Darby Twp, 1880)
SPANGLER, ELLA M. - bc 1 Mar 1876, Darby Twp; d 19 May
 1876, Darby Twp.,
SPRAGE, MARY - bc 1798, VA; bl. (Muhlenburg Twp, 1850)
  Margaret - bc 1844, OH; bl. (1850)
  Robert - bc 1840, VA; bl. (1850)
SPRIGGS, DENNIS - bc 1820, PA; bl laborer. m Mary (_____).
 (Circleville, 1860)
  Mary - bc 1825, VA; bl. (1860)
  Margaret - bc 1835, OH; bl. (1860)

SPRIGGS, DENNIS - bc 1810, VA; bl farm laborer. m Harriet
(_____). (Muhlenburg Twp, 1870)
　　Harriet - b 1820 or 1823, VA; d 15 Aug 1878, Muhlen-
burg Twp. of consumption. bl. (1870)
SPRIGGS, SARAH m Alexander Brown & lived in Circleville.
STAFFORD, LOUIS - bc 1796, KY; bl carman. (Harrison Twp,
1880)
STAFFORD, TRUFE - b 1811 or 1816, KY; bl drayman. m Mary
(_____). (Circleville, 1850-1860)
　　Mary - b 1822, OH; bl. (1850-1860)
　　Laura - bc 1847, OH; bl. (1860)
STAMP, DAVID - bc 1830, OH; bl laborer. m Sarah (_____).
(Circleville, 1860)
　　Sarah - bc 1836, OH; bl. (1860)
　　Eddie - bc 1859, Circleville. bl. (1860)
　　Linn - bc 1857, OH; bl. (1860)
　　Malachi - bc 1850, OH; bl. (1860)
　　Richard - bc 1852, OH; bl. (1860)
STANHOPE, JOHN - bc 1846, OH; bl. (Circleville, 1870)
STANHOPE, WILLIAM - bc 1847, OH; bl. (Circleville, 1870)
　　Harriet - bc 1819, PA; bl. (1870)
STANLEY, JOSEPHINE m Allen Jones & lived in Walnut Twp.
STANLEY, NELSON - b Feb 1840, OH; bl plasterer. parents
both b OH. m 1st, Elizabeth (Sterling); 2nd, Margretta
(_____). (Circleville, 1870-1900)
　　Elizabeth - b 1838, VA; d 13 Feb 1886, Circleville of
　　　paralysis. mul. parents both b VA. (1870-1880)
　　Margretta - b Feb 1841, VA. parents both b VA.
　　　(1900)
　　Barney - b 1870, Circleville. bl. (1870)
　　Charles Wesley - b June 1877, Circleville; d 18 Jan
　　　1879, Circleville of whooping cough. --parents
　　　listed as Nelson and Jada (Walker) Stanley--
　　George W. - bc 1872, Circleville. bl. (1880)
　　Mary E. - b 1862 or 1867, OH; bl servant. (1870-
　　　1880)
　　Nelson - b 30 Apr 1874, Circleville.
　　Susan R. - b 30 Apr. 1874, Circleville. bl. (1880)
　　Vauna M. - bc 1871, Circleville. bl. (1880)
　　William - b Mar 1864, OH; bl. (1870-1880) --see
　　　separate listing--
STANLEY, WILLIAM lived in Circleville, 1890s.
　　Dorothy - b Feb 1894, Circleville. (1900)
STANUP, ELLEN m Ferdinand Parker & lived in Circleville.
STANUP (also STONUP and STANHOPE), GEORGE - bc 1809, VA; bl
　　laborer. m Catherine (_____). (Circleville, 1840-1870)
　　Catherine - bc 1839 or 1842, OH; listed bl & mul.
　　　parents both b VA. (1870-1880)

Alice - bc 1864, OH; bl. (1870)
Eliza - b 1856, OH; listed bl & mul domestic servant. (1870-1880)
Elnora - bc 1867, OH; bl. (1870)
George A. - b 1858, OH; bl farm laborer. (1870-1880) --see separate listing--
STANUP/STANHOPE, GEORGE - b 1811 or 1814, OH; mul farmer and laborer. m Hannah (_____). (Circleville, 1850-1860)
    Hannah (also Harriet) - b 1806, 1809 or 1811, PA; d 2 May 1876, Circleville of debility. listed bl & mul. (1850-1870).
    Henry - b 1833 or 1837, OH; d 8 Mar 1869, Circleville of consumption. mul laborer. (1850-1860)
    John W. - b 1843, OH; listed bl & mul laborer. (1850-1870)
    Levi - b 1844, Circleville; d 18 Oct 1868 or 6 Mar 1869, Circleville of heptic abcess. mul laborer. (1850-1860)
    William - b 1839, OH; listed bl & mul laborer. (1850-1870) --see separate listing--
STANUP, GEORGE - b Dec 1859, OH; bl hackman. parents both b OH. (Circleville, 1900)
    Catherine - b Jan 1900, Circleville. (1900)
    Gretchen - b Jan 1894, Circleville. (1900)
    Lena - b Aug 1885, OH. (1900)
    Nina B. - b Nov 1886, OH. (1900)
    Pearl - b Apr 1879, OH. (1900)
    Tabitha - b Jan 1888, OH. (1900)
STANUP, GEORGE m Rosie (Barnett) & lived in Circleville, 1880s.
    Minnie - b 10 Nov 1886, Circleville.
STANUP, WILLIAM - b Sept 1842, OH; mul plasterer. father b OH; mother b PA. m Mary E. (Redman). (Circleville, 1880-1900)
    Mary E. - b May 1844, VA; mul. parents both b VA. (1880-1900)
    Nettie Bell - b 11 Sept 1875, Circleville; d 24 Sept 1878, Circleville of typhoid fever.
STANUP, WILLIAM - b June 1874, OH; bl day laborer. mother b OH. m. Estell (_____). (Circleville, 1900)
    Estell - b 1873, OH. mother b KY. (1900)
STASHER, GEORGE - bc 1849, NC; bl servant. (Circleville, 1870)
STEPLOE, HANNAH - b 1790, VA. freed by James Steploe, Jr. in Bedford Co, VA, 26 Apr 1841. lived in Pickaway Co, 1840s.
    Maria - bc 1832, Bedford Co, VA.

113

STEPLOT, WILLIAM - bc 1842, VA; mul farm worker. parents
both b VA. m Nancy (____). (Circleville, 1880)
STEPTER, ANNIE m Mansfield Austin & lived in Circleville.
STEPTER (also STEPTOE), HOPE m Sarah (Wargo) & lived in
Muhlenburg Twp, 1880s.
    Anna - b 13 June 1880, Muhlenburg Twp.
    Hattie - b 4 May 1882, Muhlenburg Twp.
STEPTER (also STEPTOE), JOHN X. - bc 1801 or 1810, Bedford
Co, VA; d 2 July 1879, Darbyville of paralysis. bl
farmer and farm laborer. m Lucy (____). (Muhlenburg
Twp, 1870) --possibly Steploe related to Hannah freed
in Bedford County, VA, 1841--
    Lucy - b 1815 or 1820, VA; bl. parents both b VA.
      (1870-1880)
    Emma - bc 1860, VA; bl. m Thomas Peters. (1870)
    Hope - bc 1853, VA; bl farm laborer. (1870) --see
      separate listing--
    John - bc 1851, VA; bl farm laborer. (1870)
    William - bc 1865, VA; bl. (1870)
STEPTER, SALLIE L. (or Sarah) m Patrick Raglin & lived in
Darby Twp.
STEPTOE, MARGARET m Willis Morley 24 Oct 1875, Pickaway Co.
STEPTOE, WILLIAM - bc 1845, VA; bl farm laborer. m Nancy
(____). (Muhlenburg Twp, 1870)
    Nancy - bc 1847, OH; bl. (1870)
STEVENS, FRANK - b Dec 1858, OH; mul day laborer. parents
both b OH. m Mary E. (Dade). (Circleville, 1880-1900)
    Mary E. - b Aug 1861, W VA. parents both b W VA.
      (1900)
    William F. - b 22 Dec 1877, Circleville. (1900)
STEVENS, JACKSON - bc 1838, KY; bl school teacher. (Cir-
cleville, 1880)
    Lizzie - bc 1851, OH; bl. parents both b NC. (1880)
STEVENS, REUBEN - bc 1855, OH; bl farm worker. m Rebecca
(____). (Muhlenburg Twp, 1880)
    Rebecca - bc 1856, KY; bl. (1880)
STEVENS, REUBEN m Mary (Mayson) & lived in Circleville,
1880s. --may be 2nd wife of above--
    Minnie - b 26 Apr 1885, Circleville.
STEWARD (and STEWART)
STEWART, ARCHIMEDUS - bc 1819, VA; mul. m Ermine (____).
(Jackson Twp, 1860)
    Ermine - bc 1821, NC; mul. (1860)
    Benjamin S. - bc 1848, VA; mul. (1860)
    Emily J. - bc 1846, VA; mul. (1860)
    Harriet A. - bc 1852, VA; mul. (1860)
    James A. - bc 1858, VA; mul. (1860)
    James J. - bc 1850, VA; mul. (1860)

Mary F. - bc 1855, VA; mul. (1860)
Sally C. - bc 1844, NC; mul. (1860)
Thomas R. - bc 1847, VA; mul. (1860)
William D. - bc 1853, VA; mul. (1860)
STEWART, ARTHUR - b Feb 1890, Darbyville; d 7 Sept 1890, Darbyville of fever.
STEWART, BALLARD P. - bc 1852, VA; mul. parents both b VA. m Clementine (Randall), white female. (Wayne Twp, 1880)
    Bertie (or Birdie) - b 9 Dec 1873, Frankfort, Ross
      Co; d 8 Nov 1877, Wayne Twp. of diptheria.
    Dotta May - b 11 Sept 1876, Wayne Twp. mul. (1880)
    James Otto - b 10 July 1878, Wayne Twp.
STEWART, DONALDSON - bc 1808, NC; bl farmer. m Rachel
  (____). (Jackson Twp, 1860)
    Rachel - bc 1811, NC; bl. (1860)
    Charles - bc 1856, OH; bl. (1860)
    John - bc 1848, OH; bl. (1860)
    Louisa - bc 1844, NC; bl. (1860)
    Nancy - bc 1853, OH; bl. (1860)
    Parthena - bc 1843, NC; bl. (1860)
    William - bc 1850, OH; bl. (1860)
STEWART, EDWARD E. - b Feb 1857, OH; mul barber. father b NC; mother b OH. m Mary (Binzer). (Circleville, 1880-1900)
    Mary - b July 1854, OH; mul. parents both b NC. (1880-1900)
    Clara L. - b 4 Mar 1883, Circleville. (1900)
    Mina E. - b 29 Mar 1881, Circleville. (1900)
STEWART, HENRY - b 1825 or 1834, NC or VA; mul plasterer. m Sarah J. (____). (Circleville, 1850-1860)
    Sarah J. - bc 1829 or 1835, NC or VA; listed bl & mul. (1850-1860)
    Charles - bc 1859, Circleville. bl. (1860)
    John - bc 1850, Circleville. bl. (1860)
    William - bc 1855, Circleville. bl. (1860)
STEWART, HOMER - bc 1840, VA; mul servant. parents both b VA. m Martha (Jackson). (Jackson Twp, 1880)
    Florence - bc 1862, OH; mul. parents both b OH. (1880)
    Homer - b 15 June 1871, Muhlenburg Twp.
    Jane - bc 1871, OH; mul. parents both b OH. (1880)
    Sara - bc 1878, OH; mul. parents both b OH. (1880)
STEWART, JOHN - bc 1855, VA; mul servant. parents both b VA. (Circleville, 1880)
STEWART, NANCY m Henry Davis & lived in Harrison Twp.
STEWART, ROBERT - b 1832 or 1834, NC; bl mason and plasterer. m Frances (____). (Circleville, 1850-1860)
    Frances - bc 1828, OH; bl. (1860)

Edward - bc 1856, Circleville. bl. (1860)

Floyd - bc 1853, Circleville. bl. (1860)

STEWART, ROBERT - bc 1852, VA; bl laborer. (Circleville, 1870)

STEWART, SARAH m Samuel Whiting & lived in Muhlenburg Twp.

STEWART, WARNER - b 1810, NC; mul farm laborer. parents both b NC. (Muhlenburg Twp, 1870; Williamsport, 1880)

STEWART, WILLIAM - bc 1820, VA; bl farm laborer. (Jackson Twp, 1860)

STEWART, WILLIAM E. - bc 1829, VA; bl wagon maker. m Elvira (____). (Monroe Twp, 1860)

    Elvira - bc 1826, VA; mul. (1860)

    Frances A. - bc 1852, VA; mul. (1860)

    Harriet A. - bc 1858, OH; mul. (1860)

    John I. - b 1860, Monroe Twp. mul. (1860)

    Mary E. - bc 1857, VA; mul. (1860)

    Susan Y. - bc 1856, VA; mul. (1860)

STUARD, WARREN - b 1800, Ross Co; d 26 Sept 1892, Circleville of heart disease.

STOVINS, MARY - bc 1841, OH; mul. (Circleville, 1850)

STREETS, ANNIE - bc 1852, OH; bl laborer. (Circleville, 1870)

STREETS, JOHN W. - bc 1841, OH; bl laborer. (Circleville, 1860)

STREETS, LOUISA - bc 1849, OH; mul domestic. parents both b VA. (Circleville, 1880)

STREETS, REBECCA J. m Richard Davis & lived in Circleville.

STREETS, WILLIAM - bc 1835, OH; bl farmer. parents both b SC. (Circleville, 1880)

TAN (also spelled TANN)

TAN, ANDREW - bc 1810, NC; bl drayman. (Circleville, 1850)

    Margaret - bc 1835, NC; bl. (1850)

TAN, BESSIE lived in Circleville, 1890s.

    Bertha - b 27 June 1891, Circleville.

TAN, BRIT - bc 1815, NC; d 1 May 1887, Circleville of stroke.

TAN(N), BRIT - b 1830 or 1832, NC; bl laborer. parents both b NC. m Amanda (Chapman). (Circleville, 1870-1880)

    Amanda - b 1843 or 1849, VA; d 19 Nov 1898, Circleville of cancer. bl. parents both b VA. (1870-1880) --also listed as Nannie in birth records--

    Edward - b 1866 or 1868, OH; bl. (1870-1880)

    Ellen - bc 1859, OH; bl. (1870)

    Hartley William - b 9 Sept 1884, Circleville.

    Ida - bc 1873, Circleville. bl. (1880)

    John - b 1870, Circleville. bl. (1870-1880)

Lizzie - bc 1877, Circleville. bl. (1880)
Mary - bc 1843, VA; mul. (1870) --probably another
    name for Amanda--
Nancy A. - b 15 Dec 1874, Circleville; d 15 Nov 1888,
    Jackson or Wayne Twp. killed on railroad tracks.
    bl. (1880)
Nannie - b 1 Mar 1870, Circleville.
TAN, DENNIS - b 1815, NC; bl plasterer. parents both b NC.
    m Frances (Winter). (Circleville, 1870-1880)
    Frances - b 1826 or 1832, NC; bl. parents both b NC.
        (1870-1880)
    Anthony - b 1864 or 1866, OH; bl. (1870-1880)
    Barbery - bc 1852, OH; bl housemaid. (1870)
    Benjamin - bc 1869, OH; bl. (1870)
    Bidley (also Doctor) - b 1862, OH; bl laborer.
        (1870-1880)
    Dennis - b Apr 1874, Circleville. bl. (1880)
    Kate - bc 1879, Circleville. bl. (1880)
    Lucy - bc 1855, OH; bl nurse. (1870)
    Mary - bc 1854, Ross Co; d 1 June 1872, Circleville
        of dropsy. bl house servant. (1870)
    Rose (also Rozetta) - b 20 July 1871, Circleville.
        bl. (1880)
    Thomas - b 1867, OH; bl. (1870-1880)
TAN, DENNIS m Nannie Elizabeth (Bobo) & lived in Circle-
    ville, 1890s. --probably s/o Dennis & Frances Tan--
    Lenora Idell - b 24 Feb 1894, Circleville.
TAN, DOC - b Sept 1860, OH; bl day laborer. parents both b
    OH. m Caroline (White). (Circleville, 1900)
    Caroline - b Mar 1876, OH. parents both b OH.
        (1900)
    William - b Dec 1899, OH. (1900) --yet age listed
        as 4 in census--
TAN, EDWARD - b Aug 1876, OH; bl day laborer. parents both
    b OH. (Circleville, 1900)
TAN, ELIJA - bc 1823, OH; bl mason. (Circleville, 1850)
TAN, ELLIOT - b June 1895, OH. parents both b OH.
    (Circleville, 1900)
TAN, IDA - b Nov 1872, OH. father b NC; mother b VA.
    (Circleville, 1900)
    Cleonia - b 5 Sept 1891, Circleville. (1900)
    Edward - b 1867, OH; bl day laborer. father b NC;
        mother b VA. (1900)
    Hartley - b Sept 1884, OH. father b NC; mother b VA.
        (1900)
    Lizzy - b May 1879, OH. father b NC; mother b OH.
        (1900)

TAN, JAMES - bc 1825, VA; bl. parents both b VA. (Circleville, 1880)

TAN, JAMES - bc 1850, VA; bl farm laborer. (Wayne Twp, 1880)

TAN, JESSE H. - b Mar 1897, Pickaway Co; d 14 July 1891, Washington Twp. Infirmary of leyonosis.

TAN, JIM - bc 1830, OH; bl laborer. (Circleville, 1880)

TAN, LUCY - d 1877 or 1878, Pickaway Co. d/o Lucy Tann.

TANN, RICHARD - b Sept 1870, OH; bl day laborer. parents both b OH. m Samantha (____). (Circleville, 1900)
> Samantha - b Mar 1875, OH. parents both b OH. (1900)

TAN, SARAH m Colin or John Cooper & lived in Circleville.

TANNER, ROSIE m Isaac Seward & lived in Darby Twp.

TARPIN, JAMES and 3 males, 4 females lived in Deer Creek Twp, 1830.

TATE, Q. H. - b Jan 1849, VA; bl farm laborer. parents both b VA. m Mary (____). (Monroe Twp, 1900)
> Mary - b Sept 1861, OH. father b VA; mother b OH. (1900)
> Clarence - b Sept 1895, OH. (1900)
> Curtis - b May 1890, OH. (1900)
> James Noah - b Aug 1883, OH. (1900)
> Johnie - b Jan 1899, OH. (1900)
> Lucile - b May 1890, OH. (1900)

TAYLOR, FREDERICK - b Mar 1859, NC; bl clergyman. parents both b KY. m Francis (____). (Circleville, 1900)
> Francis - b May 1852, MO. parents both b MO. (1900)
> Catherine - b Mar 1879, MO. parents both b MO. (1900)

TENSY, HORACE - b May 1854, OH; bl day laborer. parents both b OH. m Amanda (____). (Circleville, 1900)
> Amanda - b Oct 1864, OH. parents both b OH. (1900)
> Harry - b Aug 1889, OH. (1900)
> Hester - b Feb 1883, OH; bl cook. (1900)
> Mary - b May 1884, OH. (1900)
> Maud - b July 1882, OH; bl cook. (1900)

TENZY, HENRY - bc 1849, VA; bl farm laborer. (Jackson Twp, 1870)

TERRY, CELIA - bc 1863, OH; bl. (Circleville, 1880)

TERRY, CHARLES m Catherine (Lindsay) & lived in Washington Twp, 1880s.
> Charles - b 4 Jan 1881, Washington Twp.

TERRY, EDWARD - bc 1851, OH; bl farm laborer. parents both b OH. (Muhlenburg Twp, 1880)

TERRY, HARRIS m Amanda Collins & lived in Walnut Twp, 1880s.
> Susie - b 29 Mar 1886, Walnut Twp.

TERRY, WILLIAM - d 2 July 1883, Washington Twp. Infirmary.
THACKER, ALICE m Thomas Artist & lived in Harrison Twp.
THACKER, DELILA m Frank Green & lived in Walnut Twp.
THACKER, JAMES m Mozell (or Dell) (Russell) & lived in
    Wayne Twp, 1880s.
        Doeza Ann (or Docie A) - b 15 Dec 1885 or 1886, South
            Union Twp, Ross Co.
THOMAS, ELLEN m Palestine Irving & lived in Circleville.
THOMAS, JAMES - bc 1836, VA; mul. (Muhlenburg Twp, 1860)
        Ellen - bc 1846, VA; mul. (1860)
THOMAS, JOHN - b 1830 or 1831, VA; bl farmhand. father b
    PA; mother b VA. m Elisabeth (_____). (Muhlenburg Twp,
    1860; Scioto Twp, 1870-1880)
        Elisabeth - b 1822, VA; bl. (1860-1880)
        Julian Richard - b 1857, VA; bl. (1860-1880) --see
            separate listing--
THOMAS, JOHN - bc 1838, OH; bl. (Circleville, 1850)
THOMAS, JOHN - b Jan 1840, VA; bl farm laborer. parents
    both b VA. (Circleville, 1900)
        Elizabeth - b Dec 1883, OH. parents both b OH.
        (1900)
THOMAS, JOSEPH - b June 1865, OH; bl farmer. parents both
    b VA. m Harriet (Redman) & lived in Circleville, 1880s.
    (Washington Twp, 1900)
        Harriet (or Hattie) - b Jan 1877, OH. father b VA
            mother b OH. (1900)
        Clessie - b 13 Nov 1898, Circleville.
THOMAS, JULIAN - b 1857, VA. m Lizzie (Scott) & lived in
    Circleville, 1880s.
        Frederick - b 12 Sept 1882, Circleville.
THOMAS, LORENZO - bc 1838, MD; bl farm laborer. (Jackson
    Twp, 1870)
THOMAS, MARY - bc 1856, OH; bl. (Circleville, 1870)
THOMAS, PRISCILLA - bc 1810, MD; bl. (Muhlenburg Twp,
    1860)
THOMAS, THOMAS - b 1814, VA; d Mar 1880, Circleville of
    brain fever. bl cartman and minister. m Susan A.
    (_____). (Circleville, 1860)
        Susan A. - bc 1825, VA. mul. (1860)
THOMAS, WILLIAM - b 1843, MICH; mul farm laborer. (Jackson
    Twp, 1860-1870)
THOMPSON, ANNA - bc 1834, OH; bl cook. (Circleville, 1870)
THOMPSON, ANNIE - bc 1849, VA; bl housemaid. (Circleville,
    1870)
THOMPSON, ELIZABETH - bc 1822, VA; d 22 June 1879, Scioto
    Twp. of consumption. married.
THOMPSON, FREDERICK - bc 1856, VA; bl servant. parents
    both b VA. (Circleville, 1880)

THOMPSON, HUGH - b June 1874, OH; bl farm laborer. father
  b VA; mother b NC. (Monroe Twp, 1900)
THORNTON, HANEE - bc 1838, VA; bl farm laborer. m Margaret
  (_____). (South Bloomfield, 1870)
       Margaret - bc 1830, SC; bl. (1870)
       Temppy - bc 1853, OH; bl. m Alfred Smith. (1870)
THORNTON, HANSON - b 1831, VA; bl farmer and laborer.
  parents both b VA. m Barbara or Margaret (_____).
  (Circleville, 1860; Muhlenburg Twp, 1880)
       Barbara - bc 1838, NC; bl. (1860)
       Margaret - bc 1835, NC; mul. parents both b NC.
         (1880) --may be same as Barbara--
       Lenape - bc 1852, OH; bl. (1860)
THORNTON, JOHN - b Sept 1822, OH; bl farm laborer. parents
  both b VA. m Catherine (_____). (Muhlenburg Twp, 1880;
  Circleville, 1900)
       Catherine - b Jan 1823, KY; bl. parents both b KY or
         VA. (1880-1900)
THORNTON, JOHN - bc 1833, OH; bl farmer. (Jackson Twp,
  1860)
THORNTON, MARY - b Sept 1835, NC; bl boarding home opera-
  tor. father b VA; mother b NC. (Circleville, 1900)
THORNTON, NANCY - bc 1804, VA; bl. (Jackson Twp, 1850)
       Hanson - bc 1834, VA; bl farmer. (1850) --see sepa-
         rate listing--
       John - bc 1823, OH; bl farmer. (1850)
       Joshaway - bc 1830, OH; bl farmer. (1850)
       Rebecky - bc 1843, OH; bl. (1850)
       William - bc 1835, VA; bl farmer. (1850) --see
         separate listing--
THORNTON, SALLIE - bc 1 Jan 1873, Harrison Twp; d 28 Mar
  1878, Muhlenburg Twp of whooping cough.
THORNTON, WILLIAM - bc 1836, OH; bl farmhand. m Nancy
  (_____). (Muhlenburg Twp, 1860)
       Nancy - bc 1839, OH; bl. (1860)
       Elizabeth - bc 1858, Muhlenburg Twp. bl. (1860)
       Mary F. - b 1860, Muhlenburg Twp. bl. (1860)
TIBBS, EDWARD - bc 1839, OH; bl barber. m Ellen (_____).
  (Circleville, 1870)
       Ellen - bc 1833, OH; bl. (1870)
       Alice - bc 1859, OH; bl. m James Stewart. (1870)
       Florence - bc 1859, OH; bl. (1870)
       Samuel - b 1862, OH; bl day laborer. (1870-1880)
       Thomas - bc 1857, OH; bl. (1870)
       William - bc 1866, OH; bl. (1870)
TIBBS, EDWARD - b 1830 or 1832, KY; d 23 Dec 1896, Circle-
  ville of heart trouble. mul barber. parents both b KY.
  m Annie (_____). (Circleville, 1880)

Annie - bc 1844, VA; mul. parents both b VA. (1880)
Edna - bc 1875, OH; mul. (1880)
Minnie P. - b 1880, Circleville. mul. (1880)
TIBBS, FRANK - b 1821, VA; listed bl & mul farmer and team-
ster. parents both b VA. m Jane (_____). (Circle-
ville, 1860-1880)
    Jane - b 1829, VA; listed bl & mul. parents both b
        VA. (1860-1880)
    Elizabeth - b 1865, Circleville. mul. (1870-1880)
    Emma - bc 1862, Circleville. mul. (1870-1880)
    Flora - bc 1869, Circleville. mul. (1870)
    Frank - bc 1858, OH; bl. (1860)
    Frederick - b 1860, Circleville. listed bl & mul.
        (1860-1870)
    George - b 1866, Circleville. mul. (1870-1880)
    James - b 1855, OH; listed bl & mul laborer. (1860-
        1870) --see separate listing--
    Jane - b 12 Jan 1870, Circleville.
    John - b 1852, OH; listed bl & mul laborer. (1860-
        1880)
    Martha - bc 1851, OH; bl. (1860)
    Mildron or Mildert (probably Mildred) - b 1866, Cir-
        cleville. mul. (1870-1880)
    Narcissa - bc 1851, OH; mul housemaid. (1870)
    Olive - bc 1869, Circleville. mul. (1870)
    Peter - bc 1859, Circleville. mul. (1880)
    Samantha - b 1856, OH; listed bl & mul. (1860-1870)
    William - bc 1872, Circleville. mul. (1880)
TIBBS, JAMES - b 1855, OH; s/o Frank and Jane Tibbs. mul
    barber. parents both b VA. m Rebecca (Simmons).
    (Circleville, 1880)
    Rebecca - bc 1858, OH; mul. parents both b OH.
        (1880)
    Allen - b 6 Feb 1880, Circleville. mul. (1880)
    Cora - bc 1869, Circleville. mul. (1880)
    Roy - bc 1868, Circleville. mul. (1880)
TIBBS, JANE - bc 1849, OH; bl. (Circleville, 1860)
TIBBS, JOHN - bc 1820, KY; bl clergyman. m Ellen (_____).
    (Circleville, 1860)
    Ellen - bc 1831, OH; bl. (1860)
    Benjamin - bc 1850, OH; bl. (1860)
    Daniel - bc 1856, OH; bl. (1860)
    Lewis - bc 1846, OH; bl. (1860)
TIBBS, LAURA m Willis Haithcock & lived in Circleville.
TIBBS, MARTHA - bc 1862, OH; bl domestic servant. parents
    both b VA. (Circleville, 1880)
TIBBS, MARY - bc 1842; d 30 Sept 1867, Circleville of
    consumption.

TIBBS, MINNIE - bc 1869, OH; bl. parents both b OH. (Circleville, 1880)

TIMMONS, ALLA - b 26 Sept 1875, Darby Twp; d 29 Aug 1876, Darby Twp.

TIMMONS, OTHER - b 13 March 1877, Darby Twp; d 25 March 1877, Darby Twp.

TIPP, JOHN m Mary (_____) & lived in Circleville, 1860s.
    Mary - b 7 Oct 1867, Circleville; d. 10 Oct 1867, Circleville.

TOBYES (or TOBIAS), FLINIA - bc 1804; d 15 Feb 1884, Circleville of old age.

TODD, HULDAH - b 1811, OH; d 14 Nov 1889, Deer Creek Twp. of paralysis. widow. mul domestic servant. parents both b KY. (Wayne Twp, 1860-1880)
    Frank - bc 1844, OH; mul farm laborer. (1870)
    Isaac J. - bc 1858, OH; mul laborer. (1880)
    Jason - bc 1838, OH; mul farm laborer. (1860)
    L. Ann - bc 1851, OH; mul. (1860)

TODD, MARY m Richard Johnson & lived in Muhlenburg Twp.

TODEL, JASON - bc 1841, OH; mul farm laborer. (Jackson Twp, 1870)

TOLER, JUDY - bc 1851, NC; bl servant. parents both b NC. (Circleville, 1880)

TOLES, LEWIS - bc 1821, VA; mul farmer. (Circleville, 1850)
    Holland - bc 1834, OH; mul farmer. (1850)
    James - bc 1832, OH; mul farmer. (1850)
    Jane - bc 1848, OH; mul. (1850)
    Nancy - bc 1825, VA; mul. (1850)
    Nancy - bc 1838, OH; mul. (1850)

TOLES, WILLIAM - b July 1857, OH; bl day laborer. parents both b OH. m Maggie (_____). (Circleville, 1900)
    Maggie - b Jan 1864, ALAB. parents both b ALAB. (1900)

TOLLEN, MARTHA - bc 1839, NC; bl. (Wayne Twp, 1860)

TOO, BENJAMIN - bc 1838, OH; mul. (Wayne Twp, 1850)

TOOTLE, E. T. m Sarah (Fulton) & lived in Wayne Twp, 1870s.
    infant - b 19 March 1879, Wayne Twp.

TRIMBLE, CARRIE m Stephen A. Jones & lived in Jackson Twp.

TROLLINGER, JACOB - bc 1832, OH; mul. m Margaret (_____). (Jackson Twp, 1860)
    Margaret - bc 1839, OH; mul. (1860)
    George - bc 1859, Jackson Twp. mul. (1860)

TRUMAN, NANCY - bc 1748, VA; bl. age listed as 112 in census. (Circleville, 1860)

TURNER, ABNER - b Oct 1821, 1832, 1834 or 1835, OH; bl farmer. parents both b OH. m 1st, Catherine (_____); 2nd, Susan Ellen (_____). (Deer Creek Twp, 1900) -- each census gives different age or year of birth--

122

Catherine - bc 1837, OH; bl. parents both b VA. (1860)

Susan Ellen - b 1834, OH; listed bl & mul. parents both b VA. (1870-1880) -- also listed as Sarah in birth records--

Barnett or Bennet - b 1858, OH; bl farm laborer. (1870-1880)

Charles - b 31 Dec 1872, Deer Creek Twp; d 10 Jan 1875, Deer Creek Twp. of diptheria.

Clifford A. - bc 1878, Deer Creek Twp. bl. (1880)

Delila - b 1862 or 1864, Deer Creek Twp. bl. (1870-1880)

George - b 1854 or 1856, OH; bl farm laborer. (1860-1870)

Jesse - b 1858 or 1860, Deer Creek Twp; bl. (1870-1880)

John - b 1856 or 1858, OH; bl farm laborer. (1860-1870)

Louisa - b 1868, Deer Creek Twp. bl. (1870-1880)

Martha Elizabeth - bc 1875, Deer Creek Twp. bl. (1880)

Minerva - bc 1850, OH; bl. (1860)

Mollie - b 1880, Deer Creek Twp. bl. (1880)

Philip - b 1852 or 1854, OH; bl farm laborer. (1860-1870)

Sarah Ellen - b 1865 or 1867, Deer Creek Twp. bl. (1870-1880)

William - b Oct 1871, Deer Creek Twp. bl. (1880)

Willis - b 1850 or 1852, OH; bl. (1860-1870)

daughter - b 1 Jan 1869, Deer Creek Twp.

TURNER, ANDREW - b Mar 1844, OH; bl farm laborer. father b VA; mother b OH. m Percilla (Dutten). (Circleville, 1900).

Percilla - b Apr 1846, OH. parents both b VA. (1900)

Andrew - b Mar 1863, OH; bl day laborer. (1900)

Charles - b Apr 1888, OH. (1900)

George - b Nov 1876, OH; bl farm laborer. (1900)

Herman - b 24 Dec 1884, Circleville. (1900)

Pearly - b Feb 1884, OH. (1900)

TURNER, ANDREW - bc 1852, OH; bl farm laborer. parents both b VA. m Mary (Jackson). (Circleville, 1880)

Mary - bc 1850, OH; bl. parents both b OH. (1880)

Andrew - bc 1873, Circleville. bl. (1880)

George - bc 1878, Circleville. bl. (1880)

Harry - bc 1876, Circleville. bl. (1880)

Mary - bc 1874, Circleville. bl. (1880)

Myrtle - b 1 Jan 1887, Circleville.

William - bc 1871, Circleville. bl. (1880)

TURNER, ANNA - b 1 Apr 1876, Darby Twp; d 5 Mar 1877, Darby Twp.
TURNER, BENJAMIN - b Oct 1849, OH; bl farmer. parents both b OH. m Alice (_____). (Perry Twp, 1900)
   Alice - b Sept 1858, OH. father b OH; mother b VA. (1900)
   Bennett - b Aug 1895, OH. (1900)
   Ella - b Aug 1884, OH. (1900)
   Joseph - b July 1888, OH. (1900)
   Laura - b Feb 1890, OH. (1900)
   Maggie - b May 1892, OH. (1900)
   Martin - b Oct 1897, OH. (1900)
   infant - b May 1900, Perry Twp. (1900)
TURNER, FRANK - b 8 Feb 1880, Circleville to Lucy Willis and ___ Turner.
TURNER, GEORGE - b 1819 or 1825, VA; bl laborer. parents both b VA. (Circleville, 1870-1880)
   Benjamin - b 1863 or 1866, OH; bl. (1870-1880)
   Elizabeth - b 1869 or 1871, OH; bl. (1870-1880)
   Flora - bc 1859, OH; bl. (1870)
   Mary - b 1844 or 1846, VA; bl. (1870-1880)
   Minerva - bc 1875, Circleville. bl. (1880)
   Nancy - b 1866, OH; bl. (1870-1880)
   Sally - bc 1864, OH; bl. parents both b VA. (1880)
   Thomas - bc 1853, VA; bl laborer. (1870)
   SALLIE - bc 1820, VA; bl domestic servant. parents both b VA. (1880)
TURNER, GEORGE - b May 1864, OH; bl day laborer. parents both b OH. m Harriet (_____). (Circleville, 1900)
   Harriet - b Dec 1871, OH. father b VA; mother b OH. (1900)
   Cathleen - b Sept 1897, OH. (1900)
   Jeff - b Sept 1897, OH. (1900)
   Samantha - b Nov 1895, OH. (1900)
TURNER, GEORGE m Anna (Dervin) & lived in Circleville, 1890s.
   Jeffie - b 23 Sept 1899, Circleville.
TURNER, JEFF m Sarah E. (Hinkley) & lived in Circleville, 1890s.
   Harry - b 11 July 1891, Circleville.
TURNER, JOHN - bc 1796, VA; bl day laborer. m Sarah (_____). (Jackson Twp, 1860)
   Sarah - b 1810 or 1814, OH; bl housemaid. father b VA; mother b OH. (1860; Circleville, 1870-1880)
   Andrew - b July 1848, OH; bl farm laborer. (1860-1870; Muhlenburg Twp, 1900)
   Ann - bc 1844, OH; bl. (1860)
   Effie - b 1861, OH; bl domestic servant. (1870-1880)

Emmie - bc 1872, Circleville. bl. (1880)
George - b 1851, OH; bl laborer. (1860-1870)
George - b 1865, OH; bl. (1870-1880)
Gracey - bc 1878, Circleville. bl. (1880)
Henry Jeff - bc 1877, Circleville. bl. (1880)
Jane - bc 1846, OH; bl. (1860)
Martha Ann - b 1858, OH; bl housemaid. (1870-1880)
Rebecca - b 1853 or 1855, OH; bl domestic servant.
   (1860-1880)
Samantha - b 1867, OH; bl. (1870-1880)
Sarah E. - bc 1845, OH; bl. (1860)
Willis - bc 1853, OH; bl laborer. (1870)
TURNER, MARY m William Collins & lived in Circleville.
TURNER, MIRANDA m Isaac Dyson & lived in Harrison Twp,
   1870s & Walnut Twp, 1880s. --also listed as Amanda
   Turney--
TURNER, MOSES - b 1825 or 1829, OH; bl farm laborer.
   (Jackson Twp, 1860-1870)
      Elizabeth - bc 1820, OH; bl. (1870)
      Andrew - bc 1848, OH; bl farm laborer. (1870)
TURNER, SARAH - bc 1842, OH; bl domestic. (Jackson Twp,
   1860)
TURNER, SUSAN - bc 1843, Vinton Co; d 29 June 1883, Deer
   Creek Twp. of cancer of bowel.
TURNER, TRAVIS - b Oct 1845, VA; bl sprinkling wagon
   driver. parents both b VA. m Cressa (____). (Circle-
   ville, 1880-1900)
      Cressa - b Nov 1849, OH; bl. father b VA; mother b
         OH. (1880-1900)
      Hattie - bc 1873, OH; bl. (1880)
TURNER, TURNEY - b Oct 1892, Circleville; d 9 Mar 1893,
   Circleville.
TURNEY (many listed as TURNER and vice versa)
TURNEY, DELL m Ambrose Gibbs & lived in Circleville.
TURNEY, EDWARD m Mary (____) & lived in Circleville.
      John - b 1865, Jackson Twp; d 11 Nov 1867, Circle-
         ville of sore throat.
TURNEY, GEORGE - b 12 Oct 1882, Circleville; s/o George
   Turney.
TURNEY, GRACE lived in Circleville, 1890s.
      daughter - b 12 March 1895 to Grace Turney and ____
         Smith.
TURNEY, JAMES - b 1810, OH; mul farmer. (Circleville,
   1850; Scioto Twp, 1860).
      Margaret - b 1813 or 1820, OH; mul. (1850-1860) --
         probably spouse--
      George - b 1845 or 1847, OH; mul. (1850-1860)
      Harriet - b 1834 or 1837, OH; mul. (1850-1860)

Mary - b 1838 or 1840, OH; mul. (1850-1860)
Miranda - b 1842 or 1845, OH; mul. (1850-1860)
Sarah - b 1847 or 1849, OH; mul. m Albert or Alfred
    Coleman. (1850-1860)
William - b 1840 or 1842, OH; mul farmhand. (1850-
    1860)
TURNEY, JANE m Silas Sheridan & lived in Harrison Twp.
TURNEY, NANCY m Warren Keal & lived in Circleville.
TURNEY, NED - bc 1840, VA; mul laborer. parents both b VA.
    (Jackson Twp, 1880)
TURNEY, PARK - bc 1820, OH; listed bl & mul farmer. (Cir-
    cleville, 1850)
TURNEY, ROXANNA m William Decker & lived in Circleville.
TURNEY, SARAH ELLEN m Scott Gibbs & lived in Perry Twp.
TURNEY, TRIVOS - bc 1846, VA; bl laborer. m Irena (_____).
    (Circleville, 1870)
    Irena - bc 1848, OH; bl. (1870)
TURNEY, ZELDA m John Harris & lived in Circleville.
TYNER, ABRAHAM and 2 males, 6 females lived in Harrison
    Twp, 1840.
TYSON, ISAAC - bc 1836, OH; bl farmhand. (Scioto Twp,
    1860)

VAIL, ELLA m. Elija Bird and lived in Circleville.
VALENTINE, ANDREW (also ANDERSON) - b June 1873, OH; bl day
    laborer. father b TENN; mother b OH. m. Matilda
    (Johnson). (Circleville, 1900)
    Matilda - b Mar 1872, OH. parents both b OH. (1900)
    Andrew - b Jan 1899, Circleville; d 22 Feb 1899,
        Circleville.
    Georgia - b Mar 1894, Circleville. (1900)
    John - b 18 July 1897, Circleville; d 4 May 1898,
        Circleville of brain trouble.
    Mary - b Feb 1895, Circleville. (1900)
VALENTINE, CORA B. - b 19 Nov 1882, Washington Twp.
VALENTINE, DANIEL - b Aug 1875, Circleville; d 6 Mar 1876,
    Circleville of diarrhea.
VALENTINE, ELIAS - bc 1824, NC; bl farm laborer. m Mar-
    garet (_____). (Jackson Twp, 1870)
    Margaret - bc 1834, VA; bl. (1870)
    Margaret - bc 1866, OH; bl. (1870)
    Martha - bc 1869, OH; bl. (1870)
    Rebecca - bc 1868, OH; bl. (1870)
VALENTINE, JACKSON - bc 1842, NC; bl farm laborer. parents
    both b NC. m Mary (_____). (Scioto Twp, 1880)
    Mary - bc 1852, NC; bl. parents both b NC. (1880)
    Mary W. - bc 1875, VA; bl. (1880)
    Sarah C. - bc 1872, VA; bl. (1880)

VALENTINE, MAGGIE J. - b 1868, Circleville; d 10 June 1870,
     Circleville of fever.
VALENTINE, MARY - bc 1877, OH; d/o Emma Valentine (white).
     father b TENN; mother b Ohio. mul. (Circleville, 1880)
VALENTINE, PUMPHREY m Margaret (Jackson) & lived in Jackson
     Twp, 1870s.
          Mary - b 24 Apr 1874, Jackson Twp.
VALENTINE, WILLIAM - bc 1843, VA; bl laborer. m Frances
     (_____). (Circleville, 1870)
          Frances - b 2 Nov 1849, Circleville; d 6 Aug 1875,
               Circleville of pneumonia. mul. (1870)
          Augustus - bc 1863, OH; mul. (1870)
          Ebenezer - b 20 June 1870, Circleville; d 13 Jan
               1871, Circleville of fever.
          Maggie - b 1870, Circleville. mul. (1870)
VANMETER, DAVID - b 1845 or 1847, OH; mul board boy. (Cir-
     cleville, 1850-1860)
VANOY, EDWARD - b Jan 1836, NC; bl officer. parents both b
     NC. (Jackson Twp, 1900)
VINA, NANCY - bc 1824, OH; bl. (Circleville, 1860)
          Amanda - bc 1844, OH; bl. (1860)
          Grein (?) - bc 1841, OH; bl farm laborer. (1860)
          Washington - bc 1848, OH; bl. (1860)
VINCENT, IRWIN - bc 1839, OH; bl house servant. (Circle-
     ville, 1870)
VINES, JOHN - b Nov 1844, OH; bl drayman. parents both b
     VA. m Dora (_____). (Circleville, 1900)
          Dora - b Dec 1844, VA. parents both b VA. (1900)
VINES, REBECCA m John McMan & lived in Circleville.
VINEY, AUGUSTUS JOSEPH - b Feb 1831, VA; bl laborer.
     parents both b VA. m E. Mary (_____). (Circleville,
     1870-1900)
          E. Mary - bc 1839, NC; bl. parents both b NC.
               (1870-1900)
          Luworina (?) - bc 1866, OH; bl. (1870)
VINEY, H. WINTER - b Jan 1900, OH. parents both b OH.
     (Circleville, 1900)
VINEY, JESSE - b 1889, Circleville; d 3 Jan 1890,
     Circleville.
VINEY, JOSEPH G. - bc 1837, VA; bl drayman. parents both b
     VA. m Mary S. (_____). (Circleville, 1880)
          Mary S. - bc 1843, NC; bl. parents both b NC.
               (1880)
          William L. - bc 1866, OH; bl. (1880)
VINEY, LAWRENCE - b 1866, Circleville; d 27 Feb 1893, Cir-
     cleville of heart trouble. barber.
VINEY, MAGGIE in Washington Twp. Infirmary, 1890s.
          Mary L. - b 14 June 1897, Washington Twp. Infirmary.

VINEY, MARGARET - b Mar 1880, OH; bl domestic. parents
   both b GA. (Circleville, 1900)
VINEY, WILLIAM - bc 1814, VA; mul laborer. m Melinda
   (_____). (Circleville, 1850)
      Melinda - bc 1818, VA; mul. (1850)
      Amanda - bc 1844, OH; mul. (1850)
      James W. - bc 1847, OH; mul. (1850)
      John - bc 1838, OH; mul. (1850)
      Louisa - bc 1837, VA; mul. (1850)
      Mary G. - b 1850, Circleville. mul. (1850)
      Nancy - bc 1838, OH; mul. (1850)
      Napoleon B. - bc 1836, VA; mul. (1850)
      William G. - b 7 Apr 1841, Gallipolis; d 31 May 1877,
         Circleville of drowning. mul. (1850) --see
         separate listing--
VINEY, WILLIAM - b 7 Apr 1841; laborer. m Margaret A.
   (_____). (Circleville, 1870)
      Margaret A. - b 1842, NC; mul. parents both b NC.
         (1870-1880)
      Chauncey D. - bc 1876, Circleville. mul. (1880)
      George Washington - b 18 Jan 1870, Circleville. mul.
         (1870-1880)
      Josephine C. - b 1865 or 1867, Circleville. mul.
         (1870-1880)
      Malinda A. - b 1863, Circleville. mul. (1870-1880)
      Thornton - bc 1875, Circleville. mul. (1880)
VINSON, QUINCY - bc 1852, OH; bl farm laborer. (Jackson
   Twp, 1870)
VIRES, ALEX - b 1852; d 21 July 1899, Darby Twp. of blood
   poison.

WAJAT, ELIAS - bc 1811, NC; bl farm laborer. (Jackson Twp,
   1870)
WALDRON, JOSEPH H. or W. - bc 1827, VA; bl farmer. m
   Elisabeth (_____). (Muhlenburg Twp, 1860)
      Elisabeth - bc 1824, OH; bl. (1860)
      Mary A. - bc 1857, Muhlenburg Twp. bl. (1860)
      Matilda - b 24 Jan 1857, Muhlenburg Twp. bl. (1860)
      Parthena E. - bc 1859, Muhlenburg Twp. bl. (1860)
WALKER, HENRY - bc 1846, OH; bl farm laborer. m Margaret
   (Davis). (Harrison Twp, 1870)
      Margaret - b 1851, OH; bl. parents both b VA. (Muh-
         lenburg Twp, 1860; Scioto Twp, 1880)
      Albert B. - b 10 Oct 1874, Harrison Twp.
      Lina - b 22 Feb 1876, Harrison Twp. bl. (1880)
      May - b 1880, Scioto Twp. bl. (1880)
WALKER, JAMES - bc 1822, VA; mul carpenter. m Sarah A.
   (_____). (Harrison Twp, 1860)

Sarah A. - bc 1829, VA; mul. (1860)
Edward - bc 1851, OH; mul. (1860)
Ellen - bc 1849, OH; mul. m Ferdinand Parker.
   (1860)
Jane - bc 1856, OH; mul. (1860)
Mary - bc 1856, OH; mul. (1860)
Mildred J. - bc 1842, VA; mul. m Richard H. Irving.
   (1860)
Robert - b 1860, OH; mul. (1860)
Winfield - bc 1852, OH; mul. (1860)
WALKER, THEOPHILUS - b 1815, VA; mul farmer. m Mary
   (_____). (Monroe Twp, 1850-1860)
   Mary - b 1816 or 1820, VA; bl. (1850-1860)
   Angeline - b 1842, OH; mul. (1850-1860)
   Calvin - bc 1853, Monroe Twp. bl. (1860)
   Elizabeth - b 1850, Monroe Twp. bl. (1860)
   Henry A. - bc 1857, Monroe Twp. bl. (1860)
   James - b 1848, OH; bl. (1850-1860)
   John - bc 1836, OH; mul. (1850)
   Levi - b 1846 or 1849, OH; mul. (1850-1860)
   Martha - b 1844, OH; bl. (1850-1860)
   Matilda - bc 1854, OH. mul. (1860)
   Susan - b 1839, OH; mul. (1850-1860)
WALKER, WILLIAM E. - b Jan 1849, IND; mul farmer. father b
   France; mother b NC. m Martha (Williams) & lived in Mt.
   Sterling, Fayette Co. (Monroe Twp, 1900)
   Alice - b Feb 1890, OH. (1900)
   Andrew - b 30 Nov 1898, Monroe Twp.
   Cecil - b Nov 1896 or 1898, OH. (1900)
   Clarence - b Oct 1880, OH; mul farm laborer. (1900)
   Daisy - b Sept 1884, OH; mul housekeeper. (1900)
   Frank E. - b Aug 1896, OH. (1900)
   Gladiola - b Oct 1894, OH. (1900)
   Henry - b Nov 1892, OH. (1900)
   James - b Mar 1888, OH. (1900)
   Stella - b Oct 1875, OH; mul housekeeper. (1900)
   William - b July 1886, OH. (1900)
WALKER, WILLIAM m Martha (Rather) & lived in Jackson Twp,
   1880s. -- may be same as above--
   William - b 21 June 1886, Jackson Twp. --may be same
      as above--
WARD, ANN M. - bc 1858, OH; bl. (Circleville, 1870)
WARD, LAVINIA - bc 1811, VA; bl. (Circleville, 1860)
   Mary E. - bc 1843, OH; bl. m John Dickerson. (1860)
WARD, SPENCER - b 1848, VA; d 24 Jan 1868, Circleville of
   palsey.
WARDAM, EDWARD - bc 1839, OH; bl farmer. (Scioto Twp,
   1860)

WARE, MARY m John J. Dickerson & lived in Circleville.
WARGO (often listed as HARGO and vice versa)
WARGO, ELIJAH - b Aug 1863, Marion Co; d 10 June 1877, Deer
    Creek Twp. of lung fever. single farmer.
WARGO, JONATHAN W. - b 1860, Deer Creek Twp; d 10 Oct 1879,
    Deer Creek Twp. of fall.
WARGO, SARAH m Hope L. Stepter & lived in Muhlenburg Twp.
WARREN, ELIAS or ELLIS - b 1839, VA; bl laborer. parents
    both b VA. m 1st, Mary (____); 2nd, Eliza (____).
    (Circleville, 1870-1880)
        Mary - bc 1845, KY; bl. (1870)
        Eliza - bc 1852, OH; bl. mother b NC. (1880)
        Artis - b 1874; d 10 Sept 1876, Circleville of lung
            fever.
        Charity - b 1880, Circleville. bl. (1880)
        Charles - b 1869, Circleville. bl. (1870-1880)
        Dora - bc 1876, Circleville. bl. (1880)
        James - b 28 Feb 1871, Circleville. bl. (1880)
        Maggie - bc 1877, Circleville. bl. (1880)
        Sarah - b 1870, Circleville. bl. (1880)
WARRICK, JOHN freed in Hardy Co, W VA. Lived in Pickaway
    Co, 1838.
WASHINGTON, DAVID - b Jan 1870, OH; bl day laborer.
    parents both b KY. (Pickaway Twp, 1900)
        John - b Mar 1879, OH; bl day laborer. (1900)
WASHINGTON, GEORGE - bc 1842, VA; d 24 Jan 1877, Circle-
    ville in railroad accident.
WATKINS, GEORGE - bc 1845, OH; bl farm laborer. (Jackson
    Twp, 1870)
WATKINS, WILLIAM B. m Nancy A. (Springer) & lived in Cir-
    cleville, 1870s.
        Freeman B. - b 24 Feb 1873, Circleville.
WATSON, ALEC m Martha (____) & lived in Muhlenburg Twp,
    1860s.
        Reuben - b 19 May 1868, Muhlenburg Twp.
WATSON, DAVID - bc 1826, VA; bl farmer. parents both b VA.
    m Lovena (____). (Darby Twp, 1880)
        Lovena - bc 1826, VA; bl. parents both b VA. (1880)
        Amanda M. - bc 1862, OH; bl. (1880)
        Julia Ann - bc 1852, OH; bl house servant. (1880)
        Margaret M. - bc 1866, OH; bl. (1880)
        Mariah A. - bc 1864, OH; bl. (1880)
        William H. - bc 1856, OH; bl laborer. (1880)
WATSON, ELIZABETH m Henry Fox & lived in Harrison Twp.
WATSON, THOMAS - bc 1847, OH; mul farmer. parents both b
    VA; m Ann D. (____). (Darby Twp, 1880)
        Ann D. - bc 1857, OH; mul. father b VA; mother b OH.
            (1880)

David H. - bc 1874, OH; mul. (1880)
Martha Ann - bc 1876, OH; mul. (1880)
Qintus P. - bc 1872, OH; mul. (1880)
William A. - bc 1878, OH; mul. (1880)
WEAVER, ANNA - bc 1848, OH; bl housemaid. (Circleville, 1870)
WEAVER, DENNIS - b Apr 1873, OH; bl barber. father b NC; mother b OH. m Linda (_____). (Circleville, 1900)
Linda - b Mar 1876, KY. parents both b KY. (1900)
Charles H. - b Dec 1895, OH. (1900)
Howard S. - b Mar 1898, PA. (1900)
WEAVER, DENNY - b July 1878, Circleville; d 15 Sept 1878, Circleville.
WEAVER, EMMA - b Jan 1852, OH. parents both b VA. (Circleville, 1900) --probably wife of John Weaver, s/o William A & Mary Weaver, and who m. Emma (_____) 1870s--
Ada - b May 1876, OH; bl servant. father b NC. (1900)
Birdie - b May 1882, OH; bl servant. father b NC. (1900)
Blanche - b May 1888, OH. father b NC. (1900)
Delano - b Jan 1877, OH; bl barber. father b NC. (1900)
Ernie - b June 1889, OH. father b NC. (1900)
Fred - b May 1884, OH; bl day laborer. father b NC. (1900)
Hartley - b Sept 1879, OH; bl barber. father b NC. (1900)
Lloyd - b Aug 1892, OH. father b NC. (1900)
WEAVER, ENOCH - bc 1809, 1812, or 1821, NC; bl plasterer. m Emma (_____). (Circleville, 1850-1870)
Emma - b 1827 or 1830, NC; bl. (1850-1860) --listed as Elisabeth in 1860--
Ann M. - b 1845, NC; bl. (1850-1860)
George - b 1847 or 1849, OH; bl plasterer. (1850-1870)
George - bc 1866, Circleville. bl. (1870)
Ida - b 1856 or 1859, Circleville. bl. (1860-1870)
Joseph - b 1851, Circleville. bl plasterer. (1860-1870)
Lazarus - b 1853, Circleville. bl plasterer. (1860-1870)
Sally - b 1855, Circleville. bl. (1860)
ELIZABETH (also BETSY) - b 1772 or 1780, NC; bl. (1850-1860)
WEAVER, GRANT m Minnie (Brokaw) & lived in Muhlenburg Twp, 1890s.
Harry Edgar - b 4 Dec 1894, Muhlenburg Twp.

WEAVER, HARRISON - bc 1838, NC; bl farm worker and laborer.
m Mary (Smith).   (Circleville, 1870-1880)
    Mary - b 1845 or 1851, OH; bl worker at hotel.
        parents both b OH. (1870-1880)
    D. - b 2 May 1878, Circleville.
    Henry - b 2 Apr. 1876, Circleville. bl. (1880)
    Nellie - b 1870, Circleville. bl. (1870-1880)
    Nettie - b 1867, Circleville. bl. (1870-1880)
WEAVER, HEZEKIAH - b Aug 1860; bl porter at hotel. (Cir-
cleville, 1900)
WEAVER, JOHN m Emma (_____) & lived in Circleville, 1870s.
    Noah - b 22 Nov 1870, Circleville.
WEAVER, MARY - b 1829, Hagerstown, MD; d 9 Oct 1880,
Circleville of paralysis. married. --probably wife of
Harrison Weaver--
WEAVER, STANLEY - b 1890, Circleville; d 13 Nov 1891,
Circleville of fever.
WEAVER, TEO ANN - bc 1842, NC; d 13 Sept 1870, Circleville
of fever.
WEAVER, W. H. - bc Aug 1876, Circleville; d 25 Oct 1878,
Circleville of whooping cough.
WEAVER, WILLIAM A. - b 1815, NC; bl barber. m Mary
    (_____). (Circleville, 1860-1870)
    Mary - b 1819, NC; bl. parents both b NC. (1860-
        1880)
    Daniel - b 1852, NC; bl barber. (1860-1880)
    Dora - bc 1856, NC; bl. (1860)
    Emanuel - bc 1853, NC; bl. (1860)
    Emma D. - b 1857 or Aug 1859, NC; d 2 Mar 1877,
        Circleville of consumption. bl. (1860)
    Georgiana - bc 1843, NC; bl. (1860)
    Harrison - bc 1841, NC; bl barber. (1860) --see also
        separate listing--
    Henrietta - b 1847 or 1848, NC; bl. m Charles Goff.
        (1860)
    James - bc 1843, NC; bl laborer. (1870)
    John - b 1837, NC; bl barber and laborer. (1860-
        1870)
    Julia - bc 1850, NC; bl. (1860)
    Lincoln - b 1861, Circleville. bl. (1870-1880)
    Mary - bc 1852, NC; bl. (1860)
    Missouri - bc 1846, NC; bl. m Robert Hollingsworth.
        (1860)
    Noah - bc 1857, NC; bl. (1860)
WEAVER, WILLIAM H. - b 1835 or 1839, NC or TENN; bl laborer
and servant. parents both b TENN. (Circleville, 1860-
1870)
WEAVER, WILLIAM - bc 1840, NC; bl farm laborer. (Jackson
Twp, 1870) --possibly same as above--

WEAVER, WILLIAM - bc 1844, OH; bl. (Circleville, 1860)
WEAVER, WILLIAM - bc 1849, OH; bl house servant. (Wayne
    Twp, 1870)
WEINMAN, JAMES m Amanda (Hill) & lived in Circleville,
    1880s.
        child - b 27 Dec 1897, Circleville.
WELLS, MORGINS - bc 1842, Iowa; bl farm laborer. m Mehela
    (_____). (Scioto Twp, 1870)
        Mehela - bc 1836, GA; bl. (1870)
WESLEY, JOHN - bc 1869, NC; bl. (Circleville, 1860)
WHEATLEY, HENRY m Margaret (_____) & lived in Muhlenburg
    Twp, 1880s.
        Johnny - b 25 Nov 1880, Muhlenburg Twp.
WHEATLEY, MARY - b 1836, KY; d 15 Dec 1880, Circleville of
    pneumonia.
WHITE, ALBERT - bc 1834, OH; bl barber. m Frances (_____).
    (Circleville, 1860)
        Frances - bc 1836, OH; mul. (1860)
WHITE, JOHN and 2 males, 3 females lived in Circleville,
    1840.
WHITE, JOHN - b Mar 1838, OH; bl laborer. father b VA;
    mother b OH. m Lucinda (_____). (Circleville, 1860-
    1900)
        Lucinda - b Sept 1840, OH; bl housemaid. father b
            VA; mother b OH. (1860-1900)
        Mary - bc 1863, Circleville. bl. (1880)
        Samuel H. - b 1860, Circleville. bl. (1860-1880)
        Walter - bc 1870, Circleville. bl. (1880)
        LOUISA - b 1812, 1814 or 1817, Ross Co, OH; d 15 Aug
            1889, Circleville of dysentery. bl. parents both
            b VA. (1860-1880)
WHITE, JOHN - bc 1850, OH; bl laborer. father b VA; mother
    b OH. (Circleville, 1880)
WHITE, MOSES - b 23 May 1824, TENN or VA; d 9 Sept 1875,
    Circleville of pneumonia. bl teamster. (Circleville,
    1870)
        Cynthia - bc 1844, KY; bl. (1870) -probably spouse-
WHITAKER, W. S. m Dolly (Scott) & lived in Circleville,
    1870s.
        S.B. - b 12 May 1878, Circleville.
WHITEN (also interchanged with WHITING)
WHITEN, HENRY - b 1796, VA; bl farmer.   m Amelia (_____).
    (Jackson Twp, 1840-1860; Muhlenburg Twp, 1870) --pos-
    sible first wife Mary, b. 1805, OH)
        Amelia ("Milly") - b 1810, OH; bl. parents both b
            VA. (1840-1870; Muhlenburg Twp, 1880)
        Julian - bc 1834, OH; bl. (1850)
        Reason - bc 1828, OH; bl. (1850)

Samuel - b 1839, Jackson Twp; bl farm laborer.
    (1850-1860) --see separate listing--
WHITEN, JOHN - bc 1870, OH; mul. parents both b OH.
    (Circleville, 1880)
WHITING, ETHYL - b Oct 1896, OH. father b IND; mother b
    KY. (Monroe Twp, 1900)
WHITING, JORDAN - b 1874, OH; bl farm laborer. parents
    both b OH. (Monroe Twp, 1900)
WHITING, SAMUEL - b 1839, OH; bl farmer. parents both b OH.
    m Sarah (Stewart). (Jackson Twp, 1850-1860; Muhlenburg
    Twp, 1870; Monroe Twp, 1880)
        Sarah - bc 1842, OH; bl. (1870)
        Alfred L. - b Aug 1873, Muhlenburg Twp; bl. (1880)
        Edward - b 29 Sept 1870, Muhlenburg Twp; bl. (1880)
        John E. - b 1869, Muhlenburg Twp; bl. (1870-1880)
        Joseph - bc 1877, Muhlenburg Twp; bl. (1880)
        Rosella - b 1867, Muhlenburg Twp; bl. (1870-1880)
        William - b 1865, Muhlenburg Twp; bl. (1870-1880) --
            see separate listing--
WHITING, WILLIAM - b Nov 1865, OH; bl farmer. parents both
    b OH. m Catherine (____). (Monroe Twp, 1900)
        Catherine - b June 1871, OH. parents both b OH.
            (1900)
        Arnold - b Sept 1893, OH; bl. (1900)
WHITSON, BENJAMIN - bc 1838, OH; bl farm laborer. m Jane
    (____). (Scioto Twp, 1880)
        Jane - bc 1848, OH; bl. father b OH; mother b TENN.
            (1900)
        Charles - bc 1870, OH; bl. (1880)
        Elnora - bc 1868, OH; bl. (1880)
        Mandela - bc 1877, OH; bl. (1880)
        Nettie - bc 1879, Scioto Twp; bl. (1880)
        Sarah - bc 1873, OH; bl. (1880)
WHITSON, CHARLES - bc 1812, VA; bl farmer. father b PA;
    mother b Germany. m Catherine (____). (Muhlenburg
    Twp, 1880)
        Catherine - bc 1825, VA; bl. parents both b VA.
            (1880)
        Henry L. - bc 1863, OH; bl farm laborer. (1880)
        Jennie A. - bc 1865, OH; bl farm laborer. (1880)
WHITTACO/WHITTICO
WHITTACO, ELIZABETH - bc 1830, VA; d 8 Feb 1888, Washington
    Twp Infirmary. bl. married. parents both b VA.
    (Circleville, 1880)
        Margaret - bc 1847, VA; bl servant. (1880)
WHITTACO, FRANCES m. Robert Fowler & lived in Muhlenburg
    Twp.

WHITTACO, JOHN - bc 1817, VA; mul laborer. parents both b
    VA. m Susan (____). (Darby Twp, 1880)
        Susan - bc 1831, VA; mul. parents both b VA.   (1880)
        Blanche - bc 1878, VA; mul.   (1880)
        George - bc 1876, VA; mul.   (1880)
        Isabel - bc 1861, VA; mul.   (1880)
        Margaret - bc 1852, VA; mul.   (1880)
        Mena - bc 1868, VA; mul.   (1880)
        Robert - bc 1871, VA; mul.   (1880)
        Wade - b 1860 or 1862, VA; listed bl & mul servant.
            (1880)
WHITTACO, VINCENT - bc 1799, VA; d 12 July 1891, Washington
    Twp Infirmary of dropsey. bl farm laborer and shoe-
    maker. m Diana (____). (Jackson Twp, 1850)
        Diana - bc 1826, PA.   (1850)
WHITTACO, VINCENT - bc 1822, OH; bl farm laborer.   (Jackson
    Twp, 1860)
WHITTACO, WINSTON - bc 1820, VA; bl laborer. parents both
    b VA. m Charity (____). (Wayne Twp, 1880)
        Charity - bc 1830, NC; mul. parents both b NC.
            (1880)
WHITTINGTON, HARRY - b Dec 1870, OH; bl blacksmith.
    parents both b VA. m Genetta (Hazelwood). (Circle-
    ville, 1900)
        Genetta (also "Nettie") - b Aug 1874, OH. father b
            NC; mother b VA. (1900)
        Homer - b 11 May 1894, Circleville; bl. (1900)
WHITTINGTON, HASEL - b Sept 1837, OH. parents both b VA.
    (Circleville, 1900)
        Allen - b Dec 1878, OH. parents both b VA. (1900)
        Cora - b Feb 1875, OH. parents both b VA. (1900)
WHITTINGTON, HENRY - b 1836 or 1838, VA; bl plasterer. m
    Harriet (Allen). (Circleville, 1860-1880)
        Harriet- b 1838, OH; bl. (1860-1880)
        Allen - b 10 Dec 1878, Circleville; bl. (1880)
        Carrie - b 22 Feb 1874, Circleville; bl. (1880)
        Harriet - b 1 Oct 1872, Circleville; bl. (1880)
        Harry - b 1871, Circleville; bl. (1880)
        James - b 1864, Circleville; bl. (1870-1880)
        Jesse M. - b 5 Dec 1876, Circleville; d 11 July 1877,
            Circleville of spasms.
        John C. - b 1862, Circleville; d 25 June 1885, Cir-
            cleville from fall from window. bl day laborer.
            (1870-1880)
        Mary - b 1886, Circleville; d 14 June 1882, Circle-
            ville of consumption. (1870-1880)
        Thomas - b 1868, Circleville; bl. (1870-1880)
        William H. - b 1859, Circleville; bl hotel worker.

WHITTINGTON, JOSEPH - bc 1843, OH; bl. (Circleville, 1870)
    Cora - bc 1869, Circleville; bl. (1870)
    Elizabeth - bc 1857, OH; bl. (1870)
    Maria - bc 1862, OH; bl. (1870)
    Nannie - bc 1864, OH; bl. (1870)
    Willis - bc 1868, OH; bl. (1870)
WHITTINGTON, LAVERTA m James Jackson & lived in Circleville.
WHITTINGTON, THOMAS - b June 1867, OH; bl laborer. parents
   both b OH. m Gracie (____). (Circleville, 1900)
    Gracie - b June 1879, OH. parents both b OH. (1900)
WHULTRY (?), HENRY - bc 1843, KY; bl day laborer. parents
   both b OH. m Mary A. (____). (Muhlenburg Twp, 1880)
    Mary A. - bc 1839, KY; bl. parents both b KY.
     (1880)
    Albert - bc 1869, OH; bl. (1880)
    Amanda - bc 1863, KY; bl. (1880)
    Catherine - b 1880, Muhlenburg Twp; bl. (1880)
    Ellen - bc 1872, OH; bl. (1880)
    Henry - bc 1878, OH; bl. (1880)
    Mary - bc 1875, OH; bl. (1880)
    William - bc 1865, OH; bl. (1880)
WILKES, JOSEPH - bc 1769, VA; bl. (Muhlenburg Twp, 1860)
WILL, ISAAC - bc 1851, VA; bl farm laborer. (Muhlenburg
   Twp, 1870)
WILL, ROBERT m Sarah (Nye) and lived in Circleville, 1860s.
   Robert E. - b 17 Nov 1869, Circleville.
WILLIAMS, ALBERT - b June 1860; bl worker on public (?).
   parents both b OH. (Pickaway Twp, 1900)
    Rufus - b Oct 1876, OH; bl day laborer. (1900)
WILLIAMS, BERTHA - b Feb 1891, OH. parents both b OH.
   (Circleville, 1900)
    Lenora - b Feb 1893, OH. parents both b OH. (1900)
    Viola - b Nov 1894, OH. parents both b OH. (1900)
WILLIAMS, DAISY - b 1890, Bourneville, Ross Co; d 2 Oct
   1892, Circleville of heart disease.
WILLIAMS, EDMON had daughter Sarah by Sarah Henry.
WILLIAMS, FANIA (fem) - b Feb 1863, OH; bl housekeeper.
   father b VA; mother b SC. (Circleville, 1900)
    Saidid - b Apr 1862, OH. father b VA; mother b SC.
     (1900)
WILLIAMS, GEORGE - b 1836, Circleville; d 21 Jan 1876,
   Circleville of pneumonia. married.
WILLIAMS, HENRY - bc 1826, OH; bl. (Muhlenburg Twp, 1850)
WILLIAMS, JOHN - bc 1825, OH; bl. (Muhlenburg Twp, 1850)
WILLIAMS, LOUISA - bc 1837, OH; bl housemaid. (Wayne Twp,
   1870)
WILLIAMS, LUCY - b 13 July 1875, Circleville; d 25 Jan
   1876, Circleville of lung fever.

WILLIAMS, MANSON - b 1823, VA; bl gardener. m Emma
(____). (Circleville, 1860)
    Emma - bc 1820, VA; bl. (1860)
WILLIAMS, MARY- bc 1837, OH; mul domestic. m Harvey Jack-
son. (Monroe Twp, 1860)
WILLIAMS, NATHANIEL lived in Darby Twp, 1860s.
    child - b 1 Aug 1867, Darby Twp.
WILLIAMS, SARAH m Harry Hill & lived in Deer Creek Twp.
WILLIAMS, SARAH m William T. Farrow.
WILLIAMS, SUSAN - bc 1826, NC; bl. (Circleville, 1850)
    Margaret - bc 1836, NC; bl. (1850)
    William - bc 1835, NC; bl. (1850)
WILLIAMS, WILLIAM - bc 1836, OH; bl plasterer. m Susan
(Johnson). (Circleville, 1860)
    Susan - bc 1841, bl. (1860)
    Alfretta - b 1860, Circleville; bl. (1860)
    Caroline - b 9 Jan 1872, Circleville.
    Josephine - b 1858, Circleville; bl. (1860)
WILLIAMS, ____ (fem)- b Apr 1872, OH. parents both b OH.
(Circleville, 1900)
    Betty - b Oct 1888, OH. parents both b OH. (1900)
WILLIAMSON, CHARITY - b Apr 1829, NC. parents both b NC.
(Circleville, 1900)
WILLIS, THOMAS - bc 1850, VA; bl farm laborer. m Lucy
(____). (Jackson Twp, 1870)
    Harvey - b 1 Feb 1878, Circleville.
WILSON, HATTIE - b Mar 1880, OH; bl domestic. (Circle-
ville, 1900)
WILSON, JOSEPH m Anne (Wilson) & lived in Circleville,
1890s.
    Lester - b 25 Mar 1899, Circleville.
WILSON, MARY - b Sept 1866, OH; bl domestic. father b VA;
mother b OH. (Circleville, 1900)
WILSON, ROLF - b June 1886, OH. parents both b OH. Cir-
cleville, 1900)
    Clarence - b Mar 1898, OH. parents both b OH. (1900)
    Jennie - b Jan 1891, OH. (1900)
    Leona - b May 1893, OH. (1900)
    Walker - b Aug 1888, OH. (1900)
WILSON, SOFA - bc 1861, OH; bl cook. parents both b VA.
(Circleville, 1880)
WINFIELD, JAMES - bc 1863, OH; bl laborer. parents both b
OH. (Darby Twp, 1880)
WINGATE, PERRY and 2 females lived in Washington Twp, 1820.
WINGO, PRESLEY - bc 1847, OH; mul farm laborer. parents
both b OH. m Mary (____). (Darby Twp, 1880)
    Mary - bc 1844, NC; bl. parents both b NC. (1880)
    Emma F. - bc 1872, OH; bl. (1880)

Frank - bc 1874, OH; bl. (1880)
Mary Elizabeth - bc 1871, OH; bl. (1880)
WINTERS, CATHARINE - b Dec 1863, OH. parents both b VA.
(Circleville, 1900)
WINTERS, FRANCES m Dennis Tann & lived in Circleville.
WINTERS, GUSTAVUS - b Aug 1861, OH; bl farm laborer.
father b VA; mother b OH. (Jackson Twp, 1900)
WINTERS, JOHN - b 1812 or 1819, VA; bl whitewasher or black
mason. m Julia (____). (Circleville, 1860-1870)
Julia - b 1836, VA; bl. (1860-1870)
Augustus - bc 1859, Circleville; bl. (1870)
John H. - b 1851, OH; bl laborer. (1860-1870)
Lucy - b 1857, Circleville; bl. m Willis Johnson.
(1860-1870)
Mary A. - b 1859, Circleville; bl. (1860-1870)
Minnie - bc 1866, Circleville; bl. (1870)
Netta - bc 1869, Circleville; bl. (1870)
Rosetta - bc 1866, Circleville; bl. m Frank Smithen.
(1870)
William - b 1854, OH; bl. (1860-1870)
WINTERS, JOHN - bc 1853, OH; mul groomsman. father b VA:
mother b OH. , (Circleville, 1880)
WINTERS, LUCY - b 1797, 1802, or 1804, VA; d 21 Sept 1875,
Circleville of debility. bl. (Circleville, 1850-1870)
WINTERS, NANNIE - bc 1866, OH; mul servant. parents both b
VA. (Circleville, 1880) --may be Minnie d/o John &
Julia Winters--
WISE, ALEXANDER - b VA; d 19 Aug 1868, Circleville of lung
disease. listed as illegitimate child.
WISE, ____ - b Apr 1868, Circleville; d 18 June 1868,
Circleville in accident. c/o Mary Wise.
WOLF, JAMES W. m Ella (Moyer) and lived in Salt Creek Twp,
1890s.
Charles E. - b 13 Feb 1895, Salt Creek Twp.
WOODARD, LEWIS- bc 1846, OH; bl house servant. m Mary
(Hargrove). (Circleville, 1870)
Mary - bc 1848, OH; bl. (1870)
Harriet - b 2 Jan 1882, Circleville.
WOODS, HENRY - bc 1854, OH; bl barber. parents both b OH.
m Mary (____). (Circleville, 1880)
Mary - bc 1853, VA; mul. parents both b VA. (1880)
WOODS, MARY - bc 1868, OH; mul. (Circleville, 1870)
WOODS, PARIS - bc 1827; bl servant. (Circleville, 1860)
WOODS, WILLIAM - b 1875, Circleville; d 16 Jan 1891, Cir-
cleville of typhoid fever.
WOODY, LOUIS - bc 1852, VA; bl laborer. m Mary (____).
(Circleville, 1880)

Mary - bc 1853, OH; bl. father b VA; mother b OH.
(1880)
William - bc 1875, OH. (1880)
WOODY, MARY - b July 1845, OH. parents both b VA. (Circleville, 1900)
WOPLINGTON, IDA m Andrew Mayo & lived in Walnut Twp.
WORK, WILLIAM m Julia F. (Whitson) & lived in Muhlenburg
Twp.
Charles Henry - b 19 Oct 1881, Muhlenburg Twp.
WORLEY, JOHN m Sarah (_____) & lived in Darby Twp, 1870s.
Emma - b 16 June 1876, Darby Twp.
WORLEY, WILLIS - b Mar 1852, NC; bl farmer. parents both b
NC. m Margaret (Steptoe). (Circleville, 1870; Darby
Twp, 1880; Muhlenburg Twp, 1900)
Margaret - b June 1857, VA. parents both b VA.
(1870-1900)
Alice - b Dec 1887, OH. (1900)
Ambrose - b Jan 1881, Darby Twp; bl farm laborer.
(1900)
Charles F. - b Aug 1885, OH. (1900)
Daniel Boone - b Dec 1875, OH; bl farm laborer.
(1880-1900)
James E. - b 1 Sept 1878, OH; bl farm laborer.
(1880-1900)
Mansfield - b Sept 1892, OH. (1900)
Margaret - b 24 Oct 1875, Pickaway Co. (1880)
Martha M. - b 19 Jan 1895, Muhlenburg Twp. (1900)
Theodore - b May 1890, OH. (1900)
Theora - b May 1890, OH. (1900)
William W. - b Apr 1883, OH; bl day laborer. (1900)
WRIGHT, BLANCHE - b July 1884, OH. father b OH; mother b
VA. (Circleville, 1900)
WRIGHT, ELIZABETH - b 1831, Gallipolis; d 3 Dec 1873, Wayne
Twp. of paralysis.
WRIGHT, GEORGE m Lucy (Legow) & lived in Monroe Twp, 1880s.
Floyd - b 22 May 1887, Monroe Twp.
WRIGHT, JAMES - b 1826, Mangiluck, VA; d 24 May 1898,
Circleville of suicide. mul drayman. parents both b
VA. m Louisa (Norman). (Circleville, 1860-1880)
Louisa - b 1838, OH; mul. (1860-1880)
Catherine - bc 1866, Circleville; mul. (1870)
Fanny D. - b 3 Jan 1878, Circleville.
James A. - b 1859, Circleville; mul. (1860-1870)
Jennie - b 28 Aug 1840, Circleville; mul. (1880)
Kate - bc 1868, Circleville; mul. (1880)
Lydia - bc 1870, Circleville; mul. (1880)
Malinda (Linna) - bc 1868, Circleville; mul. m
William Bass. (1860-1870)

Norman - b 1863, Circleville; mul drayman. (1860-1880)

Servisia - bc 1875, Circleville; mul. (1880)

Sherman - b 1865, Circleville; mul drayman. (1860-1880)

WRIGHT, LIZZIE M. - b 30 Apr 1873, Circleville; d 19 Feb 1876, Circleville of clot in head.

WRIGHT, MARIA - b July 1823, VA. parents both b VA. (Circleville, 1900)

WRIGHT, MARY C. m William H. Smith & lived in Circleville.

WRIGHT, NICHOLAS - bc 1822, DEL; bl carpenter and wagon maker. m Priscilla (____). (Wayne Twp, 1860; Circleville, 1870)

    Priscilla - bc 1830, VA or OH; bl. parents both b VA. (1870)

WRIGHT, RICHARD - b 1854, Harrisburg, Pickaway Co; d 8 Dec 1886, Circleville of consumption. bl farm laborer.
parents both b OH. m Mary (____). (Circleville, 1880)

    Mary - bc 1853, OH. father b MD; mother b VA. (1880)

    Ida - bc 1879, Circleville; bl. (1880)

    Mary - bc 1878, Circleville; bl. (1880)

WRIGHT, WILLIAM - bc 1855, OH; mul livery stable worker.
parents both b VA. m Susan (____). (Wayne Twp, 1880)

    Susan - bc 1856, OH; mul. mother b MD. (1880)

WRINGLE, HARMON - bc 1851, OH; bl. (Wayne Twp, 1870)

WYATT, CHARLES E. - b 1877 or 1877, Circleville, s/o Susan Wyatt & Wesley Mitchell.

WYATT, ELIZABETH - b July 1833, NC; bl. parents both b NC. (Circleville, 1870-1900)

    Blue E. - bc 1852, OH; bl housemaid. (1870)

    Martha - bc 1862, OH; bl. (1870)

    Nettie - b 1866, Circleville; bl. (1870-1900)

    Penella - b Jan 1889; bl housekeeper. parents both b NC. (1900)

    Susan J. - bc 1859, OH; bl. (1900)

WYATT, GEORGE - bc 1840, OH; bl. parents both b NC. m Lotta (Holmes). (Circleville Twp, 1870)

    Lotta - bc 1844, KY; bl cook. parents both b KY. (1870)

    Joan - b 2 Mar 1875, Circleville.

WYATT, GEORGE - bc 1846, OH; bl. (Wayne Twp, 1860)

WYATT, GEORGE - b July 1875, Circleville; d 20 Feb 1876, Circleville of diarrhea.

WYATT, IRA - bc 1833, NC; bl laborer. m Lizzie (____). (Circleville, 1860)

    Lizzie - bc 1832, NC; bl. (1860)

    Abbe B. - bc 1856, OH; bl. (1860)

Harriet A. - bc 1849, OH; bl. (1860)

Susan A. - bc 1858, OH; bl. (1860)

WYATT, JAMES W. - bc 1876, OH; bl. father b NC; mother b
VA. (Circleville, 1880)

Daisey - bc 1878, OH. father b NC; mother b VA.
(1880)

WYATT, JERRY m Ella (Franks) & lived in Circleville, 1880s.

Ella - bc 1859, Circleville; d 4 Mar 1892, Circleville of consumption

WYATT, JONAS - b May 1850, OH; bl drayman and day laborer.
parents both b NC. m Annie (_____). (Circleville,
1880-1900)

Annie - b Mar 1854, VA; bl. parents both b VA.
(1880-1900)

WYATT, JULIA - bc 1851, OH; mul domestic. m Richard
Redman. (Circleville, 1860)

WYATT, MARY L. - b 5 Feb 1889, Circleville; d 26 Feb 1890,
Circleville of consumption.

WYATT, MURPHEY - b 1805 or 1808, Hartford Co, N.C.; d 3 Apr
1870, Circleville of chills. mul drayman. m Patsey
(_____). (Circleville, 1850-1860) --also listed as
Nathan Wyatt--

Patsey - b 1810 or 1815, NC; mul. (1850-1860)

Albariah - bc 1845, Circleville; mul. (1860)

Armicia - b 1839 or 1841, NC; mul. (1850-1860)

Henry - b 1835 or 1839, NC; mul. (1850-1860)

Ira - b 1833, NC; mul. (1850) --see separate
listing--

Penna - b 1834, NC; mul. (1850-1860)

WYATT, MURPHEY - bc 1818, NC; bl drayman. m Rebecca
(_____). (Circleville, 1860)

Rebecca - b 1819, NC; bl. parents both b NC.
(Circleville, 1860-1880)

Amanda - b 1853, OH; bl housemaid. parents both b
OH. m James Miller. (1860-1880)

George - b 1847, OH; bl laborer. (1860-1870)

James P. - bc 1840, NC; bl. (1860)

Jerry - b 1851, OH; bl laborer and plasterer.
parents both b OH. (1860-1880)

Jonas - b 1855 or 1859, Circleville; bl laborer.
(1860-1870)

Julia - bc 1849, OH. (1860)

Mary J. - bc 1845, OH; bl. (1860)

William - b 1843, OH; bl laborer. (1860-1870)

WYATT, WILLIAM- b 1842, OH; bl laborer. m Ida (_____).
(Circleville, 1880) --probably s/o Murphey & Rebecca
Wyatt--

Ida - bc 1858, OH; bl. mother b VA. (1880)
George E. - b 15 Apr 1876, Circleville; bl. (1880)
Josie M. - bc 1879, Circleville; bl. (1880)

YATES, ELLA - b Sept 1887, Circleville; d 22 May 1888, Circleville.
YATES, NATHAN - bc 1856, OH; mul laborer. father b VA. (Circleville, 1880)

www.ingramcontent.com/pod-product-compliance
Lightning Source LLC
Chambersburg PA
CBHW070451090426
42735CB00012B/2513